Fencing Lessons

By Susan Kemmerer

Schoolhouse Publishing
659 Schoolhouse Road
Telford, PA 18969
215-721-9293
www.shpublishing.com

Published by
Schoolhouse Publishing
659 Schoolhouse Road
Telford, PA 18969
215-721-9293
www.shpublishing.com

Dedication

This project was ten long years in the making, mainly because life got busy, raising and homeschooling kids. This study sat on the shelf, waiting, for months at a time between writings. But life has a way of making kids grow up, and eventually I had time to write again. My youngest daughter became my test subject and editor for this study. She went through the study several times, first as a student, and later as an editor. She invested herself into its pages, reading it with a critical eye, and helping me to improve it. She was consistently kind and apologetic when making corrections – wanting to encourage me at the same time she was pointing out mistakes. To my baby girl, Rebecca. You truly inspire me to do better and to be better. I love your wisdom and kindness, your passion and your creativity. Thank you for all your help! I love you!

About *Fencing Lessons*:

Fencing Lessons is designed for your students to develop a deep love for the Word of God and for God Himself. The title comes from the idea that God's Word is our spiritual sword (Ephesians 6:17), so it is important for us to learn how to use it effectively. The study of the use of a sword is called fencing. Each lesson is broken down into four sections:

Sword Drill is a simple exercise to help your student not only memorize the books of the bible (for quick and easy access), but also to help him/her learn a little about each book.

Sword Play exercises are puzzles, riddles, word searches, and quizzes that use God's Word. As your students play the games and solves the puzzles, they are becoming more familiar with God's Word, helping them to hide His Word in their hearts.

Fencing Practice is a short Bible study based on a particular passage (the same passage used in the **Sword Play** exercise).

Thrust and Parry is the most important part of the lesson. It teaches the student to apply God's Word to his/her own life, so he's not like the man in James 1:23 who looks in the mirror, then forgets what he's seen.

The first 13 *Fencing Lessons* are about the importance and power of God's Word. Lessons 14-38 are about God Himself, His omnipotence, omniscience, and omnipresence. Lessons 39-47 are about God's love. He IS love. Lessons 48-59 study many of God's other attributes, including His holiness, justice, righteousness, truth, purity, and wisdom. Lessons 60-70 study the "Roman Road" – a look at basic gospel truths that lead to salvation. A solid grasp of these truths will help your student to share the gospel with other people. Lessons 71-90 are a study of Christian living. As believers, our lives *should* look different than the world's. These lessons will help your student to grasp and own this fact by applying God's Word to everyday situations, while avoiding 'easy grace.'

I've attempted to phrase all the questions throughout *Fencing Lessons* in such a way that your students will be able to answer them regardless of the version of the Bible they use. I specifically used ESV and KJV in creating *Fencing Lessons*, but also consulted other translations as well to verify that your students should be able to answer the questions and solve the puzzles regardless of the version they use.

Fencing Lessons can easily be adapted for use as a family devotional with the ***Fencing Lessons Family Devotional*** (available from Schoolhouse Publishing and other bookstores).

A note about answers: I would encourage you to allow your student easy access to the answer key. *Fencing Lessons* shouldn't be stressful to your student, only fun and challenging. If a puzzle isn't making sense or a riddle is too hard after looking up the scripture, allow them to look up the answer. He/she will still be familiarized with and learn God's Word.

A note about doctrine: ***Fencing Lessons*** focuses on basic tenets of Christian faith: the infallibility of the Word of our triune God, the effect of sin on all men through Adam and the need of all men to be saved, salvation by grace through faith in the atoning work of Jesus alone, the reality of a final judgment followed by heaven or hell, and so on. All lessons are brief enough to allow you, the parent or teacher, to flesh out the lessons to fit with your church's teaching on a particular doctrine.

I pray this study will impact your students' lives for His Kingdom and for His glory.

A Note to YOU, the Student

I won't make this long, because if you're like my own kids, I know you don't want to read this. More schoolwork! Please bear with me, though.

I was raised in an unchurched family who came to know the Lord miraculously when I was a young teen. The difference that His Lordship made in our lives was astounding. And as a result I know that I know that I know that God is real and alive and powerful. I know what a wretched sinner I was and the miracle of God's amazing grace. And I have decided to follow Jesus, no turning back.

My husband, on the other hand, was raised in the church. He doesn't remember ever not loving Jesus, though he committed his life to the Lord during his childhood. He struggles to fully comprehend the depths of his depravity and the heights of God's grace, because he's always been 'a good boy.' I don't know your story, but it's probably similar to one of these two. **Fencing Lessons** will help you to embrace the truth of who YOU are apart from Christ and who YOU are IN Christ.

Please approach this study prayerfully. Never open your bible without first beginning that inner dialogue with your heavenly Father. Pray. Your bible is FULL of power; explosive, creative, life-giving power. Cherish it.

Don't be put off by the 'obviousness' of many of the questions and answers. They may be obvious to you, but aren't obvious to young believers. If they are easy or obvious to you, continue to answer them and count it as warm-ups or exercises. Guard your heart, your attitude, and take the opportunity to pray for other students across this nation who are learning these concepts for the first time. Remember, every athlete needs to warm up before an event, and a Christian is no exception. Keep your negative attitudes in check and know that "man does not live by bread alone, but by every word that proceeds from the mouth of God" (Matthew 4:4, Deuteronomy 8:3). Enjoy the meal, even if it's something you've tasted many times before.

I want you to know that I am praying for you. It is not a mistake or 'just a parental order' that you are taking this course. Believe that God is in this, just as He is in every mundane moment of your life, if you are serving Him. I am praying that you will experience the full and glorious life that true discipleship will give you. I am praying for you.

~Susan Kemmerer

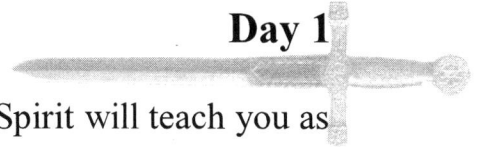

Begin with prayer. A suggestion: Ask that the Holy Spirit will teach you as you study God's Word.

Sword Drill

The first five books of the Bible are called *The Pentateuch* or *The Law*. List their titles in order:

G _ _ _ _ _ _, *E* _ _ _ _ _, *L* _ _ _ _ _ _ _ _, *N* _ _ _ _ _ _,

D _ _ _ _ _ _ _ _ _ _

Sword Play

The words, phrases, and their synonyms in the puzzle below are taken from Hebrews 4:12. They all describe God's Word. They will be horizontal, vertical, diagonal, forward, or backward in the puzzle.

Word Bank

active	dividing	powerful
alive	full of life	purpose-filled
breathing	hardworking	quick
busy	living	severing
cutting	piercing	sharp
discerning	pointy	

```
s  w  e  r  t  y  y  s  u  b  u  i  o  p  t  p
a  q  d  h  a  r  d  w  o  r  k  i  n  g  t  i
f  u  l  l  o  f  l  i  f  e  d  f  g  n  d  e
g  i  h  j  k  l  z  x  c  a  v  b  n  i  i  r
n  c  m  y  q  w  a  a  c  t  i  v  e  t  s  c
i  k  e  l  r  t  y  y  u  h  i  o  p  t  c  i
d  a  a  e  s  f  g  h  t  i  j  k  s  u  e  n
i  l  i  v  i  n  g  l  z  n  x  c  h  c  r  g
v  i  v  i  b  n  m  q  w  g  i  e  a  r  n  h
i  v  l  l  u  f  r  e  w  o  p  o  r  t  i  s
d  e  l  l  i  f  e  s  o  p  r  u  p  y  n  o
u  i  o  p  a  d  s  e  v  e  r  i  n  g  g  e
```

Fencing Practice

What is your most-valued possession – the one item that you enjoy taking with you everywhere you go?...Your own special "treasure" that you don't think you could do without? Let's put it this way: If you knew you were going to be taken and kept hostage for, oh…two months, and you were given the opportunity to take one thing with you, what would it be? Would *your Bible* come to mind?

For the next 13 lessons, we'll be studying about God's Word. As you study and learn what an amazing treasure you have in God's Word, you will find the Holy Spirit working in your heart so that your Bible will begin to move up your priority list to become one of your most-prized possessions.

In your Bible, read Hebrews 4:12. In the *first* sentence of that verse, God's Word is described by three adjectives (or describing words). What are those three adjectives? Write those three adjectives below, *one on the first line of each row*. Behind each of these adjectives, write 2 or 3 synonyms (or words that mean the same thing). Refer to your word search word bank on the previous page for ideas.

_____ : _____

_____ : _____

_____ : _____

Now, complete the sentences below by first writing in those same three original adjectives (above) listed in Hebrews 4:12 in the *first blank* of each sentence. Then complete each sentence by copying the two synonyms you chose for each adjective in the remaining two blanks.

1. My Bible, which is God's Word, is _____, _____, and _____.

2. My Bible, which is God's Word, is _____, _____, and _____.

3. My Bible, which is God's Word, is _____, _____, and _____.

Thrust and Parry

Because we are human, we are all-too-easily prone to allowing *things* to take the place of God and His Word in our lives. List one or two things that demand your attention to take first place in your life. It can be an item, a person, an ambition, a hobby, etc.

_____

_____

As you go through *Fencing Lessons* you will have many opportunities to know firsthand the piercing power of God's Word in your life and heart. You will experience the activity of God's powerful Word to strengthen you in your faith and your Christian walk. Becoming a fencing expert takes time and practice and a willingness to surrender to The Master and the surgical precision of His Mighty Word. Are you willing to take up the challenge?____

Memory work: Copy the first line of Hebrews 4:12, up to the word *sword*.

_____

_____

_____

_____

_____

Prayer suggestion: Ask God to illuminate (or show you) what has taken first place in your heart. Ask God to help you to make Him and His Word first in your life.

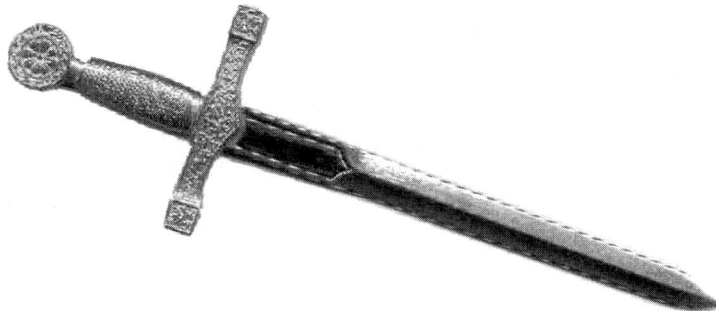

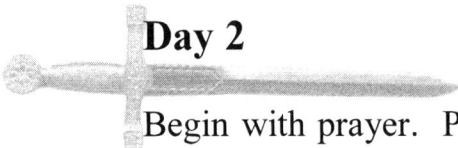

Day 2

Begin with prayer. Pray that your heart will be open to the work of God's Word.

Sword Drill

The Pentateuch or *The Law* was given by God to His people, most likely through **Moses**. List the titles of those 5 books in order:

G _ _ _ _ _ _, *E* _ _ _ _ _ _, *L* _ _ _ _ _ _ _ _ _, *N* _ _ _ _ _ _,
D _ _ _ _ _ _ _ _ _ _

Sword Play

The following words are taken from Isaiah 55:10-11. They describe the purpose of God's Word, and the promise of His Word's success. Use the words in the word bank below to complete the clues, then fill in the puzzle.

accomplish	heaven	purpose	sprout
bread	mouth	seed	water

Across
3. To begin growing: _____
4. To achieve: _____
7. God's home: _____
8. A food: _____

Down
1. What words come out of: _____
2. A plan or reason for: _____
5. What a plant grows from: _____
6. What we drink: _____

Fencing Practice

Yesterday you read how God's Word is alive, quick, powerful, active, and sharp. His Word is always busy doing *something*. Think of things that you are busy doing: school, chores, sports, music, playing, socializing. Tomorrow we will look again at Hebrews 4:12 to see specifically what His Word is actively doing *in you*. Today, though, we want to step back and look at a bigger picture.

In your Bible, read Isaiah 55:10-11. Isaiah compares *the duty* or purpose of God's Word to rain or snow. He lists the many things that rain does once it falls. List four of those things mentioned in this passage:

- _____
- _____
- _____
- _____

In the same way, God's Word works in us: it waters us, causes fruit to grow in our lives, and feeds us. The end of verse 11 gives a promise about God's Word. What is that promise? _____

_____

_____

Thrust and Parry

Look again at the list of things you wrote that describe the purpose of rain. Since God's Word serves a similar purpose in our lives, use the same words and phrases from the list above to complete the sentences below. You may need to rephrase a little. The first one is done for you. And remember, God promises His Word *will succeed* in your life…

God's Word will *water me* _____.
God's Word will _____.
God's Word will _____.
God's Word will _____.

Your memory verse is Hebrews 4:12. Like yesterday, write the first line in that verse, up to the word *sword*. _____

_____

_____

_____

Prayer suggestion: Pray that God will cause you to grow and produce fruit for Him.

Day 3

Begin with prayer. A suggestion: pray that God's Word will feed and water you today.

Sword Drill

The Law, also called the _____ forms the first five books of the Bible. List the titles of those 5 books in order:

G _ _ _ _ _ _, *E* _ _ _ _ _, *L* _ _ _ _ _ _ _ _, *N* _ _ _ _ _ _,
D _ _ _ _ _ _ _ _ _

Sword Play

The answers to the following riddles are words found in Hebrews 4:12. They may be used differently in the riddles than they are used in the verse, so use your imagination.

I am emotional. The Bible says I am easily deceived. Apart from Christ I am hard and full of sin. What am I?

_____

I make movement possible. I turn like a hinge. I am the connection between two immovable parts. What am I?

_____

I am the ***description*** of many things: a mind full of knowledge and wisdom, someone's tongue when he or she frequently uses harsh words, or a surgeon's scalpel. I am a word that describes all of these. What am I?

_____

I originate in the heart. I am a powerful tool – to build up or tear down. I am a mighty weapon – for good or evil. I have emotional "taste" – salty, sweet, bitter. I can be written or spoken. What am I?

_____

Fencing Practice

Turn in your Bible to Hebrews 4:12. You may want to underline this verse in your Bible. We learned in the last lesson that God's Word (your Bible) waters us, feeds us, causes us to sprout and grow. But how does it do that? The second part of this verse uses a word that describes *how* God's Word accomplishes His purposes in us. There is a word in Hebrews 4:12 that means *to penetrate* or *to stab into*. What is that word? _____

God's Word cuts right through the surface of our lives to the very center of our existence. List the six words in Hebrews 4:12 that describe what's below the surface of your life – the place where God's Word is working in you:

- _____
- _____
- _____
- _____
- _____
- _____

Thrust and Parry

It may seem a little weird to realize that God's living, active Word is right now working in you – working on your thought life and even *discerning* (perceiving, figuring out) what your heart *intends* to do *before* you do it! Think about your day today and check off your *thoughts* on the following:

	Yes	No
I intend to do my schoolwork.	_____	_____
I intend to do it well.	_____	_____
I intend to do my chores today.	_____	_____
I intend to do them cheerfully.	_____	_____
I intend to get along with my siblings today.	_____	_____
I intend to be kind and encouraging toward them.	_____	_____
I intend to honor and obey my parents today.	_____	_____
I intend to obey them cheerfully.	_____	_____

Look at your list. You may *think* you are going to try to do well today, but the *intentions* of our hearts are often different, so by the end of the day we find we've been lazy with our work, grumbling about chores, and mean to our siblings! But, even though *we* might not know all of this ahead of time, God does! *He knows the intentions of our hearts* and *still* loves us. His Word is busily working in your heart to change you! Fill in the blank with an encouraging word or phrase from Hebrews 4:12.

God's Word is _____.

Memory verse: Copy the first line of Hebrews 4:12 (up to the word *sword*) below:

_____
_____
_____
_____
_____

Prayer suggestion: Thank God that He loves you even though He knows all the thoughts and intentions of your heart. He is so good to us!

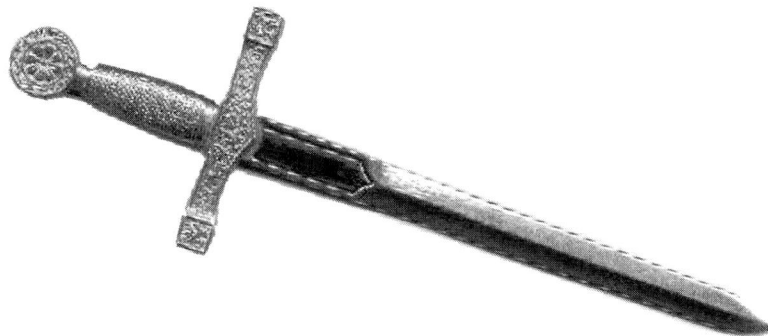

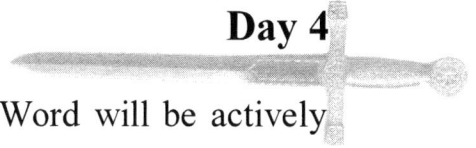

Begin with prayer. A suggestion: pray that God's Word will be actively working inside the deepest parts of you.

Sword Drill

The Law, also called the _____ forms the first five books of the Bible. List the titles of those 5 books in order:
G _ _ _ _ _ _, *E* _ _ _ _ _ _, *L* _ _ _ _ _ _ _ _, *N* _ _ _ _ _ _,
D _ _ _ _ _ _ _ _ _ _

Sword Play

The following multiple choice quiz is based on Matthew 4:1-4. Circle the correct answers.

1. Jesus was led to _____ (verse 1):

the wilderness,
Jerusalem,
His parents' house,
the temple

2. Who led him there? _____ (verse 1):

His disciples,
Joseph,
the Spirit,
the devil

3. Why was he led there? _____ (verse 1):

to preach,
to pray,
to be tempted,
to fight

4. How long was He there? _____ (verse 2):

40 days,
2 weeks,
Sunday (the Sabbath),
while He was growing up

5. According to the verse, what was apparently on the ground there? _____(verse 3):

sand,
scorpions,
stones,
cactus

6. He was told to turn these into _____. (verse 3):

weapons,
tax money,
angels,
bread

7. Jesus answered that man lives by _____. (verse 4):

eating healthy,
God's Word,
exercise,
spiritual warfare

Fencing Practice

If you haven't already done so, turn to Matthew 4:1-4 and read it. This is the beginning of the story of Jesus' temptation. Notice that when Jesus answers Satan, he *begins* his answer with a short phrase. What is that phrase? _____ Oh-h-h! *Where* is it written? In the *Pentateuch*! Jesus quotes Deuteronomy 8:3 to the devil!

Do you remember what Satan told Jesus to do?...He told Jesus to turn _____ into _____. Now that doesn't sound too bad to me! What's wrong with making a little bread when you're hungry? But Jesus understood something. Sure, it's not wrong to eat bread when you are hungry. But, Satan was trying to get to His heart...make Him *not* trust God to provide. I can just picture Satan whispering to Jesus' heart, "You poor man. So-o-o hungry. I thought your Father *loved* you and was going to take care of you. But you're so-o-o hungry. What kind of Father starves his child? Why don't you just turn a few of these stones into some nice, soft, crusty bread. Mm-m-m! You'll feel so much better if you take care of yourself."

Here's the important part of the lesson. Jesus knew His own heart, and He knew God's Word. He answered that "man doesn't live by bread alone." Bread only feeds your body – and someday your body will die. But, there's a more important part of you that needs to be fed. If you are a believer, it's the part of you that will live forever. And, according to Jesus (and the Pentateuch), what feeds *that* part of you? _____

Thrust and Parry

Think of all the food you've eaten today – even snacks. List all the food you can remember that you ate just today:

_____	_____	_____
_____	_____	_____
_____	_____	_____
_____	_____	_____
_____		

Now, list all the "spiritual food" you've fed yourself today. This would include things like scripture that you read, worship songs you sang or listened to, prayers you participated in (especially if they contained God's Word), or sermons you listened to:

_____	_____	_____
_____	_____	_____
_____	_____	_____
_____	_____	_____
_____	_____	_____

Because we are human, we easily forget that there's more than just a body that needs feeding. Do you feel a little embarrassed by your lists? If you do, that's a *good* thing. That is evidence of the Holy Spirit working in your heart to grow a love of God's Word in you!

Memory verse: Again, copy the first line of Hebrews 4:12 (up to the word *sword*) below:

_____
_____
_____
_____
_____

Prayer suggestion: Pray that God will help you to love His Word so much that you'll want to feed on it every day.

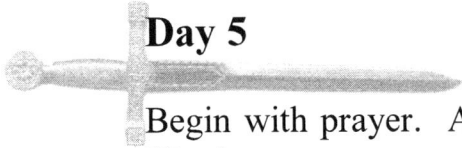

Day 5

Begin with prayer. A suggestion: Pray that you will be hungry for God's Word.

Sword Drill

List the first five books of the Bible (which form the _____) in order: *G* _ _ _ _ _ _, *E* _ _ _ _ _, *L* _ _ _ _ _ _ _ _ _, *N* _ _ _ _ _ _, *D* _ _ _ _ _ _ _ _ _ _

Sword Play

The words and phrases in the word search puzzle below are taken from Psalm 19:7-11. They all describe God's Word. The words could be vertical, horizontal, diagonal, backward, or forward.

Word Bank

better than gold	perfect	rules	testimony
clean	precepts	statutes	true
commandment	pure	sure	
law	right	sweeter than honey	

```
d  k  f  h  b  c  x  d  r  u  o  l  q  n  x  y
l  l  k  y  f  s  t  a  t  u  t  e  s  a  e  z
l  t  e  s  t  i  m  o  n  y  r  t  s  n  k  r
a  u  i  p  p  v  f  d  x  d  h  k  o  s  r  i
w  s  z  e  r  e  e  t  n  c  k  h  g  t  s  g
r  p  e  r  f  e  c  t  a  l  n  d  y  e  c  h
e  d  v  u  k  p  c  x  m  a  c  e  l  p  o  t
t  f  s  s  l  b  b  e  h  t  y  u  x  s  m  n
i  f  g  h  o  v  d  t  p  u  r  e  l  y  m  r
t  x  z  v  l  r  r  w  q  t  m  d  h  k  a  s
p  r  b  w  t  e  s  o  l  k  s  v  y  a  n  i
i  b  e  t  t  e  r  t  h  a  n  g  o  l  d  a
s  z  h  e  y  w  a  a  d  t  r  s  p  n  m  w
f  g  e  x  y  c  l  e  a  n  o  i  e  d  e  j
r  w  j  v  s  a  i  i  g  c  h  u  y  q  n  c
s  y  s  o  e  t  h  g  b  f  d  e  u  r  t  m
```

Fencing Practice

Turn in your bible to Psalm 19:7-11. Today we want to especially look at *verses 7-9*. There are *at least* five different words that mean the same thing as "God's Word" in this passage. List these five **synonyms** here, in order, from the passage:

_____

_____

_____

_____

_____

There are also *at least* five different **adjectives** that *describe* those five synonyms listed above. List these **adjectives** here, in order, from the passage:

_____

_____

_____

_____

_____

There are also four *purposes* listed here – four things that God's Word accomplishes in us. List these four **verbs** here, in order, from the passage:

_____

_____

_____

_____

Thrust and Parry

You are going to paraphrase Psalm 19:7-9. In the sentences below, copy the lists you just made (above) based on Psalm 19:7-9. In the first blank, write the first **synonym** from your list. In the second blank, write the correct **adjective**. In the third blank, write the correct **verb** from your list. You may need to change the form of the verb so that it makes sense in the sentence: **reviving** will become **revives**, etc. *The first one, taken from verse 9, is already done for you as an example:*

1. My Bible, which contains God's ____rules____, is _____true_____. It ___is righteous___. (vs 9)

2. My Bible, which is God's _____, is _____.
It _____ me. (vs 7)

3. My Bible, which is God's _____, is _____.
It makes me _____. (vs 7)

4. My Bible, which is God's _____, is _____.
It _____ my heart. (vs 8)

5. My Bible, which is God's _____, is _____.
It _____ my eyes. (vs 8)

Memory verse: Again, copy the first line of Hebrews 4:12 (up to the word *sword*) below:

_____

_____

_____

_____

_____

Prayer suggestion: Pray that God's Word will be sweeter than honey and better than gold to you.

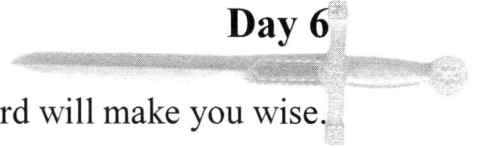

Begin with prayer. A suggestion: Pray that God's Word will make you wise.

Sword Drill

The second five books of the bible tell the history of ancient Israel. Listed in order, they are: *J* _ _ _ _ _, *J* _ _ _ _ _, *R* _ _ _, *1 & 2 S* _ _ _ _ _.

Sword Play

The answers to this true-false quiz are all taken from Psalm 19:7-11. Circle either T (for true) or F (for false).

1. God's law revives my appetite.   T or F

2. God's testimony makes simple, childish people like me wise.   T or F

3. God's precepts make my heart rejoice.   T or F

4. God's commandments are like a light to the eyes.   T or F

5. God's rules (statutes) are irritating and a pain in the neck.   T or F

6. I should desire God's Word more than I desire $1,000,000.   T or F

7. God's Word should be sweeter to me than a bag full of my
   favorite candy.   T or F

8. God's Word is like an alarm system, warning me of danger.   T or F

9. There isn't much reward in keeping God's Word, but at least
   you know God is pleased.   T or F

Fencing Practice

Read Psalm 19:10-11. Verse 10 describes just how much we should love God's Word. We should desire God's Word more than _____. When David wrote this psalm, he wanted to make sure we understood just how precious God's Word is. He didn't just stop with the word *gold*, though gold is precious enough. He said God's Word should be desired more than what *kind* of gold? _____ gold. Now, David didn't even stop there!

He *really* wanted to make sure we understood. Did he say we should desire God's Word more than *a piece* of fine gold? No! We should desire God's Word more than _____ find gold!

David, being the smart guy that he was, really wanted to make sure we "got it." So, he said God's Word is sweet….Not just sweet, but sweeter than _____...Not just sweeter than honey, but sweeter than honey from the _____.

Don't you think that if we *really* believed David's statement, then God's Word by itself would be treasure enough? If you owned something that was sweeter than honey and more precious than lots of fine gold, wouldn't you be content with that? But God, through David, promises even more! *Not only* is God's Word sweeter than honey and more precious than fine gold, but if we *keep* it (*do what it says*), we get a (vs 11) _____ _____.

Thrust and Parry

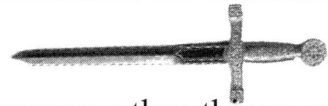

Because we're human it's easy for us to treasure other things more highly than we treasure God's Word. As a teenager, one of my favorite hobbies was reading novels. When I learned that I should desire God's Word more than any earthly treasure, and it should be sweeter than any exciting adventure story, I decided to train myself to treasure His Word. I made a resolution that *before* I picked up a novel to read, I would *first* spend at least a little time reading my Bible. God used this resolution to grow my love for His Word.

Think of something you enjoy doing every day and write it here: _____. Could you practice treasuring God's Word by reading (or listening to on your device) a verse or chapter from your Bible *before* you engage in that activity – even if it's several times a day?

Memory verse: Copy the rest of Hebrews 4:12 here (starting **after** the word *sword*): _____

_____

_____

_____

_____

Prayer suggestion: Pray that you will love God's Word more every day.

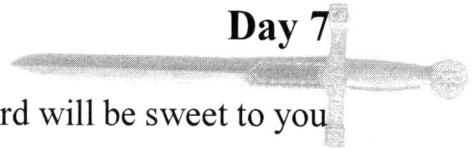

Begin with prayer. A suggestion: Pray that God's Word will be sweet to you today as you study.

Sword Drill

The book of *Joshua* tells the story of the children of Israel entering the Promised Land under the leadership of Joshua. List the second five books of the Bible in order: *J* _ _ _ _ _, *J* _ _ _ _ _, *R* _ _ _, *1 & 2 S* _ _ _ _ _.

Sword Play

The words in the in the word box below are all different types of lights. Use them to fill in the clues below, then use the clues to complete the puzzle on the next page.

candle	lamp	oil lamp	sun
fire	moon	searchlight	torch
flashlight	nightlight	streetlight	

Across:
5. Lights the night sky: _____
6. Fill with fossil fuel, then light the wick: _____
9. Brightens roads: _____
10. Lightens a birthday cake: _____
11. A dim light in a dark room, for sleeping: _____

Down:
1. This lightens a room: _____
2. Lightens the daytime sky: _____
3. Powerful light for seeking something: _____
4. A handheld light: _____
7. A primitive light made by dipping a rag-wrapped pole in fuel: _____
8. Fueled with wood when camping: _____

Fencing Practice

Just think of all the wonderful things you've already discovered about God's Word! Your Bible, God's Word, is living, active, powerful, sharp, watering you, feeding you, growing you, changing you, reviving you, making you wise, making you rejoice, is better than gold, sweeter than honey, warning you, and rewarding you! Wow! What an incredible treasure! But wait – there's more!

Turn in your Bible to Psalm 119. If you take a moment to page through all of Psalm 119, you'll notice a few things. First, how many verses are there in Psalm 119? _____ This Psalm is the longest chapter in your Bible. Did you notice how this Psalm is broken down into sections, each headed with an odd word? Those headings are actually letters of the Hebrew alphabet. What is the first heading before verse 1? _____ This is the Hebrew letter A. If you could read the *Aleph* section of Psalm 119 in the original Hebrew language, you would find that each line in that section begins with an A. Each line in the *Beth* section begins with a B in Hebrew. However, once the psalm was translated into English, it was no longer an *acrostic* poem.

If you take the time to read this Psalm, you'll find that the entire thing is about…do you want to take a guess what Psalm 119 is about? _____ _____ If you guessed "God's Word," you're correct!

Look at Psalm 119:105. What is the Hebrew letter heading that section? _____. And to what two things does this verse compare God's Word? A _____ and a _____.

Thrust and Parry

Life would be very difficult without light. We have lights for every occasion. There are special lights for helping you watch your step in a dark auditorium, to help you see your gas gauge when traveling in a car at night, to reflect off your bike when you ride it at night. Dentists have special lights to see into your mouth. Mechanics have special lights to look under the hood. Teachers use laser lights to point to important information on the board.

Right where you are sitting, count how many different lights you see: _____ God has given us the most important light of all. It lightens our path as we walk through life on our journey to heaven. It shines in front of our feet so every little rock and stumbling block can be avoided. What is this amazing light, according to Psalm 119:105? _____

Memory work: Copy the rest of Hebrews 4:12 (starting after the word *sword*): _____

_____

_____

_____

_____

Prayer suggestion: Pray that God will help you to love God's Word so that its light will always help you.

Day 8

Begin with prayer. Pray that God's Word lighten your path today.

Sword Drill

After _ _ _ _ _ _ led God's people into the Promised Land, they were ruled by *Judges* like Gideon, Deborah, and Samson. List the second five books of the Bible: *J _ _ _ _ _, J _ _ _ _ _, R _ _ _, 1 & 2 S _ _ _ _ _.*

Sword Play

Circle the correct answer from Psalm 119:9-16 for each question below.

1. How can a young man (or woman) keep his way pure? (verse 9)
   -by listening to the pastor
   -by not watching TV
   -by living according to God's Word
   -by being homeschooled

2. How do you seek God? (verse 10)
   -on the condition that He does what I want
   -with your whole heart
   -by going to church on Sunday
   -when you are in trouble

3. What prayer does the Psalmist pray in verse 10?
   -that God would keep him from wandering from His commands
   -that God will give him his heart's desires
   -that God will make him rich and wise
   -that God will heal him

4. Where does the psalmist store God's Word? (verse 11)
   -in a scroll on a shelf where he can see it
   -in his heart
   -in his head
   -in a museum

5. Why does the psalmist store God's Word? (verse 11)
   -so it doesn't get lost
   -so it will gain interest and make him rich
   -so that he'll be wiser than his friends
   -so that he won't sin against God

6. The psalmist delights in God's Word as much as he delights in… (vs 14)
   -all riches
   -a delicious banquet
   -his own wisdom
   -being powerful and popular

7. Where will the psalmist fix his eyes? (verse 15)
   -on his own heart
   -on the skies
   -on God's ways
   -on holy men

8. What will the psalmist meditate on? (verse 15)
   -God's precepts
   -Sunday's sermon
   -the gossip from town
   -how his brother offended him

9. What will the psalmist delight in? (verse 16)
   -lovely ladies
   -a bountiful meal
   -God's statutes
   -fellowship with the saints

10. What won't the psalmist forget? (verse 16)
    -to pray each morning
    -to tithe
    -to go to church on Sunday
    -God's Word

Fencing Practice

When you look at the adults around you, and you see the areas in their lives where they struggle, you need to remember that they were once young like you. Their lives were simple. They went to school and played sports and hung out with their friends. So, why do they now struggle with things like alcoholism, anger, cigarette addiction, grouchiness, negativity, laziness, spending problems, and so on? Did they intend to be like this when they grew up? Of course not! But that's the nature of sin. It catches you and entangles you when you don't expect it. Here's the question: how can you make sure that you won't have those same struggles when you grow up? How can a young person keep his or her way pure? Psalm 119:9 tells you the answer:

Here is one more tremendous blessing that you reap from your Bible, which is your treasure. If you *live* it now, you will keep your way pure! Wouldn't it be wonderful if scientists could invent a vaccine that would keep you from the disease of sin? After all, sin is the biggest problem in life! Well, God did give us a sin immunization of sorts. It's your Bible. Now, owning a Bible and letting it sit on your shelf won't get you anywhere. Hiding it or *storing* it in your heart and *living* by it, though, gives you an amazing gift. It sort of immunizes you from sin! Why did the psalmist hide God's Word in his heart? (verse 11) _____

_____

Of course our only true salvation from sin is faith in the saving power of Jesus Christ, but once you are saved (given your life over to God and repented of your sin), you can experience victory over sin struggles through the power of God's Word!

Thrust and Parry

The man who wrote this psalm was very self-perceptive. He understood the deceitfulness of his own heart. Even though he had a tremendous love for God and was obviously a believer, he realized how easily he could slip from truth. What did he pray in the second part of verse 10?

_____

_____

Why do you think he prayed that? _____

_____

Learn a lesson from this psalmist and allow God to show you the weakness of your own heart. Don't make the mistake of believing that you'll never slip! Pray, like the psalmist, that you won't wander from God's commands.

Memory work: Copy the rest of Hebrews 4:12 (starting after the word *sword*):

_____

_____

_____

_____

_____

Prayer suggestion: Pray that God will help you to keep His commandments today.

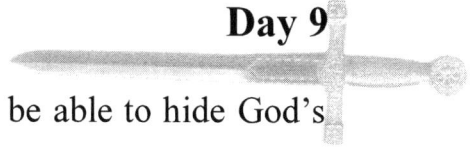

Begin with prayer. A suggestion: Pray that you will be able to hide God's Word in your heart so that you won't sin against Him.

Sword Drill

After the *J* _ _ _ _ _ (like Gideon and Samson) ruled Israel, God allowed Israel to have a king. The book of *Ruth* tells the story of the Moabite great-grandmother of King David. List the second five books of the Bible in order: *J* _ _ _ _ _, *J* _ _ _ _ _, *R* _ _ _, *1 & 2 S* _ _ _ _ _.

Sword Play

The words that answer the following riddles are all found in 2 Timothy 3:14-17. *Each answer consists of a single word.*

When you are in me, you can't wait to grow out of me. When you are out of me, you wish you could be back in me again. In me, you are considered immature and foolish. In me is the perfect time to memorize God's Word and to believe. What am I? (vs 15)

_____

I am an *adjective* (a describing word). I have been used to describe philosophers and presidents and owls. So you think you have *knowledge*? What good is that if you don't know how to apply that knowledge in the right time in the right place? If you can be this, you are me. What am I? (vs 15)

_____

I am the breath of God, the mind of God, the heart of God. I am a treasure, because when you truly have me, you have God. I am a light leading you to God. I feed you and water you. I have creative force. What am I? (vs 16)

_____

I am a word of action. I am fitted, rigged, and uniformed with appropriate gear. I describe someone who is ready with everything they need to do the job. I am prepared. What am I? (vs 17)

_____

Fencing Practice

If you haven't already done so, turn in your Bible to 2 Timothy 3:14-17 and read it. Paul has written this letter to his young friend, Timothy. Timothy was an amazing young man, full of wisdom and faith. The question is, how did he get to be so full of wisdom and faith at such a young age? Verse 15 tells us one reason: _____.
Did you notice that the Scriptures (God's Word, your Bible) makes you wise enough to lead you in a certain direction. Toward what does God's Word lead you according to verse 15? _____.
Paul tells Timothy why Scriptures make you wise enough to lead you to salvation. It is because they are _____ by God (vs 16).

Paul also says that Scripture is *profitable*. This means that it gives you more than what you started with. It gives you more than you invest in it. In four ways God's Word gives you more than you invest and leaves you with more than you started. In what four ways is Scripture profitable according to 2 Timothy 3:16?

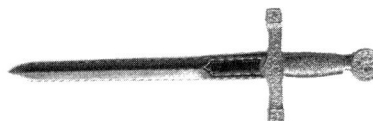

_____

_____

_____

_____

Thrust and Parry

It won't do you much good unless you know what those four words mean. Draw a line from the word in the first column to its definition in the second column to its synonym (a word meaning the same thing) in the third column.

Teaching	-a scolding for a fault	-improvement
Reproof	-equipping to fulfill a job	-reprimand
Correction	-imparting knowledge or skill	-preparation
Training	-making something right or better	-instructing

Complete the following sentences using the words and synonyms listed on the previous page in the ***Thrust and Parry*** exercise. Fill in the first blank below with *a form* of one of the words in the first list. Fill in the second blank *with its synonym* from the third list (from 2 Timothy 3:16), so that each sentence makes sense. The first one is done for you.

1. God's Word, my Bible, _____*teaches*_____ me and _____*instructs*_____ me, imparting knowledge and skill to me.

2. God's Word, my Bible, _____ me and _____ me, scolding me for my faults.

3. God's Word, my Bible, _____ me and _____ me, making me right and making me better.

4. God's Word, my Bible, _____ me and _____ me, equipping me to fulfill my purpose.

Memory work: Copy the rest of Hebrews 4:12 (starting after the word *sword*):

_____

_____

_____

_____

_____

Prayer suggestion: Pray that when God's Word "scolds" you, you will allow your heart to be corrected rather than hardening your heart.

Day 10

Begin with prayer. A suggestion: Pray that God's Word will teach and train you today as you study.

Sword Drill

The book of *R* _ _ _ tells of David's great-grandmother and also of our Kinsman Redeemer. *1* and *2 Samuel* tell the story of Kings Saul and David and the prophet, Samuel. List the second five books of the Bible in order: *J* _ _ _ _ _, *J* _ _ _ _ _, *R* _ _ _, *1 & 2 S* _ _ _ _ _.

Sword Play

The phrases in the word search puzzle below are taken from Proverbs 4:5-9. They all describe warnings of ignoring wisdom and promises of getting wisdom (God's Word, your Bible). The phrases can be vertical, horizontal, diagonal, backward, or forward.

Phrase Bank

crown you	embrace her	honor you
do not forget	exalt you	keep you
do not forsake	get insight	love her
do not turn away	get wisdom	prize her
	guard you	

```
q  d  h  i  k  y  t  r  e  w  s  f  g  j  n  v  d
l  m  o  p  e  m  b  r  a  c  e  h  e  r  r  g  b
z  c  n  n  m  u  y  r  d  c  t  s  w  q  p  l  u
t  g  o  k  o  f  g  u  a  r  d  y  o  u  l  k  g
l  o  r  l  k  t  b  f  s  m  t  p  w  a  z  p  e
i  u  y  d  d  c  f  l  m  j  u  o  y  p  e  e  k
g  p  o  r  t  c  v  o  p  c  h  f  r  p  m  x  a
e  y  u  b  v  e  d  s  r  p  o  i  u  y  t  a  s
t  b  v  e  o  s  r  o  d  g  l  t  z  c  k  l  r
i  n  n  g  i  z  w  h  g  r  e  j  b  y  t  t  o
n  h  h  w  a  n  p  i  v  j  j  t  s  w  d  y  f
s  g  t  i  y  b  b  l  o  v  e  h  e  r  s  o  t
i  e  c  o  k  h  r  w  a  k  g  v  b  e  w  u  o
g  x  u  p  r  i  z  e  h  e  r  g  e  i  l  e  n
h  c  e  q  l  b  y  x  i  e  d  p  g  a  r  m  o
t  k  y  k  y  a  w  a  n  r  u  t  t  o  n  o  d
```

Fencing Practice

If you picked up a sword, it would not automatically make you a mighty warrior. There would be training involved, and conditions to meet. If you wanted to use that sword as a mighty warrior would, you would need to exercise with it, train with it, learn about your enemy and his strategy, sharpen it and keep it protected. If you did these things, it would protect you, guard you, keep you safe, and essentially become an extension of you. Proverbs 4:5-9 tells us the same thing about the Sword of the Spirit, God's Word. Simply owning a Bible and reading a verse in Sunday School doesn't make you a sword-wielding warrior. There are conditions you'll need to meet to become a warrior of wisdom. There are also promises that are yours if you meet the conditions.

Verses 5-6 list at least four conditions you'll have to meet in order to become a wisdom warrior. What are these four conditions? (Hint: Three of them begin with "Do not...")

_____

_____

_____

_____

What are the two promises that are yours if you meet these conditions? (Hint: See verse 6.)

_____

_____

There are two more conditions to becoming a wisdom warrior hidden in verse 8. What are these two conditions:

_____

_____

What are the four promises that are yours if you meet these two conditions? (Verses 8-9)

_____

_____

_____

_____

After reading verse 9, you might think, "Whatever! I'm not wearing any garland of flowers!" However, think about this for a moment. If you were to walk into a palace, how would you know who the king was? Obviously he's the guy wearing the crown, right? How can you tell who the princess is, or the star athlete? They're the ones wearing the garland, right?

And that's what wisdom does for you. If you become a wisdom warrior, when you walk into a situation, people will recognize immediately that you are someone to be trusted, someone you can depend on – because wisdom sits on a person like a crown or a garland. Cool, eh?

Thrust and Parry

What does a policeman wear that shows he's protecting the law? _____ What does a nurse wear to show she's protecting your health? _____ What does a soldier wear to show he's protecting your freedom? _____ What does a king wear to show he's in authority over many people? _____ What does an Olympic champion wear to show he's the best athlete? _____ What does a fireman wear to show he's protecting your safety? _____ What can you "wear," according to today's scripture, to show you are a young man or woman of God? _____

Memory work: Copy the rest of Hebrews 4:12 (starting after the word *sword*):

_____

_____

_____

_____

_____

Prayer suggestion: Pray that you will become a young man or woman of wisdom by keeping, loving, and prizing God's Word, your Bible.

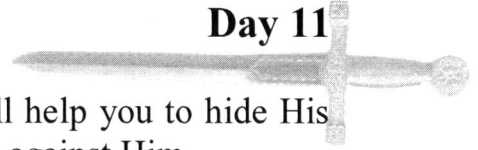

Begin with prayer. A suggestion: Pray that God will help you to hide His Word in your heart as you study, so that you won't sin against Him.

Sword Drill

The next four books of the Bible tell more of the history of the nations of Judah and Israel. List these four books of the Bible in order:

1 K _ _ _ _, 2 K _ _ _ _, 1 C _ _ _ _ _ _ _ _ _, 2 C _ _ _ _ _ _ _ _ _.

Sword Play

The answers to the following true-false quiz are found in Proverbs 8:10-11 and Proverb 8:32-36. Circle T for true and F for false.

1. Given the choice, you should choose to read your Bible over getting silver.

T   or   F

2. Though knowledge is important, you should always choose gold and silver first, because you can use it to help poor people.   T   or   F

3. With your Birthday money, you can buy either a new Bible (since yours got lost) or a new smartphone. Since you'll be learning enough Bible in this Bible study, you should choose the smartphone.   T   or   F

4. Four wheelers, snow mobiles, designer clothes and jewelry, a fast car, a new game system, to get married some day and have kids – desiring and enjoying these is what life is all about.   T   or   F

5. Jet skis, great vacations, Ipods, computer systems, stereo equipment, cell phones, hanging out, a high-paying job and a nice house – all great stuff, but as great as these are, I should *first* strive to gain wisdom.   T   or   F

6. Guys who keep God's ways tend to be cursed with a very dull and boring life. It's not worth it. Have fun while you're young.   T   or   F

7. One way to be wise is to listen to instruction.   T   or   F

8. Listening to wisdom is one way to be blessed.   T   or   F

9. Watching, waiting, and listening are boring activities, and you'll faint from boredom in this life if that's all you do.   T   or   F

10. You discover life by doing crazy and daring things, and taking chances. God smiles on the person who parties hard and has a good time.   T   or   F

11. I want to find life. I want God's favor. I better find wisdom! T   or   F

12. If you want to ruin your life, just neglect getting wisdom.   T   or   F

13. Hating education, knowledge and wisdom is the same as loving your own death.   T   or   F

Fencing Practice

I imagine there are many wonderful things you desire in this life. Many teens desire to someday be married, have children, have a successful career, and earn enough money to enjoy things in this life. Perhaps you want to have a nice car, cool electronics, good friends, fun vacations, stylish clothing, a great education, and a pleasant home. These are all good things. There is nothing wrong with desiring them. Some of them, like marriage, children, and friends, are particularly blessed by God. As pleasant and good as these things are, Proverbs 8:10-11 tells us there are three things that are even more desirable than these. What are those three things?

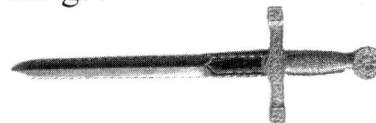

_____

_____

_____

Take a look at that short, 3-word list you just made. Hmmm. When you compare those three things with the things you desire – how do they rate? Would you rather have those things you desire, or would you prefer wisdom? If you are like the typical young person, it's probably hard to imagine that reading your Bible is better than getting that new dirt bike or wardrobe. But that's what God says! This is one of those things that you need to accept and believe by faith. You may not exactly feel like wisdom is better than riches, but you can, by faith, know that it's true. You can begin to make choices in your life that, by faith, will lead to wisdom.

Don't be surprised if you find this difficult. Our flesh certainly doesn't want to seek wisdom. No, our flesh prefers to be entertained, and pampered, and beautified, and excited. Seeking wisdom is hard work. But, believe it by faith, it is the best thing you can do.

Thrust and Parry

Make a list of ten things you desire. They might be things you want now and things you want in the future. Write those ten things below.

_____	_____
_____	_____
_____	_____
_____	_____
_____	_____

Now, rewrite the list of three things listed in Proverbs 8:10-11 that are so precious:

_____

_____

_____

The writer of Proverbs 8 really wanted to make sure you were shocked with how valuable wisdom and knowledge are. He said that wisdom, instruction, and knowledge are so valuable, that if you took all those wonderful things that you desire (see your list of ten things above), and compare them to the second list from Proverbs 8:10-11, the second list is the greatest treasure. This is one reason why your parents are so concerned about taking you to church, making sure you do well in school, and encouraging you to spend time in personal devotions. They are helping you to find the priceless treasures of wisdom, knowledge, and instruction.

Complete the sentences below by listing those same three words listed in Proverbs 8:10-11 in the *first* blank of each sentence, and filling in the 3 things you desire most (from your list of ten) in the *second* blank of each sentence.

I should desire _____ more than I desire _____.
I should desire _____ more than I desire _____.
I should desire _____ more than I desire _____.

Memory work: Copy Psalm 119:105 below: _____

_____

_____

_____

Prayer suggestion: Pray that God will help you to desire wisdom and knowledge more than you desire anything else.

Day 12

Begin with prayer. A suggestion: Pray that God's Word will teach and train you today as you study.

Sword Drill

The next four books of the Bible tell more of the history of the nations of Judah and Israel. *1 & 2 Kings* tell about the kings of those nations. List those 4 books: *1 K _ _ _ _*, *2 K _ _ _ _*, *1 C _ _ _ _ _ _ _ _ _*, *2 C _ _ _ _ _ _ _ _ _*.

Sword Play

The following words are all taken from Proverbs 8:32-36. Use the words from the word bank to complete the clues, then fill in the puzzle with the same words.

death	instruction	neglect
favor	life	waiting
hate	listen	watching
injures		

Across

3. When you find the Lord, you obtain _____
4. Hear _____; don't neglect this.
6. You are blessed if you are _____by His doors.
8. If you hate God, you love _____.
9. If you find God, you find _____.

Down

1. You are blessed if you are _____daily at His gates.
2. "And now, O sons, _____ to me…"
4. The one who fails to find God _____ himself.
5. Hear instruction; don't _____ it.
7. All who _____ God, love death.

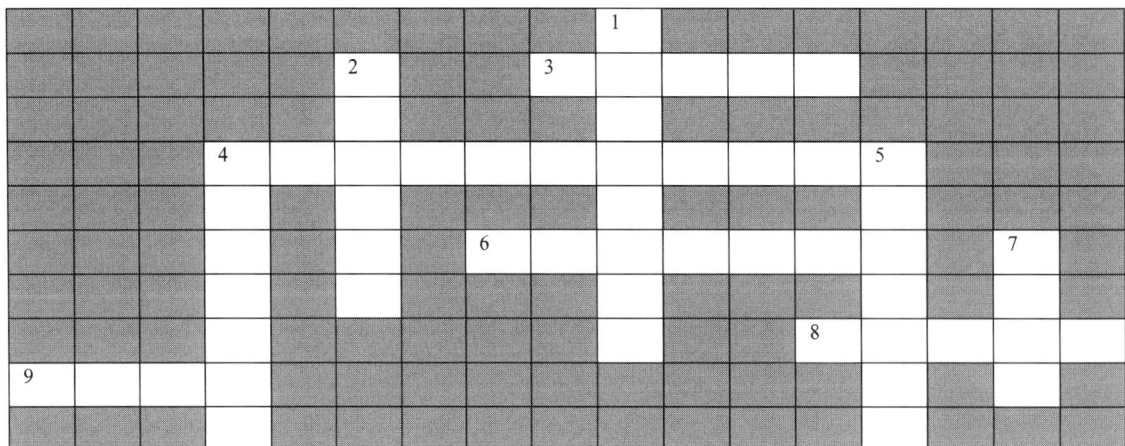

Fencing Practice

If you haven't already done so, turn in your Bible to Proverbs 8:32-36. Take a moment to read through it now....You might have noticed that the first part of the passage gives you a command, the second part gives you a promise, and the last part gives you a warning.

What are you commanded to do in the first part (vss. 32-33)? _____ What is the promise given in the second part (vss. 34-35)? _____ What is the warning given in the last part (vs.36)? _____
_____

I want you to notice something else very important in this passage. Verses 32-34 (where you are commanded to listen, hear, and be wise) are directly tied to the promise. If you listen, hear, and obey, you are blessed. But – and this is really wonderful! – listening, hearing, and doing God's Word are also the same as finding God Himself! So, how do you find God according to this passage? _____
_____.

Listening to and doing God's Word not only causes you to discover God, but is also evidence of His favor! When someone *favors* you, it means you are their *favorite*; they enjoy your company and delight in you. How would you like to have Him delight in you and favor you? (You can read this in verse 35.) So, how do you obtain favor? _____ The opposite is also true. Failing to find God is equated to injuring yourself. Failure to love God's instruction (His Word) is the same as hating Him and loving death! (Check out verse 36 to read this for yourself.) Please remember that the good works we do don't insure our salvation. Jesus alone saves us. Rather, our obedience to and delight in His Word are evidence that we are indeed saved.

Thrust and Parry

In verse 33 of this passage, we are commanded to *not* neglect instruction (God's Word). What does *neglect* mean? _____
_____ Take the neglect test on the next page to see if you are neglecting instruction.

Neglect Test

1.	I listen to my parents.	Yes	No
2.	I listen to my church teachers.	Yes	No
3.	I try to read my Bible daily.	Yes	No
4.	I try to pray daily.	Yes	No
5.	I look forward to going to church.	Yes	No

According to your answers (I hope you answered honestly!), would you say that you are blessed and obtaining favor from the Lord, because you are not neglecting God's Word (verses 34-35)? Would you say you are injuring yourself through neglect (verse 36)? The awful thing about neglect is that we don't usually realize we are injuring ourselves until it is too late. Don't fall into that trap. What kind of injuries might occur to your body and soul by neglecting God's Word? Use your imagination: _____

_____

If you *are* neglecting God's Word, then do something about it now, before you and your life are damaged. If you don't have the desire to read God's Word, you can start by asking God to *give you* the desire to love His Word and read it. That's a prayer that God delights to answer! Then, pick up your Bible and read a verse. Ask your mom or dad to help you come up with a plan. Don't give up! I am in my 50s, and I still struggle with this – but it's a treasure worth struggling for!

Memory work: Copy Psalm 119:105 below: _____

_____

_____

_____

Prayer suggestion: Pray that God will help you to love His Word.

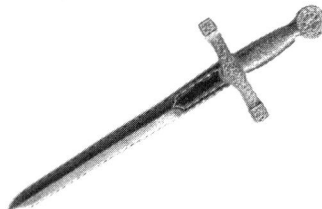

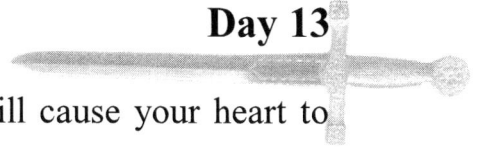

Begin with prayer. A suggestion: Pray that God will cause your heart to desire and love His Word.

Sword Drill

The books of *1 & 2 K_ _ _ _* tell of the kings of Israel and Judah. List the third 4 books of the Bible in order:
1 K _ _ _ _, 2 K _ _ _ _, 1 C _ _ _ _ _ _ _ _ _, 2 C _ _ _ _ _ _ _ _ _.

Sword Play

In the first part of this Sword Play, you will be using John 1:1-14 to find your answers. This is a wonderful passage that explains to us who Jesus is. In this passage, a number of things are compared. The author (John) concludes they are equal, or comparable. Draw a line from the things in the first list to their comparisons in the second.

List One
The Word (vs 1)…..

The Life (vs. 4)…

Receive Him (vs. 12)…

The Word became flesh (vs. 14)…

We see His glory (vs. 14)…

List Two
…become a child of God…

…was God.

…as of the only Son of the Father.

…was the light of men.

…and dwelt among us.

John 1:1-14 also contrasts a number of things, using opposites to illustrate the points. Match the contrasts below by referring to the verses indicated.

List One
All things were made through Him (vs. 3)…

The light shines (vs. 5)…

He was in the world (vs. 10)…

He came to His own (vs. 11)…

Not born of flesh (vs. 13)…

List Two
…the darkness cannot overcome it.

…born of God.

…His own did not receive Him.

…the world didn't know Him.

…Nothing was made without Him.

Fencing Practice

In this lesson we are going to switch gears. So far we've been learning what a precious treasure God's Word is. In subsequent lessons, we are going to learn what a treasure Jesus is. But, this lesson ties these two topics together. You are going to find out that they are really the same. When you treasure the one (God's Word), you treasure the other (Jesus).

If you aren't already there, turn in your Bible to John 1:1, and then fill in the blanks:

In the beginning was the _____.
The _____ *was with God.*
The Word _____ _____.
What?? Let's look at that again and write it one more time:
The Word _____ _____.

Wow! That's amazing! Does that mean that the Bible you are holding in your hands is a god and you should worship it? No, of course not. However, your Bible is the *living* word of God (remember your memory work of Hebrews 4:12). It is His thoughts and His expressions and His ideas. It is His powerful, active, living wisdom. It is the essence of God. His Word (thoughts, expression, revelation) is a picture of God. His Word was embodied (given a body) in Jesus (John 1:14). Jesus is an exact representation of God as He is revealed in His Word. Jesus, being God, as the Word, was with Him in the beginning (John 1:1) and then became flesh. In other words, if you could take the words (all-knowing thoughts, boundless wisdom, and living activity) in your Bible and give them a human body, you would have Jesus (which is exactly what happened). And Jesus *is* God, but He's also *with* God, showing that He is both separate from and the same as God. Confusing, eh? That's because our human minds aren't capable of understanding such things. It's a mystery!

Let's look again at some of the truths in this passage and fill in the blanks.

Verse one says that _____ was in the beginning, and that _____ was with God, and _____ was God.

Verse two says that *He* was *with* God in the beginning. Who is *He*?_____

Verse three says that _____ were made through *Him*. Think about Genesis 1:1. According to Genesis 1:1, who created the heavens and earth? _____ What does that tell you about God and His Word-made-flesh? _____

Verse 14 (if you haven't already figured it out) tells us that the Word became _____ and dwelt among us. Who is this talking about? _____. Can you see all the connections? It is a mystery!

Thrust and Parry

What does all of this have to do with you? Well, you already know what a precious treasure God's Word is, but now you know why. When you hold the Bible in your hands – and I'm not talking about the paper and leather and ink that is used, but the *words* in it – you are holding the very breath of God, the heart of God, the mind of God in your hands.

Because God's Word is so precious, you should treat it with reverence. It is holy, living, active. It should loom large in your heart and in your life. You should hide it in your heart. Your lips should speak it with reverence (not jokingly).

Fill in the blanks below:

In the beginning was the _____ .
The Word was with _____ .
The Word was _____ .
The _____ *was made flesh and* _____ *among us.*
God's _____ is a treasure.
I will speak God's _____ with reverence.
I will read God's _____ as often as I can.
I will hide God's _____ in my heart.
I will believe God's _____ .
I thank God for His _____ .

Memory work: Copy John 1:1 below: _____

_____

_____

_____

Prayer suggestion: Thank God for His Word.

Day 14

Begin with prayer. A suggestion: Thank God for His Word. Pray that He will help you to love it and understand it.

Sword Drill

1 & 2 C _ _ _ _ _ _ _ _ retell the story of the Kings of Israel and Judah. List the third 4 books of the Bible in order:
1 K _ _ _ _, 2 K _ _ _ _, 1 C _ _ _ _ _ _ _ _ _, 2 C _ _ _ _ _ _ _ _ _.

Sword Play

Now that you have a better understanding of how precious God's Word is, it's time to learn about the *subject* of God's Word: God Himself. Turn to Psalm 33 and read verses 6-9. Use these verses to find the answers to the multiple-choice questions below. Circle the correct answer.

1. According to verse 6, the LORD created by…
   *powerful incantations.
   *angelic hosts.
   *His Word.
   *the process of evolution.

2. Verse 6 states that He created the *heavens* and their *hosts*. *Heavens* and *hosts* probably refers to:
   *the sun and its planets.
   *the moon and stars.
   *angelic armies.
   *all of the above.

3. The LORD's power over *all* the elements of Earth is demonstrated in verse 7 by showing His control of _____.
   *water.
   *storms.
   *jars.
   *storehouses.

4. *According to verse 7,* what is one way God demonstrates His sovereignty over water?
   *He stops them.
   *He gathers them in a heap.
   *He causes storms.
   *He causes drought.

5. One example of this power is in Exodus 14:21-22 where God used _____ to lead His children through the Red Sea on dry ground.

*Moses

*Joshua

*Noah

*Jesus

6. After verses 6 and 7 demonstrate God's amazing power, verse 8 concludes that our reaction to God should be…

*to read our Bible and pray.

*to go to church every Sunday.

*to get baptized.

*to fear and stand in awe of (or revere) Him.

7. Verse 8 tells us *who* should fear Him.

*Christians and Jews

*All the inhabitants (people) on Earth

*Innocent children

*Anyone who hears His Word

8. What does it mean *to fear* the LORD?

*To honor and respect

*To love and obey

*To be afraid of

*All of the above

9. Verse 9 tells us again *why* we should fear Him:

*Because just by speaking the Word, He created.

*Because He is the judge of nations.

*Because He keeps account of all our sin.

*Because He lives in heaven.

Fencing Practice

Psalm 33:6-9 is a simple lesson in fearing the LORD. We fear Him in part because He is the creator. Maybe you've studied the theory of evolution that teaches that the universe came into existence through a giant explosion (called The Big Bang) and the resulting evolution of non-living chemicals into all living things. This is, of course, nonsense. Have you ever seen an explosion? Perhaps you saw images of hijacked airplanes crashing into the World Trade Towers on September 11, 2001. Maybe you've seen a race car crash during the Indy 500. But, here's a question for you: have you ever seen an explosion that resulted in beauty, life, and order? What was the result of

every explosion you have ever witnessed? Describe it here: _____
_____

Yet the enemies of God want you to believe that there is no God, and all the world around you was the result of an explosive evolutionary accident! If they can get you to believe their lies, will you be honoring the creator God? ____ Of course not!

Let's fill in the facts:
- *God created the heavens by His _____ (verse 6).*
- *As creator, He has power over all the elements, such as _____, which He can heap up or store as He desires (verse 7).*
- *Every single _____ on Earth should _____ Him and stand in awe of Him (verse 8).*
- *We should fear Him because He **is** the creator. He merely _____, and everything came to be (verse 9).*

Thrust and Parry

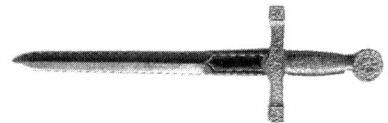

Take a moment, regardless of the weather, to step outside. Then complete the following statements.
- Describe today's weather: _____
  _____
- _____ created today's weather.
- Describe the plant life you saw outside: _____
  _____
- _____ created the plants.
- List any creatures (bugs, birds, animals) you saw: _____
  _____
- _____ created every creature.
- If you saw people, what were they doing? _____
  _____
  _____
- _____ created all mankind.

God gave us five senses for a reason. Let all these sensations move your heart to worship our creator God:
- The *scent* of rain-damp earth was created by God. I will **fear** Him.
- The *sight* of rainbow-colored flowers was created by God. I will _____ Him.

- The *feel* of a gentle breeze was created by God. I will _____ Him.
- The *sound* of the bird song and the insect hum was created by God. I will _____ Him.
- The *taste* of a raindrop on my tongue was created by God. I will _____ Him.

Memory work: Copy John 1:1 below:

_____

_____

_____

Prayer suggestion: Praise our creator God for His awesome power. Tell Him that you honor, love, obey, and fear Him.

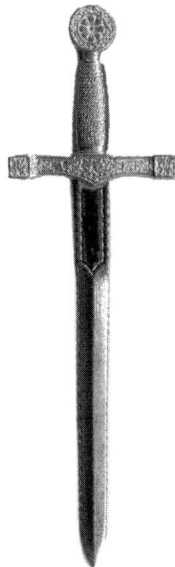

Day 15

Begin with prayer. A suggestion: Tell God that, as the creator, you love and honor Him.

Sword Drill

Both *1 & 2 K* _ _ _ _ and *1 & 2 C* _ _ _ _ _ _ _ _ _ _ tell the history of the kingdoms of Israel and Judah. List the next four books in order:
1 K _ _ _ _, *2 K* _ _ _ _, *1 C* _ _ _ _ _ _ _ _ _, *2 C* _ _ _ _ _ _ _ _ _.

Sword Play

Use this key to discover the important truths below, as found in Isaiah 40:25.

A	B	C	D	E	F	G	H	I	J	K	L	M	N	O	P	Q	R	S	T	U	V	W	X	Y	Z
1	2	3	4	5	6	7	8	9	10	11	12	13	14	15	16	17	18	19	20	21	22	23	24	25	26

__ __ __ __ __ __ __   __ __   __ __ __,   __ __ __ __ __ __ __
14 15 20 8 9 14 7   1 20   1 12 12'   14 5 9 20 8 5 18

__ __ __ __ __ __ __   __ __ __   __ __ __ __ __ __ __ __ __,   __ __
22 9 19 9 2 12 5   14 15 18   9 14 22 9 19 9 2 12 5'   9 19

__ __ __ __ __ __ __ __ __   __ __   __ __ __.
3 15 13 16 1 18 1 2 12 5   20 15   7 15 4

__ __ __ __ __ __ __   __ __   __ __ __ __ __   __ __   __ __ __.
14 15 20 8 9 14 7   9 19   5 17 21 1 12   20 15   8 9 13

Fencing Practice

If you haven't already done so, turn to Isaiah 40:25. The word *equal* means *the same as*. To you and me, the words in Isaiah 40:25 are obvious: there is *nothing* or *no one* equal to, likened to, comparable to, or the same as God! There never has been and there never will be.

God, through Isaiah, asks a *rhetorical question*: "Who is like me?" A rhetorical question is one that is asked just to make a point. You aren't expected to actually answer a rhetorical question because the answer is obvious. What is the obvious answer to the rhetorical question God asks in Isaiah 40:25? _____!

Thrust and Parry

Besides God (the Father, the Son, the Holy Spirit), in your opinion…

…who is the most powerful person that ever existed? _____

…what is the strongest force or power on earth? _____

…who or what is the wisest, smartest person/thing that ever existed?
_____

…who is the kindest, most generous person who ever existed?
_____

…who is the wealthiest person who ever existed? _____

…who is the most beautiful person who ever existed? _____

…who is the most famous person who ever existed? _____

Now, complete the statements below by rewriting your list of chosen names (in order) in the appropriate blanks below.

- God is more powerful than _____.
- God is stronger than _____.
- God is wiser and smarter than _____.
- God is kinder and more generous than _____.
- God is wealthier than _____.
- God is more beautiful than _____.
- God is more famous than _____.

Copy the question God asks in Isaiah 40:25 here: _____
_____
Answer His question here: _____!

Memory work: Copy John 1:1 below: _____
_____
_____

Prayer suggestion: Praise God for how amazing He is; for His power, love, and wisdom.

Day 16

Begin with prayer. A suggestion: Thank God for His power, loving kindness, and wisdom.

Sword Drill

The next four books of the Bible continue the history of God's people. List the titles of the four books after *2 Chronicles* here:

E _ _ _, N _ _ _ _ _ _ _, E _ _ _ _ _, J _ _.

Sword Play

The answers to the following riddles are found in Psalm 77:12-15.

1. I am a thinking word (something you do). It's a good idea to do me – especially if the subject is *God and the amazing things He does.* "Consider," "ponder," and "muse" are other words that mean the same as me.

    What am I? _____

2. The answer to me is obvious, since God is a holy, wonder-working, redeeming God. I am another rhetorical question. Write me:

    _____

3. I am not at all normal. I am seldom seen or experienced. The only way I will occur is if God intervenes in the normal sequence of events and causes something unexpected and unnatural to occur.

    What am I?_____

4. I am a word that is very special to an enslaved person. If someone does this to an enslaved person, they are ransomed and set free. All their obligations are fulfilled.

    What am I? _____

5. I am the object of God's love. He has paid a great price for me. I can be this by faith and adoption.

    Who am I? _____

Fencing Practice

If you haven't already done so, turn to Psalm 77:12-15 and read it. This passage asks another rhetorical question: Can you think of any god as great as our God? Obviously not!

Our God is truly amazing! If we take time to think about, meditate on, ponder, and muse on Him, we won't forget just how awesome He is. According to verse 12, what are we supposed to think about, meditate on, and ponder? _____ and _____.

In verse 14 what is the first thing listed that our amazing God does? _____. Read the second part of verse 14. Does God play hard-to-get, hiding so that it is hard to learn about Him? No! He *wants* you to learn about Him and to be amazed by Him! He *wants* you to be captivated and dazzled by His might. He *wants* you to trust Him completely and have faith in Him. *That's* why He displays His power all around us!

In verse 15 we are told of another miraculous thing God does. He *redeems* us. This is something else we should meditate on: His redemption. Because of your sin, you belong to Satan. You are a *slave* to your own sin. You could never, ever – not in a million years – ever pay enough to buy your freedom. But our *great* God redeems us – pays the price! Now *that* is a miracle worth remembering!

Thrust and Parry

In many countries of the world, people worship false gods made of stone. Some people worship nature: the sun, trees, animals. We are all tempted to worship idols – even you! In America, though, our gods are much more dangerous, because they don't resemble traditional gods; therefore, we don't recognize them as such.

An idol is anything to which we devote time, money and energy that rightly belongs to God. If there is something in your heart that takes first place before God, *that* is an idol. American idols are often good things, but they've taken first place in our lives. They include things such as popularity, power, money, a career, personal independence, health, and beauty.

Though I'm not saying *you* have turned these into idols, I want you to list three things (other than God Himself) such as people, possessions, or ideals, that you love very, very much.

_____

_____

_____

Now rewrite one of those three words in the first blank of each of the sentences below, and write the word "God" in the second blank of each sentence.

- Though I love _____, it cannot perform miracles, nor redeem me, so _____ will be first in my life.
- Though I love _____, it cannot perform miracles nor redeem me either, so _____ will be first in my life.
- I even love _____ a whole lot, but it can't perform miracles or redeem me either, so _____ will be first in my life.

Memory work: Copy John 1:1 below: _____

_____

_____

Prayer suggestion: Thank God for the things you love. Ask Him to help you to love Him the most.

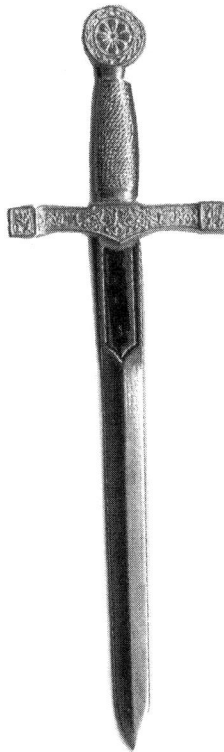

Begin with prayer. A suggestion: Thank God for the things you love most. Ask Him to help you to love Him most.

Sword Drill

The book of *Ezra* tells of the rebuilding of the temple after the nation of Judah was conquered. List the titles of the four books after *2 Chronicles* here: *E _ _ _, N _ _ _ _ _ _ _, E _ _ _ _ _, J _ _.*

Sword Play

Throughout the following lessons, we are going to try to discover who God is and why we should fear Him. Find the following words, taken from Isaiah 6:1-3, in the word search puzzle below. Each of these words is used to describe God or what it's like to be in God's presence.

Almighty	Holy	Seraphim
Exalted	Lifted up	Six wings
Glory	Lord of hosts	Throne
	Train filled the temple	

```
z  s  y  l  o  r  d  o  f  h  o  s  t  s  g  y  n  b  p  r
s  e  t  e  p  h  e  n  k  e  m  m  e  r  e  r  f  r  g  d
t  r  a  i  n  f  i  l  l  e  d  t  h  e  t  e  m  p  l  e
m  a  o  n  i  c  a  g  r  n  h  a  c  e  r  e  b  u  o  e
c  p  c  a  h  a  n  n  a  o  h  c  a  l  e  b  j  d  r  o
r  h  d  a  n  b  e  n  l  r  j  a  m  i  n  j  o  e  y  h
n  i  j  o  s  h  u  y  a  h  c  h  a  r  l  e  s  t  c  h
r  m  i  s  t  o  p  d  e  t  l  a  x  e  h  e  r  f  j  a
s  i  x  w  i  n  g  s  m  e  s  r  i  l  e  y  c  i  o  l
t  i  n  d  w  a  y  n  e  r  a  y  t  h  g  i  m  l  a  c
```

Fencing Practice

Did you ever wonder what God looks like? A number of men in the Bible were given glimpses of God. Today, we're going to look at the prophet Isaiah's description of God. If you haven't already done so, turn to Isaiah 6:1-3 and read it.

In verse 1 you'll see God sitting on a throne. What does this tell you about God? _____. Verse 1 uses two words to describe

Him as He sits on His throne. He is _____ and _____ up.
In verse 2 we see He is surrounded by seraphim (burning, cleansing angels).
How are they described in verse 2? _____

_____

Verse 3 tells us what they are doing: _____.
What are they calling? _____

_____

Do you think you would enjoy having a vision of God like Isaiah did? _____

Thrust and Parry
      You've already learned that *to fear* the Lord means to stand in awe of
God, honor and obey God, and even to be afraid of God. When Isaiah found
himself (in his vision) standing before God, he had a very strong reaction.
Read Isaiah 6:5 to discover Isaiah's reaction. What was his reaction? _____

_____

      Based on his reaction, would you say Isaiah feared the Lord? _____
Have you ever been so awed and amazed by a person's presence that you were
utterly dismayed? In America, where we have such freedom and equality, it's
hard to imagine this kind of reaction. However, Isaiah gives us a great picture
of what it looks like to fear the Lord.
      To finish today's lesson, let's take a look at the Lord's reaction to
Isaiah's fear of the Lord. Read verses 6-7.
      The seraphim touched Isaiah's lips with a burning coal and told him
two things about what the burning coal represented. What are those two
things?   _____

               _____

Memory work: Copy John 1:1 below: _____

_____

_____

Prayer suggestion: Ask God to help you fear Him. Thank Him for forgiving
your sins.

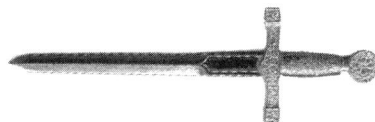

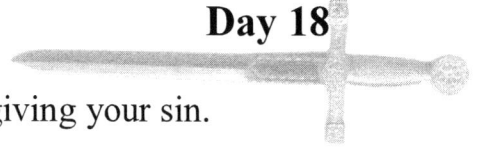

Begin with prayer. A suggestion: Thank God for forgiving your sin.

Sword Drill

The book of *E* _ _ _ tells of the rebuilding of the temple after the nation of Judah was conquered. The book of *Nehemiah* tells of the rebuilding of Jerusalem's walls. List the titles of the four books after *2 Chronicles* here: *E* _ _ _, *N* _ _ _ _ _ _ _, *E* _ _ _ _ _, *J* _ _.

Sword Play

The next eight lessons are going to teach you that God is *omnipotent* (om NI puh tent) – which means He has the freedom and power to do *anything* that is consistent with His nature. Omnipotent means He is **all-powerful**, while His nature is **all-good** and **all-loving**. That's what it means when we say "God can do *anything* that is consistent with His nature." Though He is all-powerful, He will *never* do anything bad or evil.

Using Deuteronomy 32:39, match the first part of each statement to the second part.

I am He….   …and I heal.

I kill…   …There is no god beside me.

I wound…   …out of my hand.

None can deliver…   …and make alive.

Define *omnipotent*: _ _ _ - _ _ _ _ _ _ _ _

Fencing Practice

Wouldn't it be frightening if God were all-powerful, but also capable of being mean, unconcerned, petty, or cruel? Praise God that He is all-powerful *and* kind, concerned, and loving!

According to Deuteronomy 32:39…

…are there *any* gods equal to Him (or "beside Him")?   Yes or No

…is life and death in God's hands?   Yes or No

…is wounding and healing in His hands?   Yes or No

…is deliverance in His hands?   Yes or No

Is it hard for you to sometimes trust in *both* God's power *and* His goodness? Perhaps you've lost someone you love in a tragic accident or to disease. If you haven't lost a loved one yet, you will someday. Someday even you will die. Death seems so ugly, we can't help but ask, "Why?" "Why does a good, all-powerful God let good people suffer and die? Is He *really* all-powerful *and* all good?

I can tell you, He *is* all-powerful *and* all good. You *can* trust Him. Yes, every one of us will die someday – either by sickness or accident. Some of us will die young and some of us will die when we're old. But, in His power, He defeated death. In His goodness, He made a way for you to live forever – regardless of how long or short your earthly existence is.

Thrust and Parry

A number of years ago I lost a baby in a miscarriage. Some well-meaning individuals, when they tried to comfort me, said they should have prayed more for me. Then my baby wouldn't have died. They said Satan had stolen the life of my baby. This really frightened me! I got panicky every time I thought about it! If only I had prayed harder. If only I had battled Satan. Maybe my baby would have lived. I was so sad and scared!

Then, a godly, older woman reminded me of Deuteronomy 32:39. She asked, "Is life and death in *your* hands?"

Of course not!

"Is life and death in Satan's hands?"

Of course not!

Life and death are in *God's* hands – and His hands are so good! He is
_ _ _ _ _ _ _ _ _ _ (the word for "all-powerful").

Understanding this passage encouraged me as I grieved the loss of my baby. How?

It comforted me. Either way my baby was dead, but how comforting to *know* this:

Was his death my fault or responsibility? _____

Was his death due to Satan's power over us? _____

Was the day of his death appointed by our omnipotent, loving God before the foundations of the world? _____

Remember when you face death – either your own or that of a loved one – that life is *not* in your hands, nor Satan's hands, nor anyone's hands. Death is assured. The day appointed for each one of us to die is in the hands of our omnipotent, all-kind God. And, if you belong to Him, you *will* live again! Death is defeated! I will trust both my life and my d _ _ _ _ to God.

Memory work: Copy Jeremiah 32:17a (up to "...outstretched arm..."): ___

_____

_____

_____

Prayer suggestion: Thank Him that your life is in His omnipotent, all-loving hands.

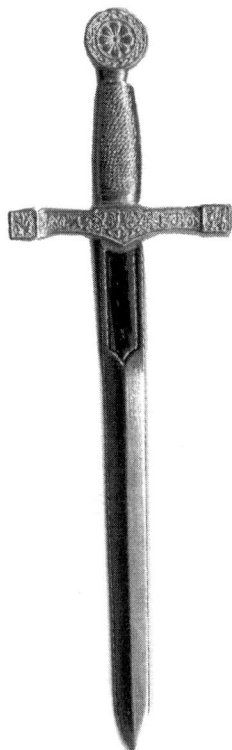

Day 19

Begin with prayer. A suggestion: Pray that God will help you to trust Him with your life.

Sword Drill

The book of *N _ _ _ _ _ _* tells of the rebuilding of the walls of Jerusalem. The book of **Esther** tells of the story of Purim, when God's people were saved from destruction by Queen Esther. List the titles of the four books after **2 Chronicles**: *E _ _ _, N _ _ _ _ _ _ _, E _ _ _ _ _, J _ _.*

Sword Play

You'll need to turn to Jeremiah 32:17-19 to find the answers to these True-False questions. According to *this passage:*

1. God made the heavens and earth.   True or False

2. God made the heavens and earth through a great explosion followed by evolutionary processes.   True or False

3. God made the heavens and earth by His great power and outstretched arm.
                                                                                              True or False

4. *Nothing at all* is too hard for our God!   True or False

5. According to verse 18, God shows loving kindness only to Americans and Jews.   True or False

6. God shows loving kindness only to those who go to church.
                                                                                              True or False

7. God shows loving kindness to thousands of people.   True or False

8. Our great and mighty God has a name: LORD of hosts. True or False

9. Our great and mighty God has many names. People all over the earth call Him by names like Allah, Buddha, and Mother Earth – but it's all the same God.   True or False

10. Our God is great in counsel – which means He has all wisdom and knowledge necessary for every situation.   True or False

11. Our God's eyes see all the ways of every man – but thankfully He knows nothing about what's going on inside my head!   True or False

12. Our God will make sure everyone is given a reward according to his work.
                                                                                    True or False

Fencing Practice

"Ah, Lord God…nothing is too hard for you."   Jeremiah 32:17
Don't you love to read that?
Isn't it comforting to know that?

"N _ _ _ _ _ _ is too _ _ _ _ for You!"

The mighty, omnipotent God who made the heavens and earth (verse 17), also shows loving kindness to you (verse 18), and watches over everything you do (verse 19)! No matter what problem you're facing, He has an answer: "You are great in c_ _ _ _ _ _ (verse 19)."

No matter what you are facing, He's greater than your problem: "You are…mighty in d _ _ _ (verse 19)."

Wow! That is omnipotence!
Our God is the cre_ _ _ _ (vs. 17).
Our God shows steadfast l _ _ _ (vs. 18).
Our God is great in wisdom and co_ _ _ _ _ (vs. 19).
Our God is mighty in d _ _ _ (vs. 19).
Nothing – absolutely *nothing* – is too h _ _ _ for our God (vs. 17)!
He is om_ _ _ _ _ _ _ _!

Thrust and Parry

Think about some of the problems you face. You're going to list those problems here.

1. What is your toughest subject in school? _____
2. Who is a person with whom you have trouble getting along?

_____

3. What is a health challenge that you (or someone you love) are facing?

_____

Now, re-list each of these problems two times in the statements below. You'll list your first problem *twice* in the first sentence, your second problem *twice* in the second sentence, and so on. Then, read your new statements out loud when you're are through.

1.   Because God is great in counsel, He knows everything about _____ and can help me in this subject. _____ is not too hard for God!

2.   Because God shows steadfast love to _____, He can help me love this person, too! Even loving _____ isn't too hard for God!

3.   Because God is mighty in deed, even health challenges like _____ are easy for Him to heal or to strengthen us and give us the courage to live with it. Even _____ isn't too hard for God!

No matter what problem you face, our omnipotent God is greater than your problem!

Do you know what your greatest problem is? It's not school, or difficult people, or financial problems, or health issues.
    It's your sin.
    Your sin completely destroyed your relationship with God, resulting in your death.
    Because of your sin, you will die.
    But, guess what!
    Even this is not too hard for our omnipotent God!
    He died for you, paid the penalty for your sin, and conquered death!

    "Ah, Lord, God...nothing is too _____ for you!"

Memory work: Copy Jeremiah 32:17a (up to "...stretched out arm..."): ___

_____

_____

_____

Prayer suggestion: Worship Him for His omnipotence. Tell Him you *know that you know* that nothing is too hard for Him.

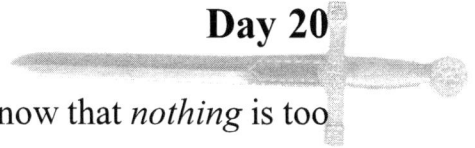

Begin with prayer. A suggestion: Tell God that you know that *nothing* is too hard for Him.

Sword Drill

The book of *E _ _ _ _* tells of the story of Purim, when God's people were saved from destruction by Queen Esther. The book of *Job* tells the story of a man who faced the worst problems imaginable – and discovered that God was bigger than his problems. List here the four books of the Bible that come after *2 Chronicles*: *E _ _ _*, *N _ _ _ _ _ _ _*, *E _ _ _ _ _*, *J _ _*.

Sword Play

All the words and phrases in the crossword puzzle below are taken from Daniel 4:34-35. They paint another picture of God's omnipotence. If you need help, check the word bank under the puzzle on the next page.

Across

3. Compared to God, these people who live on Earth are counted as nothing (verse 35). _____
4. He does as He pleases, according to _____ _____ (verse 35).
6. He does according to His will among the _____ __ _____ (verse 35).
8. His _____ endures! (verse 34)
9. All the inhabitants of _____ are counted as nothing (verse 35).
10. All those who live on earth are counted as _____ (verse 35).

Down

1. How long will God's kingdom endure? (verse 34) _____
____ _____
2. No one can stop Him. No one can _____ ___ _____. (verse 35)
5. His dominion is one that will last forever. It's _____ (verse 34)
7. Another word for a "rule" or a "reign." _____ (verse 34)

Crossword grid with numbered cells: 1, 2, 3, 4, 5, 6, 7, 8, 9, 10

Word bank:

Dominion	Generation to generation	Inhabitants	Stay His hand
Earth	His will	Kingdom	
Everlasting	Host of Heaven	Nothing	

Fencing Practice

As you already know, om_ _ _ _ _ _ _ _ means "all powerful." Daniel 4:34-35 ends the story of proud King Nebuchadnezzar of Babylon, the most powerful earthly king of that time – the conqueror of Israel. Because of his pride, God passed judgment on him. King Nebuchadnezzar would become insane and live like an animal for seven years. At the end of his insanity, King Nebuchadnezzar, conqueror of the world, finally acknowledges that *God is King!* The passage in Daniel 4 is when King Nebuchadnezzar says these words – and God restores his sanity and his kingdom.

King Nebuchadnezzar – the world's most powerful conquering king – held absolute power over all the people of the earth. The world's most powerful man came to realize that no matter how powerful he was, he was counted as n _ _ _ _ _ _ (verse 35) when compared to God.

King Nebuchadnezzar had to learn that, even though no earthly kingdom could stop him, God could! And no one could stop God or s _ _ _ _ _ _ _ _ _ _(verse 35)! King Nebuchadnezzar had to learn that someday he would die, his reign would be over and his kingdom would end, but God's dominion never ends. It is e _ _ _ _ _ _ _ _ _ _ (verse 34). God's kingdom (verse 34) will endure from g _. Why? Because our God is o _ _ _ _ _ _ _ _ _.

Thrust and Parry

Our omnipotent God is so mighty that no matter what earthly power you compare Him to – it is *nothing* next to Him! In your opinion...

What is the most powerful nation on earth today? _____

Who is the most powerful, influential person on earth today?

_____

What is the most powerful weapon on earth today? _____

Can any of these out-wit, out-maneuver, overcome, or out-last God? _____! They can't even come close!

List the three powerful things you wrote above on the lines below, then read your statement out loud.

_____, _____, and _____ are the most powerful forces on earth today, but compared to God, they are *nothing*! Our God is o _ _ _ _ _ _ _ _ _.

Memory work: Copy Jeremiah 32:17a (up to "...outstretched arm...") _____

_____

_____

_____

_____

Prayer suggestion: Worship God because He is omnipotent. Admit to Him that you are as nothing.

Day 21

Begin with prayer. A suggestion: Worship God by thanking Him for loving you even though He is everything and you are as nothing.

Sword Drill

While the book of *E* _ _ _ _ tells of the Jews' salvation by the hand of the Queen, the book of **Job** tells the story of a man who lost everything and still praised God. List the titles of the four books after *2 Chronicles* here:
E _ _ _, *N* _ _ _ _ _ _ _, *E* _ _ _ _ _, *J* _ _.

Sword Play

The code below is based on Amos 4:13. Use the key to decipher the statements below.

A	B	C	D	E	F	G	H	I	J	K	L	M	N	O	P	Q	R	S	T	U	V	W	X	Y	Z
1	2	3	4	5	6	7	8	9	10	11	12	13	14	15	16	17	18	19	20	21	22	23	24	25	26

‾ ‾   ‾ ‾ ‾ ‾ ‾ ‾ ‾.
8 5   3 18 5 1 20 5 19

‾ ‾   ‾ ‾ ‾ ‾ ‾   ‾ ‾ ‾ ‾ ‾ ‾ ‾   ‾ ‾ ‾ ‾ ‾.
8 5   13 1 11 5 19   8 9 13 19 5 12 6   11 14 15 23 14

‾ ‾   ‾ ‾ ‾ ‾ ‾ ‾ ‾ ‾.
8 5   3 15 14 20 18 15 12 19

‾ ‾   ‾ ‾ ‾ ‾ ‾ ‾.
8 5   18 5 9 7 14 19

‾ ‾ ‾   ‾ ‾ ‾ ‾   ‾ ‾   ‾ ‾ ‾   ‾ ‾ ‾ ‾,
8 9 19   14 1 13 5   9 19   20 8 5   12 15 18 4

‾ ‾ ‾   ‾ ‾ ‾   ‾ ‾   ‾ ‾ ‾ ‾ ‾.
20 8 5   7 15 4   15 6   8 15 19 20 19

Fencing Practice

If you haven't already done so, turn to Amos 4:13. This verse demonstrates God's omnipotence in two directions. He is so powerful that He can form, or create <u>m</u> _ _ _ _ _ _ _ _ _ and <u>w</u> _ _ _ (verse 13a). He controls light and darkness. He treads on, or rules over, all the heights of the <u>e</u> _ _ _ _

(verse 13b). Yet in all His creative, reigning power, He stoops down to declare to us His t _ _ _ _ _ _!

Often when we think of God's omnipotence, we think of His power as He spoke light into existence, flung the stars through space, and fashioned life. Yet one of His amazing demonstrations of power is that He cares for each of us as individuals (more than 7 billion of us!) and *wants* to be known by us.

The question is, do *you* want to know Him? Yes or No
Do *you* want to know His thoughts? Yes or No

Thrust and Parry

Our om _ _ _ _ _ _ _ _, reigning, Creator God wants us to know more about Him than just knowing about the things He does. He wants us to know Who He is, what He thinks, and how He feels.

Does that amaze you to realize that even while He reigns on high, He wants you to know what He's thinking?

Think of the people in your life. There are only certain people in your life that you allow to see inside your head and your heart. They include your family and your friends – those whom you love. Since God *wants* you to know *His* thoughts, what does this tell you about how God regards you?

_____

_____

God declares His thoughts to us in a number of different ways. Look up the following verses to remember two ways God reveals Himself and His thoughts to us.
2 Timothy 3:16 – God reveals Himself to us through _____.
Psalm 19:1 – God reveals Himself to us through _____.

When you read God's Word, do you *listen* to what He says to you? When you stand outside in God's creation, do you *listen* to what He is telling you?

Memory work: Copy Jeremiah 32:17a here: _____

_____

_____

_____

Prayer suggestion: Ask God to help you to *listen* when He speaks to you.

Day 22

Begin with prayer. A suggestion: Ask God to help you to *listen* to His voice today.

Sword Drill

The book of *J_ _* tells the story of a man who lost everything and still praised God. List the titles of the four books after *2 Chronicles* here: *E _ _ _, N _ _ _ _ _ _ _, E _ _ _ _ _, J _ _*.

Sword Play

In Jeremiah 29:11-14a, we read that almighty God knows our future. Circle the correct answers *from Jeremiah 29:11-14a*, for these questions:

1. What does God declare at the beginning of verse 11?
   *That He loves you…
   *That He has thoughts/plans for you…
   *That He's busy right now, so call back later…
   *That you're in big trouble now!

2. According to verse 11, the plans God has for your future involve…
   *Wholeness/peace; not evil…
   *Riches/wealth; not poverty…
   *Punishment; not freedom…
   *Love/friendship; not loneliness…

3. Verse 11 ends with more details about God's plans for you:
   *Obey Him or else!
   *You'll succeed in all you do…
   *It's for Him to know and you to find out…
   *He'll give you a hope-filled future with an expected end…

4. Verse 12 tells us what we're supposed to do…
   *Go to the house of the Lord…
   *Trust Him and relax…
   *Call to God and pray to Him…
   *Consult a psychic…

5. Verse 12 ends with God's action toward us:
   *He will listen to you…
   *He'll answer in His own good time…
   *He'll wake you up…
   *He will destroy your enemies…

6. God promises something in verse 13. If you seek Him…
*…You will be surprised…
*…You will find Him…
*…You're looking for something way too big…
*…You'll never find Him…

7. In verse 13 God places a condition on seekers. What is His condition?
*You must remember His words…
*You must be good…
*You have to follow your pastor…
*You have to seek Him with all your heart…

8. The beginning of verse 14 gives us the wonderful promise of Jeremiah 29:11-14a. What is it?
*You will be an angel someday…
*He will give you everything you desire…
*He will be found by you…
*You will be filled with laughter…

Fencing Practice
God's plan for your future is one more evidence that He is all-powerful, o _ _ _ _ _ _ _ _ . When you read Jeremiah 29:11-14a, it should fill you with wonder and excitement.

The great God of all the universe has a plan for you – for your future. If you are His child, then you can rest-assured that it's a *good* plan. So often, because of the culture we live in, we interpret that promise to say something that it doesn't say. Perhaps in your mind you're thinking something like this:

"Oh, good! God promises me a plan for my life; a hope-filled, good plan! That means I'm going to be happy, healthy, and wealthy!"

But, take a moment to look again at this passage. God, in this passage, doesn't promise any of these things. Instead He promises us peace (in KJV) or wholeness (in ESV). Peace or wholeness in a sin-sick world! That's a miracle! We know that because God is omnipotent, He has the power to heal and to set free and to bless with material wealth – but if, in His wisdom, He does not grant you (His child) health, wealth, and happiness on Earth, you can know He *will* grant you peace, wholeness, and even joy on Earth and a grand future and inheritance in heaven.

Thrust and Parry
On the next page underline your choice of answer in each question.

Think of it this way. Which is the bigger miracle?:
*To be healthy….OR…to have peace when you're not healthy?
*To be rich…OR…to be content when you're not rich?
*To be happy…OR…to have joy in the midst of trial and sorrow?

The great thing about God is that because He is omnipotent, He has your future all planned out. If you are His child, He has promised you a *good* future, not an evil one. Fill in the clues below with words from above.

It may include health.
    It may include p _ _ _ _ in the midst of sickness.
It may include wealth.
    It may include c _ _ _ _ _ _ _ _ _ in the midst of poverty.
It may include happiness.
    It may include j _ _ in the midst of trials and sorrow.

If you are His child, then your future *does* hold…
    *A home in h _ _ _ _ _ _ ,
    *An inh _ _ _ _ _ _ _ _ ,
    *An eternity of knowing G _ _.

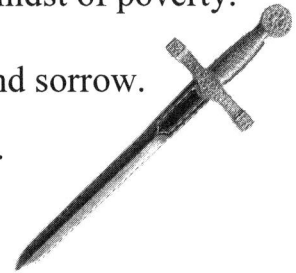

You don't have to wait until heaven to know God. Jeremiah 29:13-14a promises that if you seek Him with all your heart, you will *find* Him.

When you think of seeking Him with your whole heart, you may be tempted to think of dull, boring activities (like doing school work). But, seeking the all-powerful, amazing, astounding, creator of the world – and getting to know Him – *that's* not at *all* boring! That's an unbelievable *honor* and a mind-boggling *privilege*! Seeking God isn't a duty we *have* to do. It's an inconceivable invitation we *get* to do! Wow! The Lord of Hosts invites *you* to get to know Him!

Because God speaks to you through His Word, you'll want to be underlining verses in your Bible that are special to you. If a verse sort of leaps out at you and grabs your attention, you can be sure that's the Holy Spirit (God) speaking to you, helping you to know Him. You'll want to remember those verses by underlining them. You can even make notes in the margin of your Bible of the things you've learned. If Jeremiah 29:11-14a is special to you, then take time to underline it in your Bible right now.

Memory work: Copy Jeremiah 32:17a here: _____

_____

_____

Prayer suggestion: Thank God for His plan for you. Pray that He will help you to seek Him and to know Him.

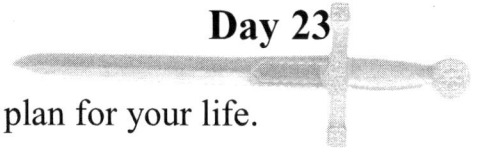

Begin with prayer. A suggestion: Thank God for His plan for your life.

Sword Drill

The next four books of the Bible are books of songs, wisdom, and poetry. *Psalms*, a worship hymnal, is the longest book of the Bible. List the books of songs, wisdom, and poetry here. *P _ _ _ _ _, P _ _ _ _ _ _ _, E _ _ _ _ _ _ _ _ _ _ _, S _ _ _ of S _ _ _ _ _ _.*

Sword Play

Acts 17:24-25 gives us another view of our omnipotent God. Below are listed a number of statements taken from Acts 17:24-25. Circle the statements that are true and cross off the ones that are false according to this passage.

He made the world.

He made everything in the world.

He is Lord of heaven and will be Lord of Earth someday.

He evolved everything in the world.

He *is* Lord of heaven and earth.

He dwells in temples and cathedrals.

He does not dwell in man-made temples and cathedrals.

He does not *need* our hands to serve Him.

He doesn't *need* anything from us.

He needs our help and cooperation.

He *needs* our hands to serve Him.

He gives life and breath.

He is the giver of all things.

He is the giver of nothing.

Man is sovereign over his own life and death.

Fencing Practice

If you haven't already done so, turn to Acts 17:24-25. I love this passage! Here's a passage that really puts us humans in our place. It's a clear reminder that God is *everything* and we (in comparison) are *nothing*.

According to verse 25, what do we need from God? _____.
What does God need from us? _____.

This is very important to understand. God does not *need* us. He doesn't need our gifts, our talents, our influence, our praise and worship, our prayers, our time, our churches, our money, our love, or our lives. If God *needed* any of these things, He wouldn't be all-powerful, would He.

Look at it this way. If God *needed* your offering and your witness to save your neighbor, it would put God in a position that was subordinate to, or lesser than you. For example, if God *needed* your offering and your witness to save the lost, you could hold that over His head and try to bargain with God: "I promise I'll witness to my neighbor if you just heal me. I don't want to suffer any more." If we could bargain with God like that, He wouldn't be omnipotent.

We need to recognize God's true omnipotence. He doesn't need us for anything, but we need Him for everything.

What are the three things listed in Acts 17:25 that God gives us?

_____
_____
_____

Thrust and Parry

Though God doesn't *need* us, because He loves us He chooses to use us in many ways. He commands us to serve Him.

How can you serve God with your money? _____
_____

Here's a question: Is it really *your* money? Whose money is it?
_____

List one of your talents – something you're good at: _____
_____

How can you serve God with this talent? _____
_____

Here's a question for you: Who blessed you with this talent?
_____

How can you serve God with your time? _____

Here's a question for you: Who gave you time on Earth? _____

Have you ever tried bargaining with God, promising you'll be good or you'll do something for Him if He'll just answer your prayer and do something for you?

Bargaining is just another way of trying to control or manipulate – and it doesn't work, does it. The reason is because God is o _ _ _ _ _ _ _ _ and doesn't *need* us.

This should give you great comfort if you're a believer, because He wouldn't be a very great God if we could manipulate His will and bargain with Him. Praise God that He doesn't *need* you or me! He is not served by human h _ _ _ _ (verse 25). Praise God that He *chooses* to be served by us and that we have the great privilege of serving Him!

Memory work: Copy Jeremiah 32:17a here: _____
_____
_____
_____

Prayer suggestion: Thank God for His omnipotence and that you *get* to serve Him!

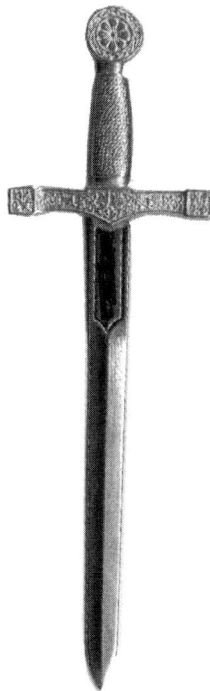

Day 24

Begin with prayer. A suggestion: Thank God that He *uses* you even though He doesn't *need* you.

Sword Drill

P _ _ _ _ _, a worship hymnal, is the longest book of the Bible. *Proverbs* is full of wise advice. List the books of songs, wisdom, and poetry here. *P* _ _ _ _ _, *P* _ _ _ _ _ _ _ _, *E* _ _ _ _ _ _ _ _ _ _ _, *S* _ _ _ *of S* _ _ _ _ _ _.

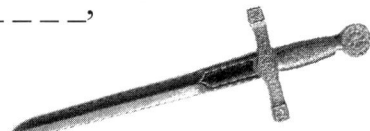

Sword Play

This simple puzzle is based on Acts 17:28a. Write each letter from the puzzle in order in the blanks below. Start with column 1, writing all the letters in column one in order. Then move to column 2, etc.

1	2	3	4	5	6	7	8	9	10	11
i	i	e	v	n	o	a	h	e	r	i
n	m	l	e	d	v	n	a	o	b	n
h	w	i	a	m	e	d	v	u	e	g

_ _ _ _ _ _ _ _ _ _ _ _ _ _ _ _ _ _ _ _ _ _ _ _ _ _ _ _
_ _ _ _ _.

Fencing Practice

The last two lessons and this lesson have taught you some wonderful truths about God's omnipotence – and about our lives as well.

In Jeremiah 29:11, you found out God has a p _ _ _ for your life – and it's a good one.

In Acts 17:25, you learned that God gives you l _ _ _ and b _ _ _ _ _ and everything else.

Today's lesson in Acts 17:28a teaches us that *in God* we l _ _ _ and m _ _ _ and have o _ _ _ _ _ _ _.

You can do nothing apart from Him. Your life is in His hands. Each breath you take is because He has ordained it. Each day you are alive is because He has granted the day to you. You cannot get away from Him. You cannot live one day longer or shorter than what He has decided. This is what it means in Acts 17:28a:

"In Him we live and move and have our being."

If you really want your mind to be boggled by God's omnipotence, then just take a moment to dwell on the fact that Acts 17:28a is true for all seven billion people on Earth – and it was true for the billions of people who have already lived and died, and it's true for all those yet to be born. Our God is amazing! Our God is o _ _ _ _ _ _ _ _!

Thrust and Parry

When you were conceived, you were given life and breath by God. You were created to live an eternity. But two possibilities exist. Either you will live forever with God…

OR

…you will live forever apart from God in eternal torment.

You cannot escape this reality. Because God is omnipotent, and because you live and move and have your being in Him, you will want to trust your life into His hands. He is o _ _ _ _ _ _ _ _ _, all-p _ _ _ _ _ _ _, and all good. Rest in His love for you. Don't fight Him. Believe me, you can't win.

And, why would you want to fight Him? How could your plans and ideas for your life possibly be better than His? Let's create an outline of who you are.

Your Profile

What is your name? _____

Who are your parents? _____

Are you adopted? _____

What is your ethnic background? _____

What color is your hair? _____ Your eyes? _____

What color is your skin? _____

What is one talent you have – or something you're good at? _____
_____

What is one handicap you have – or something you're not good at? _____
_____

What is one hobby you have? _____

Name one of your best friends: _____

Is your mom a believer? _____

Is your dad a believer? _____

Name a food you like: _____

Name a food you don't like: _____

Name something you would buy if you had $1,000 to spend on yourself: __
_____

Name someone or a charity to whom you would give $1,000 if you could:

_____

Name a place you would like to visit for vacation: _____
Name a country you'd like to visit on a short term mission trip, if you could:

_____

What might you want to be when you grow up? _____
What is one thing you'd like to do for God some day? _____

_____

Look back over your list and see how unique you are compared to everyone around you. All your unique characteristics, likes and dislikes, hopes and dreams – they are all tied up in God. You are His child – planned and created by almighty God. *He* made you like this…and what He makes *is good*.

Try to imagine two scenarios. In the first scenario, you take the outline of you, your characteristics, likes, dislikes, strengths, weaknesses, talents, hopes, and dreams – and you leave them in God's hands. You say, "In You I live and move and have my being. Use me as You will."

In the second scenario, you take your outline of you, your characteristics, talents, hopes, and dreams, and you do with them as you want, using them to please yourself. You say, "Don't tell me what to do with *my* life."

In the end, when you die, will God's plan be thwarted either way? No! He doesn't *need* us – but we *need* Him. In the end, He will win – because He's o _ _ _ _ _ _ _ _. The question is, whose side are *you* on?

Let me encourage you to leave your life in His very capable, omnipotent, always-good hands.

Memory Work: Copy Jeremiah 32:17b (the rest of the verse) here: _____

_____

_____

Prayer suggestion: Thank God for making you who you are. Give your life into His hands.

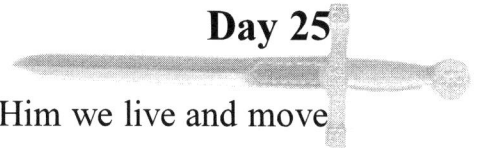

Begin with prayer. A suggestion: Praise God that in Him we live and move and have our being.

Sword Drill

The book of *P_ _ _ _ _ _* is full of wise counsel. *Ecclesiastes* is a book of wisdom, teaching that nothing in life is worth living for, except God. List the books of songs, wisdom, and poetry here: *P_ _ _ _ _,* *P_ _ _ _ _ _ _, E_ _ _ _ _ _ _ _ _ _ _, S_ _ _ of S_ _ _ _ _ _.*

Sword Play

All of the words in the puzzle below come from the lessons we've learned about our all-powerful God. There are extra words hidden as well.

```
a w r v f g c i k o l p m t s z v y t h g i m l a r
m a k e s a l l t h i n g s p o s s i b l e r s u d
i q s f r t b o q w a h o l y s p i r i t x e l n s
h x d f t w m v b a z l o r d o f h o s t s e h c y
s a c y u m w i f n b i y o u a r e g o d r n j j l
e j e k o p b n y t u f v h t c k u i d o f s a w s
d s v f o d x g i s m e l o v e m e n f a i t h m e
i e e n w o n k s t h g u o h t s i h s e k a m a v
s a r l i m e i t o f i g h t s e e i e g e n t l i
e e l l s i n n o b l v i c t o a i m e a l s a l l
b e a t h n o d r e a e a s t v i e w o w l a s e r
d d s d r i n n e f e r t t e s t m e c h o e c o u
o e t f l o w e r o f m e n n e s t l o v e r r t o
g n i n s n o s y u j b a r g e c r i e r g l o v r
o o n e c a n s i n k n o w o u t r v i c t o r y o
n n g j e s u s h d d c z q o l m o e g r e a t g f
h o m e s p u r i e e s u s l o r d p a t h w a y s
l i g h t o f t a h e w o r l d d f a i t h f u l n
j h e n e v e r l e t s g o o f m e k w n o g j p a
z u g r e a t i n c o u n s e l s a v i o m r a l l
w m d n a h s i h y a t s n a c e n o n f q o c i p
```

Almighty	In Him we live	No god besides Him
Creator	Life giver	None can stay His hand
Dominion	Lord of hosts	Omnipotent
Everlasting	Loving kindness	Plans for our lives
Great in counsel	Makes all things possible	Ruler of heaven and earth
Healer	Makes His thoughts known	Wants to be found

Fencing Practice

Turn in your Bible to Luke 1:37and read it. This is your last lesson about God's omnipotence, but never forget that *everything* God does displays his omnipotence. Luke 1:37 is tucked right in the middle of the story of the birth of Jesus. The angel Gabriel just appeared to Mary and told her she was going to have a baby – Jesus – the Son of God. He also told her that her old Aunt Elizabeth was six months pregnant with a miracle baby – John. Then Gabriel declares to Mary:

Nothing will be i _ _ _ _ _ _ _ _ with God!

Let's take a look at an utterly impossible situation. You may be a pretty good kid, but you're still not good enough for God. He is a perfectly holy God and can't tolerate *any* sin – not even a little sin. *Holy* means no sin at all. Here's the problem…the utterly impossible situation. You aren't just a little bit of a sinner (a pretty good person). You are a sinner through and through. *No matter how hard you try, you mess up. You'll never, ever be good enough for God – not in a million years.*

To make matters even worse, you're under a death penalty. *You will die for your sins…*that is, unless somehow Someone does the impossible. Since you *can't* pay the price for your sin, Someone will have to pay the price for your sin *and* make you so that you can stop sinning. But, who would do such a thing? Everyone is in the same situation as you!

That's where Luke 1:37 comes in. This impossible situation suddenly doesn't seem so impossible, does it!

Is any situation too hard for God?	yes or no
Is any problem too big for God?	yes or no
Is any sin you commit too evil for Him to forgive?	yes or no
Is it possible for you to be too unlovable for God to love?	yes or no
Is any life so messed up that God can't fix it?	yes or no
Is any sorrow or pain too deep for God to reach it?	yes or no
Is anything impossible for God?	yes or no

Thrust and Parry

You will never be able to fully appreciate God's omnipotence in saving you until you understand the total hopelessness of your situation. Put a check mark next to each sin below of which you are guilty:

o You've lied
o You've exaggerated (which is another form of lying)
o You've only told half of the truth (another form of lying)
o You've stolen

- o You've "borrowed" things without permission (another form of stealing)
- o You've been lazy
- o You've fought to be first in line or to go first in a game
- o You've taken the biggest piece for yourself
- o You've ignored your parents when they told you to do something
- o You've sneaked
- o You've been mean to your siblings
- o You've been cruel to an animal (even worms and bugs)
- o You've broken something in anger
- o You've been wasteful
- o You've sassed your parents
- o You've cheated
- o You've argued
- o You've whined
- o You've complained
- o You've said bad words
- o You've thought bad words
- o You've picked on someone
- o You've yelled at someone
- o You've threatened someone
- o You've been disrespectful of your parents behind their backs
- o You've been proud of yourself
- o You've gossiped

Look back over your list. You've probably checked off most of the items on the list if you're like the rest of the human race. If you gave the list to each person in your family, they would have it mostly checked off as well – and could no doubt add to it! Even the best-behaved person in your family will have the list mostly checked off and could add to it!

Now can you see *why* you're in an impossible situation? Praise God, we have an o _ _ _ _ _ _ _ _ God who specializes in doing the impossible! ***Nothing*** will be i _ _ _ _ _ _ _ _ _ with God!

Memory work: Copy Jeremiah 32:17 here: _____

_____

_____

_____

Prayer suggestion: Ask God to forgive you and cleanse you. Thank Him that He can do the impossible.

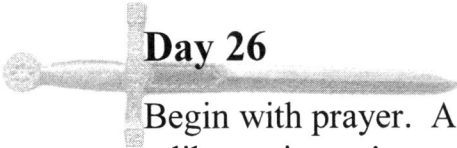

Day 26

Begin with prayer. A suggestion: Praise God that He does impossible things – like saving us!

Sword Drill

E _ _ _ _ _ _ _ _ _ _ is a book of wisdom that teaches us that nothing but God is worth living for. **Song of Solomon** is a love song that also portrays God's love for us. List the books of songs, wisdom, and poetry here.

P _ _ _ _ _, *P* _ _ _ _ _ _ _, *E* _ _ _ _ _ _ _ _ _ _ _, *S* _ _ _ *of S* _ _ _ _ _ _.

Sword Play

For the next six lessons we are going to study another amazing attribute of God. He is **omnipresent**. Read Jeremiah 23:23-24 to match the sentences below and learn what omnipresent means. Draw a line from the first part of each sentence (1st column), to the correct middle part (2nd column), to the final part (in the 3rd column).

Can a man…	…a God…	…far off
Am I…	…a God…	…in secret places
Do I not…	…hide himself…	…at hand
Not…	…I cannot…	…and earth
So that…	…fill heaven…	…see him

Unscramble the following words to get a definition of *omnipresent*:

Tno lmiietd yb sacpe or tmie.

_ _ _ _ _ _ _ _ _ _ _ _ _ _ _ _ _ _ _ _ _ _ _.

Fencing Practice

To me this is one of the most mind-boggling attributes of God. Unlike you and me, our wonderful God is not limited by space or time. I don't know about you, but my poor brain just can't comprehend that!

You and I can only be in one place at one time. God is everywhere, *simultaneously* (all at the same time) present in His fullness, in every part of His creation, all the time! There is no place anywhere where He is not.

You and I can only go forward in time, one second at a time. God isn't bound by time. He inhabits all time…past, present, and future. He doesn't just *know* the future, He *already inhabits it*, at the same time He's fully here in the present. That's because He's not limited by time like we are! Ouch! This hurts my brain! My finite mind can't comprehend our infinite God.

And that's not all. He had no beginning. He was forever and ever as far back as you could go, and then forever again. And he has no end – as far forward as you can go, and then forever again.

Our God is o _ _ _ _ _ _ _ _ _ , which means He is not l _ _ _ _ _ _ by s _ _ _ _ or t _ _ _.

Thrust and Parry

If you haven't already done so, turn to Jeremiah 23:23-24. God's omnipresence is such a comfort to us! In verse 23 He really wants you to understand that He's no far-away God, sitting up in heaven, peeking through the clouds down to earth like an astronaut in the space shuttle. No way! He's an "at hand" God.

What are some other words that mean the same as "at hand"? How would *you* say it? (You can look at Isaiah 57:15 for additional help.) God is

_____

_____

_____

When you're struggling or upset or hurt or angry, just think about it. God is *not* far away. He's not even just a phone call away. He is right here with you!

At the beginning of verse 24 (Jeremiah 23:23-24), God asks a rhetorical question. Write it here: _____

_____

Can you answer that question? Can you possibly ever get away from God? _____ Verse 24 tells us that God isn't just everywhere; He f _ _ _ _ heaven and earth! Our God is o _ _ _ _ _ _ _ _ _.

Memory Work: Copy Psalm 139:7 here: _____

_____

_____

Prayer suggestion: Praise God for His awesome omnipresence.

Day 27

Begin with prayer. A suggestion: Thank God that He is with you right here, right now.

Sword Drill

S _ _ _ _ _ _ _ _ _ _ _ _ is a love song that also portrays God's love for us. List the books of songs, wisdom, and poetry here.
P _ _ _ _ _, *P* _ _ _ _ _ _ _, *E* _ _ _ _ _ _ _ _ _ _ _, *S* _ _ _ *of S* _ _ _ _ _ _.

Sword Play

The words in this puzzle are taken from Proverbs 15:3 and from the definition of *omnipresent*. Fill in the blanks in the clues below with words from the word bank, then fill in the puzzle on the next page.

Across

4. Where the eyes of the Lord are: _____ _____
5. God is not limited by _____, which means He is everywhere at the same time.
7. Because God's eyes are in everyplace, we _____ _____ from Him or flee from His presence.
9. Whose eyes? The eyes of the _____.
11. What are the Lord's eyes doing? _____
12. He is watching both the _____ and the evil.

Down

1. This word means unlimited by space or time: _____
2. Today's Scripture is _____ 15:3.
3. The part of God that sees everything: _____
6. This word is the opposite of limited: _____
8. Opposite of "the good" is "the _____."
10. God isn't limited by _____, which means He simultaneously and fully inhabits the past, present, and future.

Word Bank		
Cannot hide	Good	Space
Every place	Lord	Time
Evil	Omnipresent	Unlimited
Eyes	Proverbs	Watching

					1							
	2								3			
4												
				5								
		6										
7							8					
							9					
			10									
11												
12												

Fencing Practice

God's eyes are in every place! He is not limited by space like us. You can only be in one place at a time. If you get up from your seat and move to another one, your first seat is now empty.

Obviously you are not omn_ _ _ _ _ _ _ _.

Have you ever tried to convince someone that you *were* omnipresent? Perhaps you briefly step away from your seat to go to the bathroom, and when you return, lo and behold, your sister or brother is sitting in *your* seat! You say:

"Get out of my seat!"

"You weren't sitting there!"

"Yes, I was! Get out!"

"Uh-uh! This seat was empty!"

"Uh-uh! It's my seat. I was here!"

"No you weren't!"

"I *was* here, but I had to go to the bathroom…"

"Sorry, but since you're not omnipresent, this seat was empty. You weren't in it. I win."

Rats! If only you were omnipresent!

Thrust and Parry

Let's apply this to your own life. Is God with you when you get up in the morning? _____ Does He see you while you eat? _____ Does He see what you eat? _____ Is He with you while you do school work? _____ Does He see you when you are being picked on? _____ Is He with you when you are picking on someone? _____ Is He with you while you're at the computer? _____ Is He with you while you're watching TV? _____ Is He with you in your bedroom? _____ Is He with you at your friend's house? _____ Does He see what you do there? _____ Does He hear what you say there? _____ Is He with you when you're texting? _____ Does He see what you're writing? _____ Is He with you when you play? _____ Is He with you when you work? _____ Is He with you when you go to bed? _____ Is there *ever* a time or place when God is not with you or can't see you? _____

Our God's amazing omnipresence should fill you with both fear (which is the beginning of wisdom) *and* comfort. You are *never* alone!

Memory Work: Copy Psalm 139:7 here: _____
_____
_____

Prayer suggestion: Praise God for His omnipresence. Thank Him for being with you all the time.

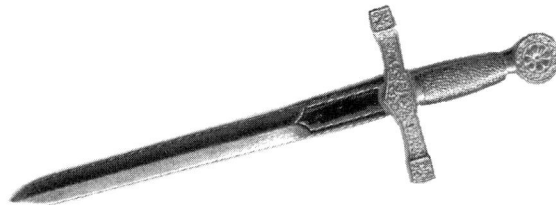

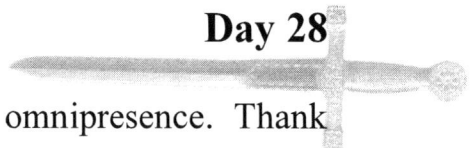

Begin with prayer. A suggestion: Praise God for His omnipresence. Thank Him for being with you now as you study His Word.

Sword Drill

The next six books of the Old Testament are written by prophets. The book of *Isaiah* has many prophecies foretelling our Savior Jesus. Write the names of those books here: *I*_ _ _ _ _, *J* _ _ _ _ _ _ _, *L*_ _ _ _ _ _ _ _ _ _ _, *E*_ _ _ _ _ _, *D*_ _ _ _ _, *H* _ _ _ _.

Sword Play

The answers to these riddles are words found in Psalm 139:7-10.

I am kind of a place – but not really. I'm actually the opposite of a place – but not really. I actually don't exist. I am the answer to the rhetorical question in verse seven.

Where am I? _____

I am a place – a wonderful, joyful place where no sin exists and no sadness. God's presence is here. It tells us so in verse eight. I am your future home.

Where am I? _____

I am a place. No one can really explain much about me, but I am a place for the dead. It may surprise you to know that God's presence is even found here. It says so in verse eight!

Where am I? _____

I am described as having wings. I am associated with alarms, showers, and roosters. Verse nine says God is here as well.

What am I? _____

I go by many names. I was filled with life on the fifth day. Black, Red, Dead, and North are a few of my names. According to verse nine, God is here as well.

What am I? _____

If you ever need a helping one of these, someone might give you one. Most folks have two. If you need leading or holding, this is what God will use – which He does all the time (see verse ten).

What am I? _____

Fencing Practice

Psalm 139:7-10 is another passage that demonstrates to us that God is o _ _ _ _ _ _ _ _ _ _. To someone who doesn't love God, this might be frightening. No matter how hard you try, it is utterly impossible to escape God's presence.

Can you escape Him in heaven? _____

Can you escape Him in Sheol? _____

Can you escape Him by jumping ahead to the next morning? _____

Can you escape Him in the depths of the ocean? _____

If you read a little further in Psalm 139, you'll find even more about His presence:

Can the darkness hide you from God (verses 11-12)? _____

Was God present with you in your mother's womb (verse 15)? _____

Is there any place or time where you can go to escape the presence of God? _____

Why? Because He is unlimited by time or space! He is our awesome o_ _ _ _ _ _ _ _ _ God!

Thrust and Parry

For an unbeliever, God's omnipresence is scary – not being able to escape God's all-seeing eyes. But, for a believer, God's omnipresence is one of the most precious and personal attributes of God. Let me ask the same questions again but from a believer's point of view.

Will God be with you in heaven? _____

Would God be with you in Sheol? _____

If time could jump forward to tomorrow, would God be there with you? _____

If you are facing something bad tomorrow, something that really scares you, is God there? _____

If you fell, physically or emotionally, to the deepest depths, is God there with you? _____

Is God with you even during the darkest times of your life? _____

Has God been with you from the moment of your conception? _____

Will He be with you until the day you die? _____

Is there any time or any place you can go where God will not be with you? _____

Why? Because He is not limited by time and space like you are. He is o_ _ _ _ _ _ _ _ _ _.

Memory Work: Copy Psalm 139:7 here: _____
_____
_____

Prayer suggestion: Praise God for His omnipresence. Thank Him that He is always with you, always leading you, and always holding you.

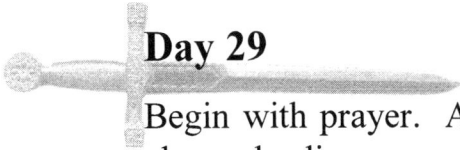

Day 29

Begin with prayer. A suggestion: Thank God that He is always with you, always leading you, and always holding you.

Sword Drill

The book of *I _ _ _ _ _* has many prophecies foretelling our Savior Jesus. The book of *Jeremiah* was written by the "weeping prophet." Write the names of the next six books after *Song of Solomon* here: *I_ _ _ _ _*, *J_ _ _ _ _ _ _*, *L_ _ _ _ _ _ _ _ _ _*, *E_ _ _ _ _ _*, *D_ _ _ _ _*, *H_ _ _ _*.

Sword Play

Solve the following code based on Psalm 139:13-16.

A B C D E F G H I J K L M N O P Q R S T U V W X Y Z
1 2 3 4 5 6 7 8 9 10 11 12 13 14 15 16 17 18 19 20 21 22 23 24 25 26

7 15 4   23 1 19   23 9 20 8   13 5   23 8 5 14   9   23 1 19

2 5 9 14 7   9 14 20 18 9 3 1 20 5 12 25   4 5 19 9 7 14 5 4

9 14   13 25   13 15 20 8 5 18 19   23 15 13 2,   5 22 5 14

2 5 6 15 18 5   9   23 1 19   6 21 12 12 25   6 15 18 13 5 4.

1 12 12   13 25   4 1 25 19   1 18 5   1 12 18 5 1 4 25

23 18 9 20 20 5 14   9 14   25 15 21 18   2 15 15 11 - 1 14 4

8 1 22 5   2 5 5 14   5 22 5 14   2 5 6 15 18 5   9   8 1 4

12 9 22 5 4   15 14 5   4 1 25!   25 15 21,   13 25   7 15 4,

1 18 5   15 13 14 9 16 18 5 19 5 14 20!

86

Fencing Practice

If you haven't already done so, turn to Psalm 139:13-16 and read it. Before you were formed or had substance, God knew you. When you were being woven together, intricately designed, a masterpiece, God was with you.

For what reason was David praising God in verse 14? _____

_____

Look back at verse 13. Who formed you, designed you, and knitted you together? _____

Now look at verse 15. You were intricately, beautifully, carefully crafted together in your mother's womb. Who was with you during this process? Who designed you? _____ Who put that design into practice and put you together? _____ Was there any part of this process when God was not present? _____ Did any part of your formation take place when God wasn't looking? _____ Does God ever, ever make a mistake? _____ Look at verse 16. Does God know your tomorrows? _____ Has God ever, ever left you any time in your life? _____ Why not? Because our God is o_ _ _ _ _ _ _ _ _ .

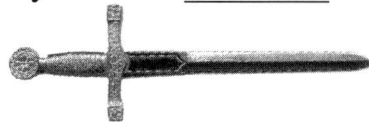

Thrust and Parry

When you look in the mirror, or when you consider your gifts and talents, there are certain things about yourself that you like. List three things that you like about yourself here: _____, _____, and _____.

Just like David did in Psalm 139, you can easily look at those three things and praise God for making you like that. But there are probably things you don't like about yourself, the way you look, or handicaps you have, or areas where you aren't talented or gifted. List three things that you don't like about yourself here: _____, _____, and _____.

Here's where your faith in God's omnipotence and omnipresence is really tested. Can you look at those three things that you don't like about yourself and *still* repeat David's Psalm? Can you thank God for the wonderful way He made you? Can you thank God for designing you the way He did? Can you thank God that He was with you, watching you, crafting every part of you?

Personalize Psalm 139:13-16 by copying those six things (the three that you like and the three that you don't like about yourself) in the spaces in the following prayer.

"You, God, formed me with these characteristics: _____, _____, _____, _____, _____, and _____. You knitted me together in my mother's womb. I praise you, for I am wonderfully, beautifully made. Wonderful are your works – *all of them*. My soul knows it! Those six things: _____, _____, _____, _____, _____, and _____ weren't hidden from you (you're omnipresent) when I was being made, intricately woven. Your eyes saw my unformed substance, including: _____, _____, _____, _____, _____, and _____ because you are omnipresent. I know you are good and all that you create is good."

Memory Work: Copy Psalm 139:7 here: _____
_____
_____

Prayer suggestion: Read your personalized Psalm 139 to God as a prayer.

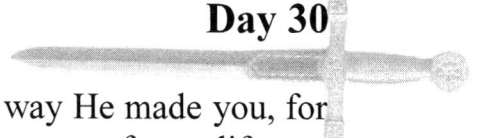

Begin with prayer. A suggestion: Thank God for the way He made you, for His good plan for you, and for being with you every moment of your life.

Sword Drill

The book of **J** _ _ _ _ _ _ _ was written by the "weeping prophet." **Lamentations** was also written by Jeremiah. Write the names of the next six books after **Song of Solomon** here: **I**_ _ _ _ _, **J** _ _ _ _ _ _ _,
L_ _ _ _ _ _ _ _ _ _, **E**_ _ _ _ _ _, **D**_ _ _ _ _, **H** _ _ _ _.

Sword Play

The acrostic below will give you an expanded definition of *omnipresent*. Use the key to fill in the missing letters.

<u>O</u> <u>M</u> <u>N</u> <u>I</u> <u>P</u> <u>R</u> <u>E</u> <u>S</u> <u>E</u> <u>N</u> <u>T</u>
  1   2   3   4   5   6   7   8   9 10 11

O u _ G _ d _ _ _ _ _ _ _ _ _ _ _ _ .
    6   1   4 8 1 2 3 4 5 6 7 8 9 3 11

M _ _ _ _ g a _ d _ v _ _ i _ g h _ l d h _ _ _ _ _ _ _ _ _ c _ .
  1 6 3 4 3   10 7 7 10 3   1   4 8 5 6 7 8 7 3 9

N _ _ l _ _ _ _ _ d b y _ _ a c _ .
  1 11 4 2 4 11 9   8 5 9

I _ h _ a v _ _ a _ d _ h _ _ l.
  10   9 9 10 10 8 9 1

P _ _ _ _ _ _ _ _ _ v _ _ l _ a v _ _ _ .
  6 1 2 4 8 9 8 11 1 10 7 9 6 7 9 2 7

R _ _ _ b _ _ , h _ _ _ w _ h _ _ _ _ _ w.
  9 2 9 2 9 6   9 4 8 4 11 2 9 3 1

E v _ _ y w h _ _ _ .
  7 6 7 6 7

S _ a y _ w _ _ h _ _ a l w a y _ .
  11 8 4 11 2 7   8

E y _ _ a l w a y _ w a _ c h _ _ g.
  9 8   8   11 4 10

N _ _ l _ _ _ _ _ d b y _ _ _ _ .
  1 11 4 2 4 11 9   11 4 2 9

T a k _ _ _ _ b y _ h _ h a _ d.
  9 8 2 9   11 9 10

Fill in this statement from Hebrews 13:5 by writing all the bold faced, underlined letters in the *Fencing Practice* part of your lesson (*below*) in the order in which you find them. Make sure you *read* it, not just pull letters from it.

_ , _ _ _ _   _ _ _ _ _   _ _ _ _ _   _ _ _.
_ _ _   _ _ _ _   _ _ _ _ _ _ _   _ _ _.
_   _ _   _ _ _ _ _ _ _ _ _ _.

Fencing Practice

If you haven't already done so, please turn to Hebre**w**s 13:5. What you w**ill** **n**otic**e** when you read it is that the first part teaches us to **vie**w money and possessions in a pa**r**ticul**a**r way. W**e** **a**re taught to keep our li**ve**s free from the _____ of _____.

Mone**y** is **n**ot evil, b**ut** lov**i**ng it is. It's too easy to **p**lace our hope and trust in money and to be**l**ieve mo**ne**y will sol**ve** all our **p**roblems. God, however, is **a** jealous God and will not share your affections with money.

But th**a**t's **n**ot all. He teaches us to practice being _____ with what we have. Go**d** is utterly c**on**fident that once **you**'ve exper**i**enced His presence – once you h**a**ve found Hi**m** – y**o**u will be totally satisfied with Hi**m**.

This is a**n** **i**mp**or**tant truth. Mone**y** and thing**s** will **n**ever satisfy you. You'll always wa**nt** more. But if you seek God and find Him, you'll be totally satisfied. It is true!

God makes it easy for you. How hard is it to find someone if that person is right next to you, with you, leading you, holding you? Not very hard at all! Our problem is that we seldom look. But, does your indifference cause God to flee? _____ He is *still* there with you!

Thrust and Parry

Do you like money? _____
Do you wish you had more? _____
Do you wish you were rich? _____

Money isn't a bad thing, but God wants you to keep your life free from the love of it. Why?

Can money save you? _____
Can money watch over you? _____
Can money be with you forever? _____

90

Can money consume you? _____

Can money control you? _____

Can money replace God in your life? _____

God tells you in Hebrews 13:5 how to keep free from the *love* of money:
1. Practice being c _ _ _ _ _ _ .
2. Remember God will never l _ _ _ _ you nor f _ _ _ _ _ _ you.

If you have *nothing* in this life – no money, no home, no toys, no food – but you have God, then you have *everything*. God's omnipresence is so amazing that *even in your weakest moments when you can hardly hang on* He will not let go of you. So, don't fill your life with money and things that money can buy. Instead seek hard after God. His presence will satisfy you more than money ever could! He is o _ _ _ _ _ _ _ _ _ _ .

Memory Work: Copy Psalm 139:7 here: _____

_____

_____

Prayer suggestion: Pray that God will help you be content with what He has provided – and that you won't be content until He has filled your heart with Himself.

Day 31

Begin with prayer. A suggestion: Ask God to fill you with so much of Himself that nothing else will make you content.

Sword Drill

L _ _ _ _ _ _ _ _ _ _ _ is another book written by the prophet Jeremiah. *Ezekiel*, a prophet, had some exciting visions of God. Write the names of the next six Old Testament books after *Song of Solomon* here: *I*_ _ _ _ _, *J* _ _ _ _ _ _ _, *L* _ _ _ _ _ _ _ _ _ _, *E* _ _ _ _ _ _, *D* _ _ _ _ _, *H* _ _ _ _.

Sword Play

The answers to the following fill-in-the-blanks are taken from your lessons on God's omnipresence and from Deuteronomy 31:6.

Abandon	Evil	Leave
Afraid	Eyes	Limited
Content	Good	Money
Courageous	Hand	Mother's
Day	Heaven	Sheol
Designed	Hide	Space
Earth	Hold	Time
Escape	Knitted	Watching
Every place	Lead	

1. Our God is in _ _ _ _ _ _ _ _ _ _. His _ _ _ _ are _ _ _ _ _ _ _ _ both the _ _ _ _ and the _ _ _ _.

2. No one can _ _ _ _ from Him. No one can _ _ _ _ _ _ His presence, since He fills _ _ _ _ _ _ _, _ _ _ _ _, and even _ _ _ _ _ _.

3. His _ _ _ _ will _ _ _ _ you and _ _ _ _ you, never letting you go.

4. He was even with you in your _ _ _ _ _ _ _'_ womb. He watched over you, _ _ _ _ _ _ _ _ _ you, and _ _ _ _ _ _ _ _ you together. Not one _ _ _ has gone by that He wasn't with you.

5. Don't waste your time on earth by worrying about _ _ _ _ _ _. Be _ _ _ _ _ _ _, because you already have the greatest treasure.

6. He is not _ _ _ _ _ _ _ by _ _ _ _ or _ _ _ _ _.

7. Be strong. Be _ _ _ _ _ _ _ _ _ _. Don't be _ _ _ _ _ _. Why? Because God is with you, holding you. He will never _ _ _ _ _ you. He will never _ _ _ _ _ _ _ you.

Fencing Practice

If you haven't already done so, turn to Deuteronomy 31:6 and read it. You might even want to underline this in your Bible. This is a startling verse, because it commands you to do something. What does it command you to do? ...be _____ and _____.

You probably already know that that's easier said than done. What things have you faced in life that scare you? If you're anything like me, you probably don't like speaking in front of a group, or making a fool of yourself, or being alone at night, or even thinking about end times. List two things that scare you: _____ and _____.

You can probably also think of things that make you feel weak, like having to say "no" to a movie that all your friends want to watch, or being annoyed by your sibling, or having to do the dishes by yourself, or stumbling on a tempting advertisement. Many things can make us feel weak and tempted to sin. List two things that can make you feel weak and tempted to sin: _____ and _____.

You might be thinking, "Yeah, right. God wants me to be strong and courageous when I face these things. That's easier said than done." And, you would be absolutely right. How is it possible that you can be strong and courageous when you face frightening or tempting circumstances? God gives you three reasons in Deuteronomy 31:6:

He is w _ _ _ y _ _ .
He will never _____ you.
He will never _____ you.

Thrust and Parry

It's so easy to forget that God helps us to be strong in the face of temptation. Look at these examples again:

Your friends want to watch a movie that you aren't allowed to watch. You might feel weak and tempted to give in and watch the movie. God says: "Be _____." He reminds you that He is with you and never leaves you.

Your sibling keeps picking on you and being annoying. You are really tired of it and are feeling weak and tempted. What you would really like to do is to yell at him and slam your bedroom door in his face. But, God says: "Be _____." He reminds you that He is with you even when you're very annoyed. You don't have to give in to the temptation to be mean to your sibling.

Your mom tells you to do the mountain of dishes by yourself. You start to moan and complain, but then you remember that God says, "Be _____." He reminds you that He never leaves you and will be with you while you are cheerfully doing your chores.

Look at the two things you wrote on page 93 that make you feel weak and ready to stumble. God wants you to be strong when you face those situations. He promises to be with you as you walk through those difficult times. What is one way you can be strong in the Lord when you are tempted in those situations? _____

Remember, God is o _ _ _ _ _ _ _ _ _ _. He is with you!

Memory Work: Copy Psalm 139:7 here: _____
_____
_____

Prayer suggestion: Pray that God will help you to be strong and courageous when you are faced with frightening circumstances or temptation.

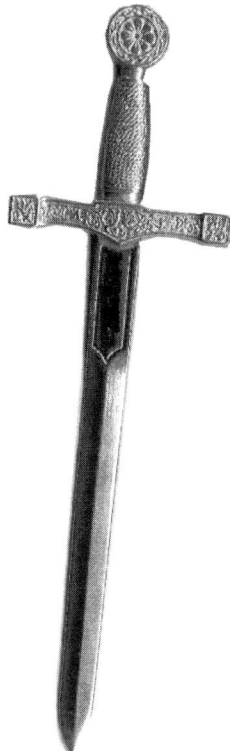

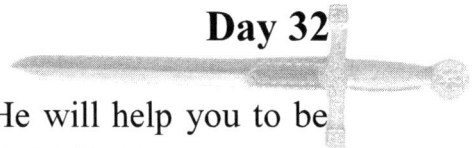

Begin with prayer. A suggestion: Thank God that He will help you to be strong the next time you are tempted. Be specific in your prayer.

Sword Drill

 E _ _ _ _ _, another prophet, had some exciting visions of God. *Daniel* had many end-time prophecies. Write the names of the next six Old Testament books after *Song of Solomon* here: *I_ _ _ _ _*, *J _ _ _ _ _ _ _*, *L_ _ _ _ _ _ _ _ _*, *E_ _ _ _ _ _*, *D_ _ _ _ _*, *H _ _ _ _*.

Sword Play

 The following multiple choice questions are based on Psalm 139:1-4. Circle the correct answer.

1. Think of how many times already today you sat down and stood up. Give a rough estimate, writing the number here: _____. How many of those times does God know about?
    a) None. He could care less about my sitting down and standing up.
    b) Only the important ones (like when I study the Bible), but not the unimportant ones (like going to the bathroom).
    c) Maybe about half; because He's far too busy to worry about the nonessentials.
    d) All of them, because He love me so much!

2. Our thoughts are the most private part of our lives. No one but you knows what goes on inside your head. What is God's relationship to your thoughts?
    a) He knows everything going on inside my head, the good, the bad, and the ugly.
    b) He is my creator and intimately understands everything about me, even what's inside of me.
    c) My hopes, fears, dreams, anxieties, loves, and hates…all of it is an open book before God.
    d) All of the above.
3. You have no idea what today will bring. You might have all kinds of plans today, but they may or may not work out. You may have hopes for your life, what you want to do when you grow up, but you have no idea whether those dreams will come to pass.

a) God has a perfect plan for you, but He can only hope you make the right choices to see that plan through. He doesn't actually know whether or not you'll choose correctly until the time comes.

b) It's impossible for God to know and understand every path of all 7 billion people on the planet. If even one of those 7 billion people chooses wrongly, it could affect the rest of the world and many generations to come!

c) *I* don't even know my tomorrows! How can *He* possibly know them?!

d) God is not bound by time like we are, so He knows perfectly my path. This includes the next few minutes, the next few years, and all my decades to come.

4. You might not always think before you speak. Perhaps things fly out of your mouth, and you realize right away that you shouldn't have said those things. Even though you don't always know what is going to come out of your mouth…

   a) …Thankfully God doesn't know either, but He can help you to patch things up when you mess up with your words.

   b) …God knows every word you will speak, even before you know it…because He knows what's in your heart.

   c) ….God gets confused when He sorts out all those words. Sometimes, you even change your mind mid-sentence! There's no way He could know all of that!

   d) …It doesn't matter unless it actually comes out of your mouth. After all, it's just your tongue!

Fencing Practice

This lesson introduces another wonderful, awesome attribute of God. Our God is **omniscient**. He is all-knowing. This makes perfect sense. God wouldn't be omnipotent (all powerful) or omnipresent (not limited by time and space) if He wasn't also omniscient. And of course, being omnipotent includes having the power of knowing all things!

If you haven't already done so, turn to Psalm 139:1-4 and read it, nice and slowly. After reading it, answer this question in your own words: How well does God know you? _____

_____

_____

Do you know what really amazes me about God's omniscience? It amazes me that He still loves me even after seeing all the "stuff" inside my head and heart! He didn't just slip into my heart at my invitation, then find He was trapped inside the life of someone with all kinds of wickedness and selfish issues! Not at all! He died for me even while I was at my ugliest. He sees all the crud in my soul, and still loves me and saves me! That is one of the reasons that God's omniscience is, to me, one of His most startling and compelling attributes. Our response to His omniscience should be, "Wow! And He *still* loves me, even after seeing what I am *really* like!"

Thrust and Parry

I would like you to imagine moving somewhere where you didn't know anyone. You were the stranger. You wanted to make some new friends. What do you look for in a friend? List at least 7 things below (characteristics, hobbies, interests) that you like in a friend:

- _____
- _____
- _____
- _____
- _____
- _____
- _____

Would you deliberately pick someone as a friend who was mean and selfish? Yes or no? _____ Would you pick someone as a friend who often ignored you and didn't want to spend time with you? _____ Would you pick someone as a friend who was your enemy? _____

It is comforting to know that even though God is omnis_ _ _ _and sees all the selfishness, anger, hatred, pride, and ugliness in our hearts, He still loves us passionately. He still chose to redeem us! Praise God! We have nothing to hide from Him…He already knows it all!

Memory Work: Copy Psalm 139:23-24 here: _____

_____

_____

_____

Prayer suggestion: Worship God for His omniscience, then thank Him that He still loves you even though He knows everything about you!

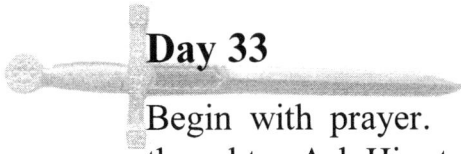

Day 33

Begin with prayer. A suggestion: Invite God to search your heart and thoughts. Ask Him to reveal any wickedness there.

Sword Drill

> *D* _ _ _ _ _ had many end-time prophecies. *Hosea* demonstrates how God faithfully loves unfaithful unlovely individuals. Write the names of the next six Old Testament books after *Song of Solomon* here: *I*_ _ _ _ _, *J* _ _ _ _ _ _ _, *L* _ _ _ _ _ _ _ _ _ _ _, *E* _ _ _ _ _ _, *D* _ _ _ _ _, *H* _ _ _ _.

Sword Play

The answers to the following true/false quiz can be found in Psalm 147:4-5. Circle T for true or F for false.

- Our God is great. He has abundant power. T F
- God flung a large, *random* number of stars across the sky. T F
- Based on His omniscience, He pre-determined the perfect, exact number of stars for the universe. T F
- Because He is omniscient, God named *only the most important stars* in the universe. T F
- Since there are billions of stars, God remembers *only* the names of the main stars. T F
- God named every star, billions of them, and remembers the name of each and every one. T F
- One definition for 'omniscient' is 'understanding beyond measure.' Another is 'all-knowing.' T F

Fencing Practice

Stars are amazing and beautiful. On a dark, cloudless night, you can see about 2,500 stars with just your eyes (no telescope). Our amazing God, who is omnis_ _ _ _ _, knows the names of each one. How easily could you remember 2,500 different names? You *might* be able to name 2,500 different people if you count all your family, your friends, neighbors, church members, sports team members, co-workers, music group members, movie and music stars, professional athletes, rulers and political leaders, and historical figures.

If you see a picture of a thin, dark-haired man with beard and a stovepipe hat, you think "Abraham Lincoln." If you see a drawing of an ancient, pregnant woman dressed in Bible-style robes, you think "Sarah, wife of Abraham." The differences in appearance, style, and setting of each individual help you to remember their names.

If, however, you look up in the night sky and see a patch of just 300 stars, from your vantage point each looks just like the other: the same shape, size, and color. What are the chances that you could correctly identify by name each of those identical-looking stars?

Do you know how many stars there are? Just in *our* Milky Way Galaxy[1], some scientists estimate there may be a trillion stars. This is a number one followed by 12 zeros. Write that number here:

1,_ _ _ , _ _ _ , _ _ _ , _ _ _

Think about it. Our incredible o _ _ _ _ _ _ _ _ _ God knows each one of them by name. But, if that isn't amazing enough some scientists estimate that there might be more than 10^{23} stars in the entire universe! That's a number one followed by 23 zeroes. Write that number here:

1 _ _ , _ _ _ , _ _ _ , _ _ _ , _ _ _ , _ _ _ , _ _ _ , _ _ _

Our o _ _ _ _ _ _ _ _ _ God knows *each one of them by name*!

Thrust and Parry

If you haven't already done so, turn in your Bible to Psalm 147:4-5 and read it. In verse 5, the psalmist tells us something about God's understanding. What does the psalmist say? _____
What do you think this means? _____
_____

- Because our God is omniscient, will you ever be able to *know* everything He knows? Yes or No
- Because our God is omniscient, will you ever be able to understand everything He understands? Yes or No

- Because our God is omniscient, will some things forever remain a mystery to you? Yes or No
- Because you have a finite mind, will you ever be able to fully comprehend our infinite God? Yes or No

This is one of those amazing things about God. If our finite minds *could* comprehend Him, then He wouldn't be infinite. Because we are finite (have limits) and He is infinite (has no limits), we must learn to be comfortable with mystery. We'll never fully understand why God does the things He does or allows the things He allows. We can't fully understand why He chooses to save His enemies, then adopts them as His children. We can, however, know this: God *is* good, *all the time*.

Memory work: Copy Psalm 139:23-24 here: _____

_____

_____

_____

Prayer suggestion: Worship God for His beautiful, starry sky. Thank Him that He knows *your* name, and loves you completely.

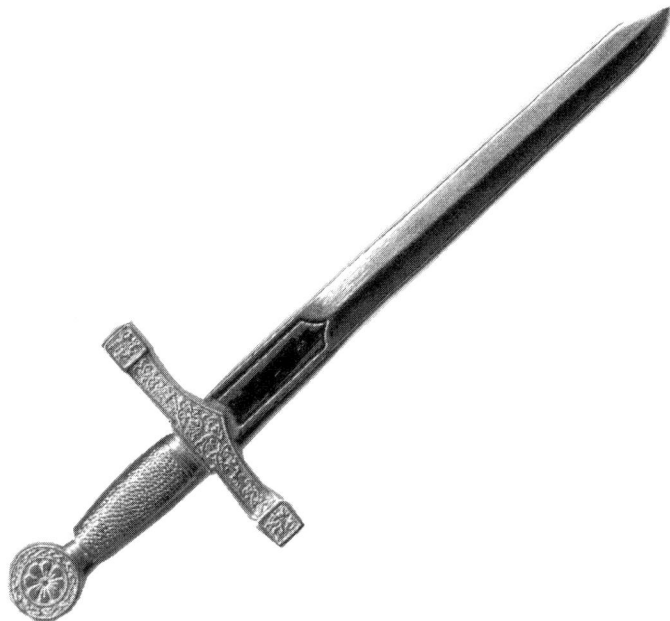

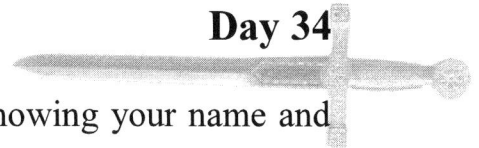

Begin with prayer. A suggestion: Thank God for knowing your name and adopting you as His child

Sword Drill

H _ _ _ demonstrates how God faithfully loves unfaithful unlovely individuals. Write the names of the next six Old Testament books after *Song of Solomon* here: *I_ _ _ _ _, J _ _ _ _ _ _ _, L_ _ _ _ _ _ _ _ _ _ _,*
E_ _ _ _ _ _, D_ _ _ _ _, H _ _ _ _.

Sword Play

The answers to the following riddles can be found in Isaiah 29:15-16.

- I am two rhetorical questions. Unbelievers often ask these. If you wanted to secretly do something sinful, you would hope the answer to these questions is "no one." The *true* answer to the questions is "God." (Verse 15)
     What questions am I?

_____

_____

- I turn and spin stuff to create something new. I can take what is seemingly worthless, and turn it into a thing of value and beauty. God is the greatest one of these of all (verse 16).
     What am I?

_____

- I am a statement…a *very* ignorant one! Evolutionists and atheists make this statement all the time. Even, sadly, many Christians make this statement of God if they fall for evolutionist teaching (verse 16).
     What statement am I?

_____

- Some hate me. Moms often don't want me in the house, on the floor. Some love me. I can be used in building materials, art work, and food vessels. Apply heat to me and I get very hard (verse 16).
     What am I?

_____

- I am another statement. This statement can be said of everyone, even those closest to you. You could say this even to your best friend, and it would be true…but, it would *not* be true if you said it of God, because He is omniscient. (Verse 16)

    What statement am I?

Fencing Practice

If you haven't already done so, turn to Isaiah 29:15-16. You are probably noticing by now that Scripture often asks rhetorical questions. This particular passage asks two rhetorical questions designed to demonstrate how ridiculous it is for anyone to believe that God is *not* omniscient. Of *course* God is omniscient. And you *cannot* hide either your plans or your deeds from Him.

Verse 16 explains just how ridiculous it is to disbelieve God's omniscience. Circle your answers to the questions below.

- Would you believe a Ford Mustang if it said to you, "I wasn't designed by a designer nor built in a factory. I *evolved.*" Yes or No?
- Picture the Empire State Building. We couldn't conceive of the building proclaiming, "There was no architect or engineer involved in my creation, nor mason, welder, or builder. There was a big BANG, and then I *evolved.*" Would you believe that statement? Yes or No?

It is even more ridiculous to believe that God did not design and create us. It is equally ridiculous to believe that the creator of us doesn't understand us. Of *course* our Creator understands us!

He not only created us, He is om_ _ _ _ _ _ _ _.

Thrust and Parry

I've invested in some high-powered software in order to run my publishing business. Despite all my efforts to figure out the software, I have only been able to master a small percentage of its capabilities. In order to take full advantage of the power of the software, I have to do one of three things:

1. Go into the software's internal help menu and ask questions. The questions are answered immediately through the software. (The designers built the answers in.)
2. Take an online course created by the designers.
3. Take a course at our local college, which is taught by someone who'd been trained by the designers.

In all three cases, it was the designers who ultimately had the knowledge to correctly and effectively teach me how to best utilize my new software. *Your* Designer also longs to correctly and effectively teach you how to best utilize the life He's given you. He's om_ _ _ _ _ _ _ _. Trust Him. Look at those three points above. Each is similar to one way our Creator (who understands us perfectly) teaches us.

- Which point (1, 2, or 3) on the previous page would most remind you of going to church and being taught by your Pastor? _____
- Which point would be most like reading God's Word, the Bible? ___
- Which point would remind you of prayer (talking directly to the designer Himself)? _____

God designed and created you. He perfectly understands everything about you. He will show you how to best use the life you've been granted. Trust Him. Pay attention to what He has to say about your life. Do what He tells you to do. He created you. He is om _ _ _ _ _ _ _ _.

Memory work: Copy Psalm 139:23-24 here: _____

_____

_____

_____

Prayer suggestion: Ask God to guide your steps today.

Day 35

Begin with prayer. A suggestion: Thank God for teaching you how to live. Ask Him to help you be a doer, not just a hearer.

Sword Drill

Joel was a prophet who talked about end times. List the first seven minor prophets here: *J _ _ _, A _ _ _, O _ _ _ _ _ _, J _ _ _ _, M _ _ _ _, N _ _ _ _, H _ _ _ _ _ _ _.*

Sword Play

Complete the following phrases by matching the first part of the phrase in the first column, with the second part of the phrase in the second column. The sentences are paraphrased from Isaiah 40:28.

Didn't you know?…   …everything, even the
                                                      ends of the earth.

Our God is…   …He is omniscient.

Our God created…   …Haven't you heard?

Our God never faints…   …and He's never
                                                      exhausted.

His understanding is   …everlasting, the
unsearchable because…   Creator.

Fencing Practice

This passage is one of my favorites. You might even want to underline it in your Bible. If you haven't already done so, turn to Isaiah 40:28, but this time read it all the way through to verse 31. When you're done reading it (and underlining it, if you want to), write in your own words what this passage teaches you about God: _____

_____

_____

_____

How wonderful to know that because God is omniscient, He knows all about your weaknesses and struggles. Because He is omnipotent, He can erase your weakness and carry you through your struggles. All you need to do is to *wait* on Him. What does that mean? When you *wait* on someone, what are you doing? _____

_____

_____

_____

Thrust and Parry

All three of the attributes we've studied so far (God is omnipotent, omnipresent, and omniscient) are implied in Isaiah 40:28. Let's review.

All-powerful = omni_ _ _ _ _ _

Not limited by space or time = omni_ _ _ _ _ _ _ _

All-knowing = omni_ _ _ _ _ _

The phrases below are taken from Isaiah 40:28. Fill in the attribute that is described by each phrase.

- Our God is an everlasting God. He is _____
- Our God is the creator God. He never grows weary. He is _____

_____

- Our God's understanding is so vast, it's unsearchable. He is _____

_____

He is so powerful that He not only created you, but He will never let you go. He is so kind and good, He will care for you during your weakest moments. He knows you so perfectly, and yet loves you anyway. Our God is omnis_ _ _ _ _.

Memory work: Copy Psalm 139:23-24 here: _____

_____

_____

_____

_____

Prayer suggestion: Thank God for His care for you. Ask Him to strengthen you today in whatever area you feel you are weakest.

Day 36

Begin with prayer. A suggestion: Ask God to help you not to grow weary (just as He promised) as you work today.

Sword Drill

J _ _ _ was a prophet who talked about end times. God sent *Amos* to the people of Israel to warn them to repent. List the first seven minor prophets here: **J _ _ _, A _ _ _, O _ _ _ _ _ _, J _ _ _ _, M _ _ _ _, N _ _ _ _, H _ _ _ _ _ _ _.**

Sword Play

All the words and phrases in the word search puzzle on the next page are taken from Proverbs 15:3 and from the attributes of God we're studying. First, fill in the blanks in the questions below (refer to the word bank for clues), then find those words in the puzzle.

1. Where the eyes of the Lord are: _ _ _ _ _ _ _ _ _ _

2. Not limited by time or space: _ _ _ _ _ _ _ _ _ _ _

3. What will you find in every place? _ _ _ _ _ _
   _ _ _ _ _ _ _

4. What God's eyes are doing: _ _ _ _ _ _ _ _ _ _ _ _

5. Opposite of good: _ _ _ _

6. A wise saying: _ _ _ _ _ _ _

7. God is _ _ _ _ all the time.

8. All-powerful: _ _ _ _ _ _ _ _ _ _

9. An old-fashioned word for "keeping watch" or "seeing."
   _ _ _ _ _ _ _ _ _

10. Having all knowledge and understanding: _ _ _ _ _ _ _ _ _ _

> **Word Bank**
> Beholding
> Every place
> Evil
> Eyes of the Lord
> Good
> Keeping watch
> Omnipotent
> Omnipresent
> Omniscient
> Proverb

```
o m n i p o t e n t c b y
a f o c p n t g w m o r l
z v e i g d x a q m b e g
t n e s e r p i n m o v n
x f v r t n g d k j p o i
e y e s o f t h e l o r d
m h r b w y v b s s k p l
k i y t n e i c s i n m o
u r p d u b j w v f o c h
l d l i o u e o s p t t e
n v a s h o k v k e r h b
r h c t a w g n i p e e k
o b e m a r k i p l k n o
```

Fencing Practice

The omniscience of God is amazing. "He knows everything about everything and everybody all the time…"[2] He doesn't have to "search for information about things, as a computer might retrieve a file; all His knowledge is immediately and directly before Him."[3] "God's knowledge is linked with His sovereignty: He knows each thing because He created it, sustains it, and now makes it function every moment according to His plan."[4]

I'm sure you are seeing how the "omni" attributes of God all work together. For God to be truly omnipotent, He must also be omnipresent and omniscient. A God who doesn't have the power to know the future couldn't be omnipotent. A God who was limited by time and space couldn't then be omniscient. Why? _____

_____

_____

_____

[2] Article, "God Sees and Knows: Divine Omniscience." The Holy Bible, English Standard Version, © 2000, 2001 by Crossway Bibles, a division of Good News Publishers, Wheaton, IL. Page 896.
[3] Ibid.
[4] Ibid.

Thrust and Parry

If you haven't already done so, turn to Proverbs 15:3 and read it. Then turn to Ephesians 1:11 and read it. (You may want to add it to your Promises list in your Bible.) When you are through reading these two verses, answer the following questions:

- Does God see you right now? _____
- As He watches you right now, what does He see? _____
_____

- Since He also sees your thoughts right now, what does He see? _____
_____

- You (if you are in Christ) have an inheritance. According to Ephesians 1:11, you were predestined to this inheritance. What does **_predestined_** mean in this verse? Look it up in a dictionary: _____
_____
_____

- How does God **_know_** who will obtain the inheritance? (See the end of Ephesians 1:11.) _____
_____

It's because He is all-powerful (om_ _ _ _ _ _ _ _), He is unlimited by time and space (om_ _ _ _ _ _ _ _ _), and He knows and understands all things (om_ _ _ _ _ _ _ _)!

Memory work: Copy Psalm 139:23-24 here: _____
_____
_____
_____
_____

Prayer suggestion: Thank God for His omniscience, that He keeps watch over you always. Thank Him that nothing about you ever escapes His attention.

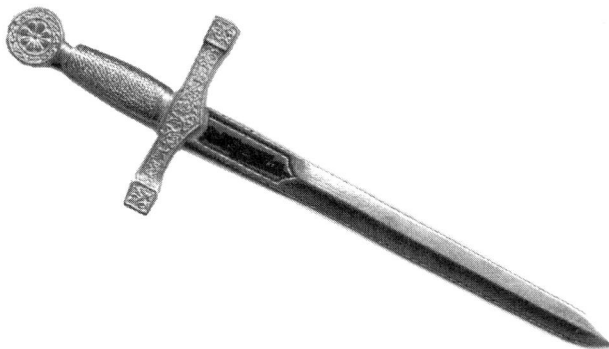

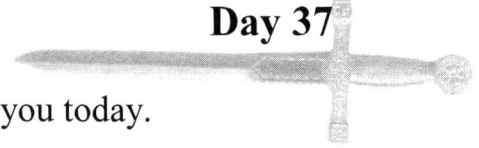

Begin with prayer. A suggestion: Ask God to search you today.

Sword Drill

God sent *A* _ _ _ to the people of Israel to warn them to repent. ***Obadiah*** reminds persecuted people that God cares for them. List the first seven minor prophets here: **J** _ _ _ , **A** _ _ _ , **O** _ _ _ _ _ _ , **J** _ _ _ _ , **M** _ _ _ _ , **N** _ _ _ _ , **H** _ _ _ _ _ _ _ .

Sword Play

The answers to the crossword puzzle on the next page are found in Isaiah 46:9-10. Fill in the blanks below, then use those words to complete the puzzle.

Across

3. What we are to remember (verse 9): _ _ _ _ _ _ _   _ _ _ _ _ _

5. Opposite of 'ending': _ _ _ _ _ _ _ _ _

6. The 'finish' of a story: _ _ _

7. Proclaiming (vs 10): _ _ _ _ _ _ _ _ _

11. Olden days: _ _ _ _ _ _ _   _ _ _ _ _

Down

1. What you are supposed to do with 'former things': _ _ _ _ _ _ _ _

2. God says, "Nothing compares to me," or "There's _ _ _ _   _ _ _ _   _ _ ."

4. God says this twice in verse 9: " _   _ _   _ _ _ ."

8. This will stand (verse 10): _ _ _ _ _ _ _

9. The book of the Bible where this passage is found: _ _ _ _ _ _

10. What his counsel will do (verse 10): _ _ _ _ _ _

Fencing Practice

If you haven't already done so, turn in your bible to Isaiah 46:9-10. We have been studying how our God knows and understands all things because He is om_ _ _ _ _ _ _ _. Isaiah 46:9-10 helps us to understand *why* God is omniscient. It's because He is omnipotent. He is the one who *declared* what the end of all things will be. He *declared* this all the way back in 'ancient times.' Of *course* He knows what will happen. He's the one who declared it!

In verse 10 He says that what He has declared, which includes His counsel, His pleasure, and His purpose, will be accomplished. According to verse 10, how much of His counsel, pleasure, and purpose will be accomplished? _____

How does He know this? Because He is om_ _ _ _ _ _ _ _.

Thrust and Parry

God obviously knows your future. He knows what you'll be doing ten years from now. He declared it from ancient times and His plan for you will be accomplished.

Not only that, but if you are in Christ, it will be a *good future*. God has declared it. It will be accomplished. Read Jeremiah 29:11. You can underline

110

it in your Bible, if you like. It's a wonderful truth! What kind of plans has God declared for you? _____ Here is a question, though. Does every believer live a long, happy, trouble-free life? _____ Of course not! I could list a number of children or Christians that I personally knew who died or were injured at a young age:

- Owen S. who died at seven months of age, needing a liver transplant.
- Andrew F. who died at age 14 in a tractor accident.
- Jimmy F. who died at age 23 in a truck accident.
- Debbie D. who was killed by a drunk driver at age 18.
- Billy H. who was accidentally shot in a hunting accident at age 15.
- Ian M. who was severely brain-damaged at age 21 from a car accident.

Perhaps you know of some young people who were injured or died at a young age. So, the question is, did God lie in Jeremiah 29:11 to those kids and their families? Of course not! In fact, God *promises* that in this world we will have troubles. (He *knows* because He is om_ _ _ _ _ _ _.) *We are not of this world.* Our wonderful future is part of another world – the world to which we *really* belong.

In the meantime, because God has declared it and *will* accomplish all that He purposes, you can know the following about your future if you are in Christ:

- On *this* earth, you will have _____ (John 16:33).
- God plans to give you _____ (Jeremiah 29:11).
- Jesus gives us _____ and who can snatch us from Him? _____ (John 10:28-29)
- In Hebrews 13:5 He promises to never _____.

How can God declare these things in Scripture? How can He know? Because He is o_ _ _ _ _ _ _ _.

Memory work: Copy Psalm 139:23-24 here: _____
_____
_____
_____
_____

Prayer suggestion: Thank God that when the tough times come in your life, He will never leave you. Thank Him that your future is secure.

Day 38

Begin with prayer. A suggestion: Ask God to fill your heart with hope, especially when your day gets tough.

Sword Drill

O _ _ _ _ _ _ reminds persecuted people that God cares for them. ***Jonah*** was a reluctant prophet who eventually did what God commanded. List the first seven minor prophets here: **J** _ _ _, **A** _ _ _, **O** _ _ _ _ _ _, **J** _ _ _ _, **M** _ _ _ _, **N** _ _ _ _, **H** _ _ _ _ _ _ _.

Sword Play

Fill in the blanks in the clues below using words from Matthew 10:29-31.
- How much are two sparrows worth? (verse 29) _____
- How many sparrows will fall to the ground without God knowing about it? (verse 29) _____
- What has God numbered? (verse 30) _____
- Is this number constant? Is it the same today as it was yesterday? ___
- Our God is o_ _ _ _ _ _ _ _ _ (all-knowing).
- This is the reason you shouldn't _____ (verse 31)
- You are of _____ _____ than _____ _____. (verse 31)

Fencing Practice

Our God is o_ _ _ _ _ _ _ _ _, and that gives us great comfort! He knows *all* about you, even how many hairs you have on your head at any given moment. What an awesome God!

This knowledge is amazing. It doesn't just show that God is smart, but it shows just how much He cares. He even knows when your pet kitty catches and eats a sparrow. If He cares for a dull little sparrow and knows how many hairs you have on your head before and after you brush it, do you have any reason to fear? _____

You may want to take a moment to underline this passage in your Bible. When things are tough, you can refer back to it.

Thrust and Parry

Think of all the things God knows.

- Does He know where you are?   Yes or No
- Does He know what's happening to you?   Yes or No
- Does He know your thoughts?   Yes or No
- Does He know your words before you speak them?   Yes or No
- Does He know your past?   Yes or No
- Does He know your future?   Yes or No
- Does He know the number of hairs on your head?   Yes or No

Can you trust a God who knows all this?

- When you go through the good times, can you trust that He knows?_____
- When you go through the successful times, can you trust that He knows and helps? _____
- When you go through bad times, can you trust that He knows and cares? _____
- When you go through tragic times, can you trust that He knows and has a plan? _____
- Can you trust His promise (because you're worth much more than a sparrow!) that your ultimate future will be good? _____

Memory work: Copy Psalm 139:23-24 here: _____

_____

_____

_____

_____

_____

Prayer suggestion: Ask God to help you to know just how much He loves you.

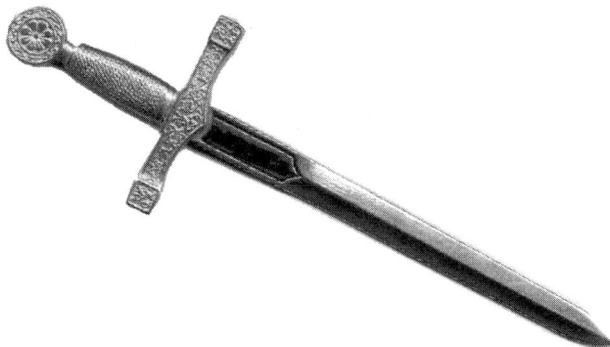

Day 39

Begin with prayer. A suggestion: Ask God to help you to know Him better as you study His Word.

Sword Drill

J _ _ _ _ was a reluctant prophet who eventually did what God commanded. *Micah* preached repentance to the Jews. List the first seven minor prophets here: **J _ _ _, A _ _ _, O _ _ _ _ _ _, J _ _ _ _, M _ _ _ _, N _ _ _ _, H _ _ _ _ _ _ _.**

Sword Play

For the next group of lessons, we are going to look at another attribute of God: His love. The answers to the multiple choice questions below can be found in Isaiah 40:11.

If you are in Christ, then God tends you. What does that mean?
- He feeds you.
- He carries you.
- He leads you.
- All of the above.

Isaiah 40:11 portrays God as _____, and you as _____.
- A mother; a baby
- A shepherd; a lamb
- A doctor; a patient
- A teacher; a student

How does God gather you, His lamb?
- With His shepherd's staff
- With a "sheep dog" (perhaps an angel)
- By speaking loudly, "Come!"
- With His own arms

What does God do with you, His lamb, once He's gathered you?
- He sends you out to the pasture.
- He carries you next to His heart.
- He tucks you safely in a barn.
- He shears you for wool.

114

What word describes how God leads you, His lamb?
- Quickly
- Competently
- Gently
- Carefully

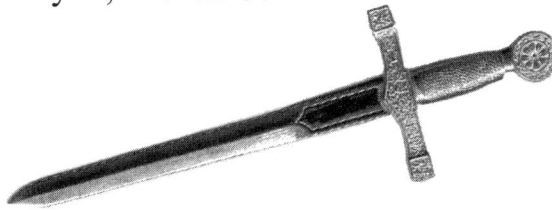

Fencing Practice

If you haven't already done so, turn in you Bible to Isaiah 40:11 and read it. You might want to underline it.

Sheep have a reputation for being stupid animals. They have poor eyesight and often aren't aware of situations right in front of them. They've been known to accidentally run into walls and actually knock themselves out.

Because sheep have no natural defense, they tend to stay in a flock. Usually a ram will serve as the leader, and the rest of the flock will blindly follow him. If the ram is removed from the flock, the rest of the flock won't be able to find their way to the pasture, even though they've gone to the same pasture every day on a clearly marked path. Without their leader, sometimes they can't even find their way out of the barn! (That's pretty stupid!)

Sheep have been known to be stubbornly stupid. If a sheep decides that the six-inch hole he sees in the fence is the way out, he may try over and over again to get out through that itty-bitty hole…even though the open gate is just a few feet away.

Sheep need a shepherd to protect them and to lead them down the right path to food and water.

Thrust and Parry

We're going to be studying many amazing verses about God's love. You might want to start a list of verses in the back of your Bible titled "God's love." As we study, you can continue to add to your list. You can refer to your list any time you want reassurance.

Isaiah 40:11 equates us with sheep. That might insult you now that you know how stupid sheep can be, but let's see if it's a good analogy after all.

- Have you ever made a poor choice even though it was obviously a poor choice? In other words, do you have "poor eyesight" like a sheep? _____
- Have you ever done something so dumb that you felt like you spiritually knocked yourself out? _____

- Have you ever given into peer pressure and followed the crowd, doing something you shouldn't have done (like the sheep blindly following their leader)? _____
- Do you ever feel like you can't find the right path for your life (even though the Bible clearly tells you the right path)?_____
- Do you ever feel like you don't know what you should do *today* and you're bored (like a sheep that can't even find its way out of the barn)? _____

In what ways is it an accurate analogy to compare us to sheep? _____

_____

_____

_____

_____

Memory work: Copy Romans 8:38 here: _____

_____

_____

_____

_____

_____

Prayer suggestion: Acknowledge that you are like a sheep and need a shepherd. Thank God for being the perfect shepherd for you despite your tendency to be like a sheep.

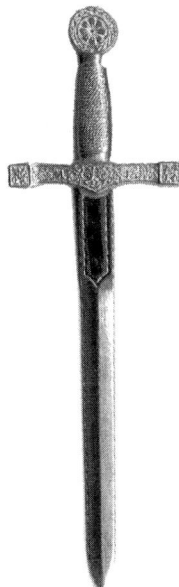

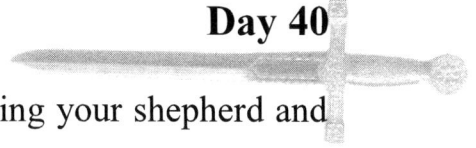

Begin with prayer. A suggestion: Thank God for being your shepherd and for leading you today.

Sword Drill

M_ _ _ _ preached repentance to the Jews. ***Nahum*** preached against the sin of the Ninevites. List the first seven minor prophets here: **J _ _ _**, **A _ _ _**, **O _ _ _ _ _**, **J _ _ _ _**, **M _ _ _ _**, **N _ _ _ _**, **H _ _ _ _ _ _ _**.

Sword Play

The answers to this true/false quiz are found in Zephaniah 3:17. Circle either T for *true* or F for *false*. (This is another great passage you can underline in your Bible or add to your list in the back of your Bible.)

- T or F God is in your midst only when you are behaving yourself.

- T or F God is mighty.

- T or F God will save you.

- T or F God *joyfully* rejoices over you. (Wow!)

- T or F His love quiets and rests you.

- T or F God occasionally hums a peaceful little tune over you.

Two of the statements above were false. Rewrite those two statements to make them true (use Zephaniah 3:17 to help you).

- _____
  _____

- _____
  _____

Fencing Practice

What strikes me most about this passage is God's *exuberance.* Religious paintings often portray Jesus and angels sweetly fluttering around, with their hands folded and their eyes cast heavenward. This passage paints for us an entirely different picture.

Our God is a loving God. He doesn't love in the same way we love. His love is joyful, mighty, exulting, and restful. Picture your reaction when your favorite team wins the championship. Picture the life, joy, and pizzazz that goes into your celebration. If you are in Christ, this is how God passionately and exuberantly rejoices over you! Isn't *that* mind boggling!

To really set this concept in your mind's eye, get up and act out God's celebratory love for you. You'll feel ridiculous, but it will help you to remember! Now, turn it around and passionately, joyfully, exuberantly worship your God in the same manner. I dare you!

Thrust and Parry

Can you picture God loudly and joyfully singing over you? It's hard for me to grasp! List five important "jobs" (for lack of a better term) that God does all the time. I've already listed two.

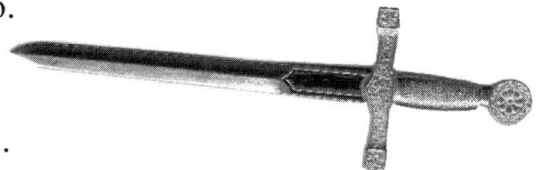

- He rules the nations.
- He keeps the planets in their orbits.
- _____
- _____
- _____
- _____
- _____

On top of all this (plus much, much more), God is busy *singing over you as an individual.* Our God is a loving God indeed!

Memory work: Copy Romans 8:38 here: _____

_____

_____

_____

_____

Prayer suggestion: Worship God. Exult and rejoice over Him. Pour out your love for Him.

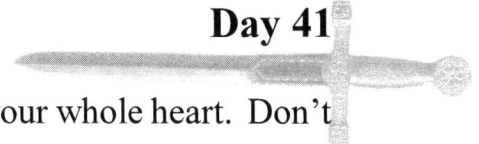

Begin with prayer. A suggestion: Worship God with your whole heart. Don't ask anything of Him. Just worship Him.

Sword Drill

N _ _ _ _ preached against the sin of the Ninevites. *Habakkuk* preached about God's faithfulness to His promises, and so can be called a forefather of the Reformation. List the first seven minor prophets here:
J _ _ _, A _ _ _, O _ _ _ _ _ _, J _ _ _ _, M _ _ _ _, N _ _ _ _,
H _ _ _ _ _ _.

Sword Play

The paragraph below is paraphrased from 1 John 3:1. The problem is that I messed it all up by substituting nine antonyms (opposites) for the correct words. You will need to replace those nine underlined words with the correct antonyms in order to fix it. The verse is written twice. The second version has blanks for you to write in your corrections.

1 John 3:1, paraphrased…

- Ignore what kind of hate the mother has for us, that we should be whispered the grownups of Satan; and so we are. The reason why the outer space doesn't flunk us is because it didn't know her.

- _____ what kind of _____ the _____ has for us, that we should be _____ the _____ of _____; and so *we are*. The reason why the _____ doesn't _____ us is because it didn't know _____.

Fencing Practice

I love this verse. (You might want to underline it in your Bible or add it to your list of verses in the back of your Bible.) God *commands* us to "see" or "behold" God's love. Do you know just how strong this love is? It's strong enough to adopt you so that now you are an *actual family member*. What does it mean "to be adopted"? _____

_____

It's one thing to say things like, "I love you like a friend," but friends come and go. They grow up, move away, or form new relationships.

Friendship is a wonderful thing, but God chooses to relate to us differently. We're more than just friends. We're *family*. We're not just *called* family. Because of God's great love, we actually *are* family. If your Bible doesn't have this phrase ("And so we are") in the actual text, check your footnotes.

So, can you *see* or *behold* God's love for you? You're His very own! "Christian" is your *new last name*. Write your full, adopted name here:

_____ _____ _____ _____
     (first)   (middle)   (last)   (new last name)

Thrust and Parry

As you go through these lessons on God's love, you're going to find that His love has nothing to do with you or your behavior. It has everything to do with Him, and the *fact* that He is faithful to His promises. It has everything to do with His own character. He *is* a God of love. Assuming you are in Christ, answer the following questions:

- Did God love you before you were saved or not until after you were saved? _____
- Did God love you before you were conceived or only after you were born and had developed your magnetic personality? _____
- Did God love you when you were an innocent baby, then stop loving you when you started sinning, then start loving you again once you were saved…or has He loved you all along? _____
- Does God stop loving you every time you fail and fall short, or has He loved you all along? _____
- Did God only start loving you once you made the decision to be saved, or did He love you when you were still His enemy? _____
- Does God love you only when you perform up to His standard, or does He love you even when you mess up? _____
- Does God just tolerate you because He's trapped by His own loving character, or does He passionately pursue you? _____

Memory work: Copy Romans 8:38 here: _____

_____

_____

_____

Prayer suggestion: Thank God that He has adopted you into His family.

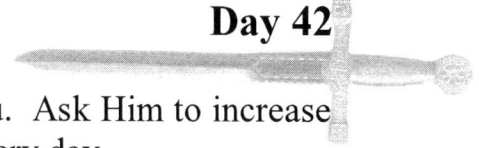

Begin with prayer. Worship God for His love for you. Ask Him to increase your "family resemblance" to look more like Jesus every day.

Sword Drill

H _ _ _ _ _ _ preached about God's faithfulness to His promises, and so can be called a forefather of the Reformation. List the first seven minor prophets here: **J** _ _ _, **A** _ _ _, **O** _ _ _ _ _ _, **J** _ _ _ _, **M** _ _ _ _, **N** _ _ _ _, **H** _ _ _ _ _ _ _.

Sword Play

To complete these puzzles, you will need to read Romans 8:37-39. This passage is so exciting. It shows how big and relentless God's love is. Complete the clues below, then use those words to fill in the mini-puzzles.

1. We aren't *just* victorious. According to verse 37 we are _ _ _ _ than _ _ _ _ _ _ _ _ _ _.

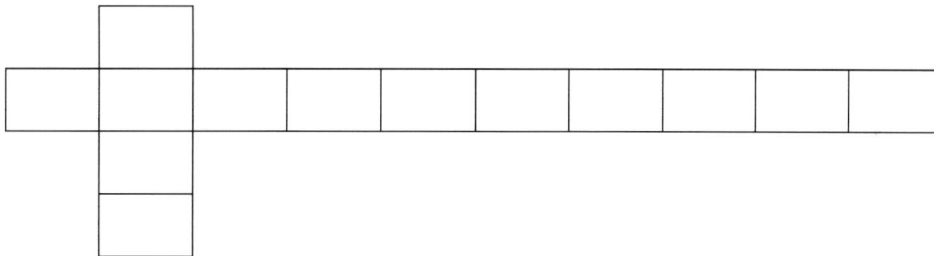

2. According to verse 38, the end of our earthly existence (also known as _ _ _ _ _) and our earthly existence (also known as _ _ _ _) can't separate us from God's love.

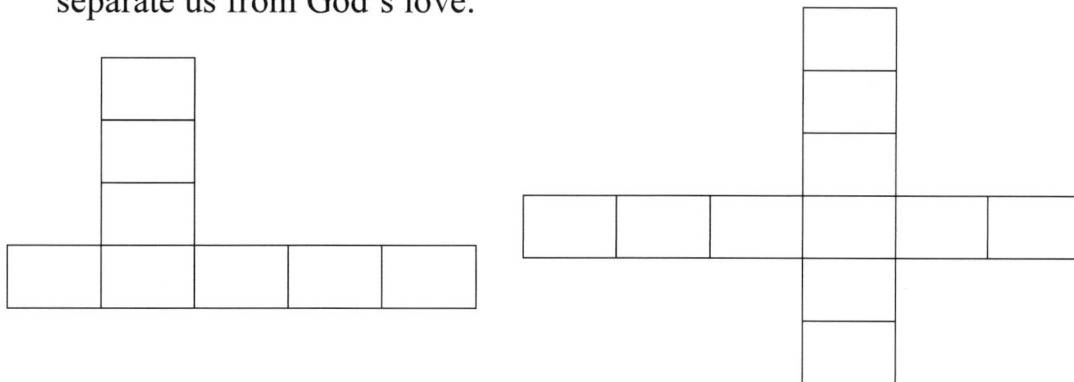

3. There are three types of beings, or entities, listed in verse 38, none of which can separate us from God's love. Write two of them here and in the puzzle above (right): _ _ _ _ _ _, _ _ _ _ _ _

4. Time can't separate us from God's love (verse 38: things _ _ _ _ _ _ _, things to _ _ _ _).

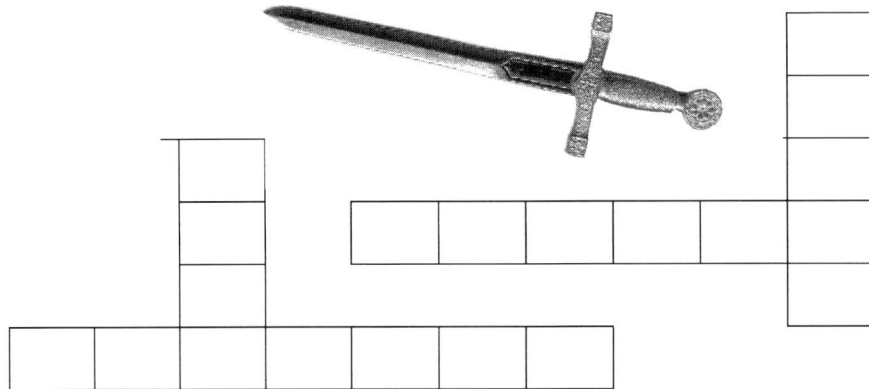

5. Space can't separate us from God's love either. Verse 39 mentions two aspects of space: _ _ _ _ _ _ and _ _ _ _ _.

Fencing Practice

You are the object of God's love. He has targeted you. His love for you is passionate and relentless. He has *proven* this to you. It is a demonstrable fact of your existence. Scripture declares it; therefore it is truth. You are loved by God.

Below list all the things in Romans 8:37-39 that *cannot* separate you from God: _____

_____

_____

_____

Thrust and Parry

Romans 8:37 tells us that we are more than conquerors. Let's think about what that means, since the Bible says that's what you are. In your own words, explain what a ***conqueror*** is. _____

_____

Now, explain in what ways *you* are a conqueror (read Romans 8:31-35 for ideas): _____

_____

_____

The last thing I want you to think about is that Romans 8:37 says that ***in Him*** you are *more than* a conqueror. Think about all you have learned, and all that God has promised you. Now, explain what it means to be *more than* a conqueror: _____

_____

(You may want to underline this verse or add it to your list in the back of your Bible.)

Memory work: Copy Romans 8:38 here: _____

_____

_____

_____

_____

Prayer suggestion: Ask God to help you to fully comprehend His love.

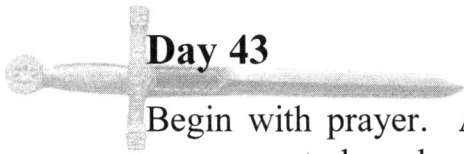

Day 43

Begin with prayer. A suggestion: Ask God to help you be more than a conqueror today when you face temptation to sin.

Sword Drill
Zephaniah prophesied to the Jews during the reign of godly King Josiah. List the last four minor prophets here: **Z** _ _ _ _ _ _ _ _, **H** _ _ _ _ _, **Z** _ _ _ _ _ _ _ _, **M** _ _ _ _ _ _.

Sword Play

The following statements are paraphrased from Lamentations 3:22-24. Match the first part of each statement with its correct ending.

The steadfast love of the Lord never….   …never come to an end.

His mercies…   …my portion.

They (His mercies) are…   …ceases.

Great is…   …hope in Him.

The Lord is…   …God's faithfulness.

I will…   …new every morning.

Fencing Practice
If you haven't already done so, turn in your Bible to Lamentations 3:22-24 and read it. What a wonderful passage this is! You may want to underline it or add it to your list in the back of your Bible.

According to this passage:
When will God's love for you end? _____
When will His mercy end? _____
The footnote in my Bible explains it like this: "*We are not consumed because God's compassion is not consumed. God's wrath toward His people will end because his compassion cannot end.*"[5]

---

[5] Quoted from the footnote on the word 'mercies' in verse 22. The Holy Bible, English Standard Version, © 2000, 2001 by Crossway Bibles, a division of Good News Publishers, Wheaton, IL. Page 1138.

Thrust and Parry

What does 'consumed' mean? _____

Do you deserve to be 'consumed'? _____ What does 'wrath' mean? _____ Do you deserve God's wrath? _____

Why is it that you don't receive those things that you deserve according to today's scripture passage? _____

_____

According to Lamentation 3:24, what is your true position? _____

_____

Verse 24 says that the Lord is our portion, or inheritance. The Hebrew word *cheleq* means *allotment, inheritance,* or *part.* Isn't that amazing! Though we deserve to be consumed by God, instead the very One from whom we need to be saved is now our *portion,* our i_ _ _ _ _ _ _ _ _, our a_ _ _ _ _ _ _, and our p_ _ _. Now, *that's* love!

Fill in the blanks with the truths of God's amazing love found in Lamentations 3:22-24.

Though I deserve _____, instead I experience God's _____. Each day in Christ is like a new day, because His mercies are _____ _____. Even when I'm unfaithful, God's faithfulness is _____. Instead of receiving God's wrath, I find that the Lord is my _____. That's why I _____ in Him.

Idea: Because my Bible is so precious to me, and God speaks to me through it, I love to write my thoughts in the margins of my Bible (and write the date) – like a conversation with God. I find it so encouraging to read back over my margin notes and remember how God spoke to my heart at that time. I also try to keep my Bible reverently neat, using a bookmark or the edge of an index card to aid me in underlining. I want to encourage you to try conversing with God through the pages of your Bible. Ask your parents to show you some of their underlined verses or margin notes.

Memory work: Copy Romans 8:*39* (new verse) here: _____

_____

_____

_____

_____

Prayer suggestion: Thank God that He is your inheritance, your portion.

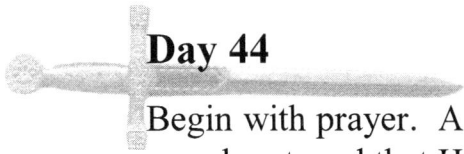

Begin with prayer. A suggestion: Ask God to help you to hide His Word in your heart, and that He would make that hidden Word active in your life.

Sword Drill

Z_ _ _ _ _ _ _ _ prophesied to the Jews during the reign of godly King Josiah. *Haggai* urged God's people to repent as they rebuilt the temple in conquered Jerusalem. List the last four minor prophets here:
Z_ _ _ _ _ _ _ _, H_ _ _ _ _, Z_ _ _ _ _ _ _ _, M_ _ _ _ _ _.

Sword Play

For the next two lessons we will be studying Psalm 103:8-14. Today we'll be looking at verses 8-11. This code is paraphrased from these verses.

A	B	C	D	E	F	G	H	I	J	K	L	M	N	O	P	Q	R	S	T	U	V	W	X	Y	Z
1	2	3	4	5	6	7	8	9	10	11	12	13	14	15	16	17	18	19	20	21	22	23	24	25	26

```
__   __ __   __ __ __ __ __.   __ __   __ __   __ __ __ __.
 9    1 13   19  9 14  6 21 12   8  5    9 19    8 15 12 25

__   __ __ __ __ __ __ __   __ __ __   __ __ __ __ __.   __
 9    4  5 19  5 18 22  5    8  9 19   23 18  1 20  8     9

__ __ __ __ __ __ __,   __ __ __ __ __ __ __,   __ __ __   __ __ __ __ __,
18  5  3  5  9 22  5     9 14 19 20  5  1  4     8  9 19   13  5 18  3 25

__ __ __ __ __,   __ __ __   __ __ __ __ __.   __ __   __ __ __
 7 18  1  3  5     1 14  4   12 15 22  5        9 20    8  1 19

__ __ __ __ __ __ __   __ __   __ __   __ __ __ __   __ __ __   __   __ __.
14 15 20  8  9 14  7   20 15    4 15   23  9 20  8   23  8 15    9    1 13

__ __ __,   __ __ __ __ __ __ __   __ __   __ __ __   __ __   __ __.
 9 20 19     2  5  3  1 21 19  5   15  6   23  8 15    8  5    9 19
```

Fencing Practice

If you haven't already done so, turn to Psalm 103:8-11 and read it. If you like, you can underline these verses and add them to your "God is love" list in the back of your Bible.

There are two things I noticed about this passage. First, it assumes quite bluntly that we're sinners deserving His anger. Second it shows just how amazing and huge and relentless His love is. Of these two, (our sinfulness, His love) which is the main focus of this passage?

_____

We know God is holy and will judge all who fall short of His perfect standard. He is the Judge. We know also that He is a God of love who goes to astounding lengths to save His children. For believers, *the emphasis is always on His love.*

Don't misunderstand. Just because He loves you endlessly, that doesn't mean He overlooks or ignores your sin. Would He still be considered perfectly Holy if He tolerated or made allowances for sin? _____ His holiness demands sinlessness. His amazing love doesn't overlook or tolerate our sin. Rather, His amazing love pays the price for our sin. There is a line in a song that says: "Your boundless love conquered my boundless sin."[6] Now, isn't *that* an amazing truth!

Thrust and Parry

Since the emphasis in this passage isn't on God the Judge, but on God the Lover of your soul, let's look at just how boundless that love is.

List the four descriptions of God found in Psalm 103:8 here:

The Lord is _____.
The Lord is _____.
The Lord is _____.
The Lord is _____.

As sinners, what do we deserve? _____

As God's children, what do we not receive (vs 10)? _____

How high are the heavens above the earth? _____

_____ How much does God love you? _____

_____How far is the east from the west? _____

How far does God remove your sins from you through Jesus? _____

_____As a believer, do you view yourself more often in the courtroom before God the Judge, or in the family room with God your Father?

_____ In light of Psalm 103:8-11, what is the correct view for unbelievers (God as judge or Father)?

_____ What is the correct view for believers?

_____

[6] "The Glories of Calvary" by Steve and Vikki Cook. © 2003 Sovereign Grace Worship (ASCAP).

Memory work: Copy Romans 8:*39* here: _____

_____

_____

_____

_____

Prayer suggestion: Worship God. Marvel that He loves you higher than the heavens are above the earth. Thank Him that He's removed your sins farther than the east is from the west. Praise God!

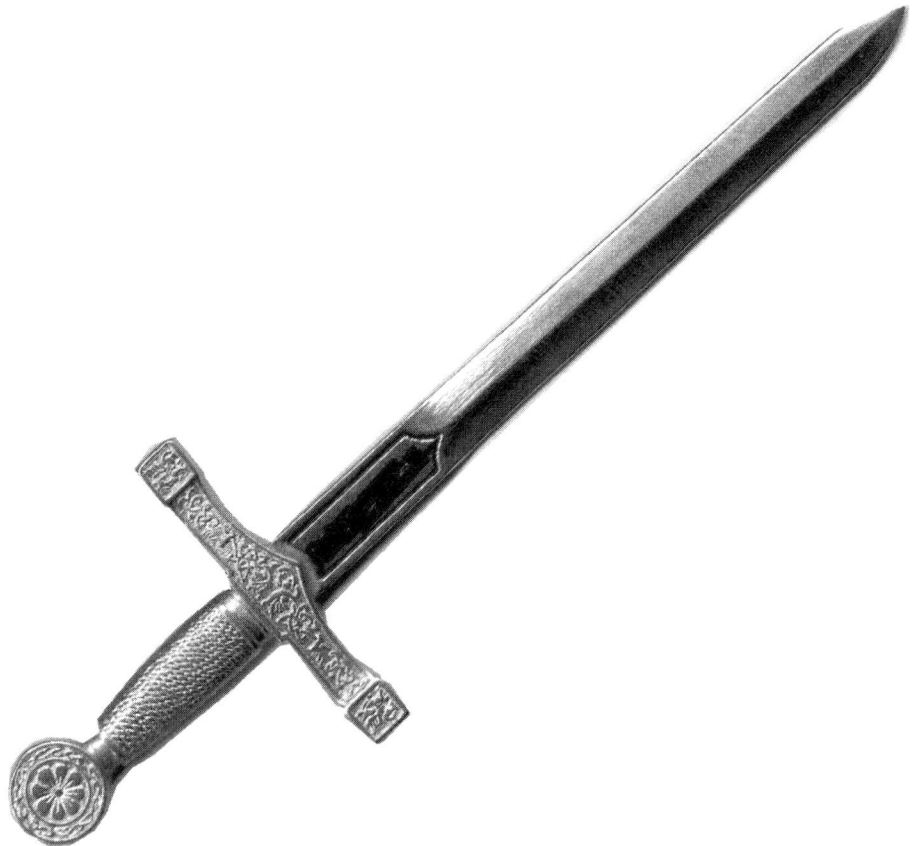

Day 45

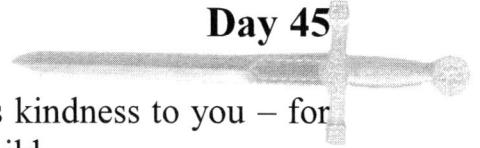

Begin with prayer. A suggestion: Thank God for His kindness to you – for being your Father and adopting you as His precious child.

Sword Drill

H _ _ _ _ _ urged God's people to repent as they rebuilt the temple in conquered Jerusalem. *Zechariah* encouraged the rebuilders to consider the future of Jerusalem. List the last four minor prophets here:
Z _ _ _ _ _ _ _ _, *H _ _ _ _ _*, *Z _ _ _ _ _ _ _ _ _*, *M _ _ _ _ _ _*.

Sword Play

The answers to the following riddles are words found in Psalm 103:12-14.

There are four of us.
You'll never be lost if you know me.
Up, down, right and left…
…but for this riddle you only need to know right and left.
I am __ __ __ __ and __ __ __ __.

I am not good.
I am your very own, and it is I who separate you from God.
But, in His goodness, He's gotten rid of me.
Just for you.
I am your __ __ __ __ __ __ __ __ __ __ __ __ __ __.

We're a pair.
Inseparable.
We're part of each other, bone of bone, flesh of flesh.
This kind of relationship can't be broken or divorced.
It is forever.
We are __ __ __ __ __ __ and __ __ __ __ __ __ __ __.

You see me when a missionary shares the gospel with a lost soul.
You see me when someone makes a meal for a starving child.
You see me in the eyes of a mom caring for her sick child.
I am another word for love.
I am __ __ __ __ __ __ __ __ __ __.

I am inconsequential, annoying, unattractive, so tiny.
I cause allergies.
People don't want me in their homes.
I am what you are formed from.
I am __ __ __ __.

Fencing Practice

Turn in your Bible to Psalm 103:8-14 and read the entire passage. If you like, you can underline these verses and add them to your "God is love" list in the back of your Bible.

Did you ever think about the difference between compassion and love? Compassion is the virtue that shares in the suffering of others. It is one aspect of love. Love is the big picture.

Just like a single diamond has numerous facets, so does love. One facet of love is the love between a husband and wife…commitment. Another is the love between friends…friendship. Another facet is the love between a father and child…nurture and protection. Another facet is jealousy. Another is compassion. These are just a few facets of love. God is like the diamond. He IS love. He demonstrates all these facets of love. Label the facets on the diamond with different facets of love.

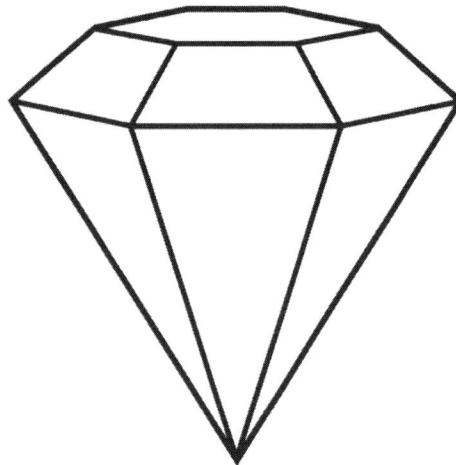

Thrust and Parry

Let's personalize today's passage. This passage reminds us of God's compassion toward us – His desire to share in our suffering.

According to verse 12 what is the first thing God does for us – in His compassion for us - in this passage? _____

_____

How far is the east from the west? _____
_____

Parents have compassion on their children. What are some of the things that compassion causes a parent to do for a child? _____
_____

Why does our Father God have compassion on us? (vs 14) _____
_____

Why does being formed by dust stir God's compassion? What do *you* think?
_____
_____

     God is our compassionate, loving Father who takes care of all our needs, including our most pressing need – our sin.

Memory work: Copy Romans 8:*39* here: _____
_____
_____
_____
_____

Prayer suggestion: Worship God! Thank Him for taking care of your most pressing need, removing your sin as far as the east is from the west.

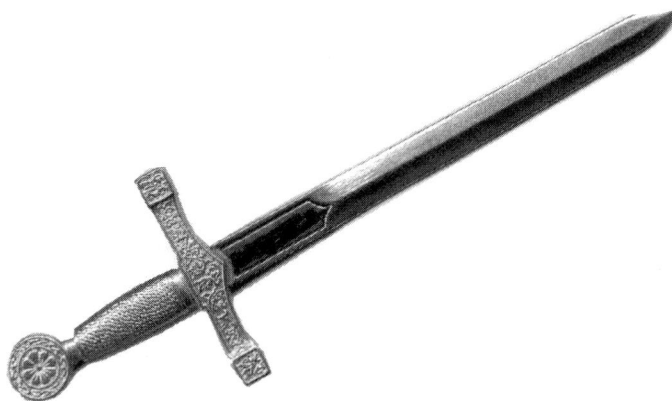

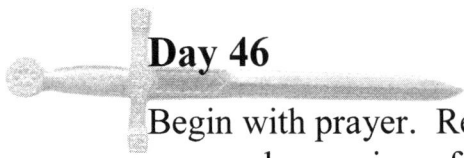

Day 46

Begin with prayer. Rejoice before God! He has had compassion on you and removed your sin as far as the east is from the west.

Sword Drill

Z _ _ _ _ _ _ _ encouraged the rebuilders to consider the future of Jerusalem. ***Malachi*** speaks to distressed people who struggle with doubts. List the last four minor prophets here:

Z _ _ _ _ _ _ _ _, *H _ _ _ _ _*, *Z _ _ _ _ _ _ _ _*, *M _ _ _ _ _ _*.

Sword Play

The following words and phrases are taken from Psalm 46:1-3. They are hidden and may be found horizontally, vertically, diagonally, running right-to-left or left-to-right..

Earth	Roaring waters
God	Sea
Mountains	Strength
Move	Tremble
Not fear	Trouble
Refuge	Very present help

```
w  l  v  o  y  g  h  e  g  o  d  j  p  o  m  b  r
d  z  h  e  f  c  x  i  k  m  h  y  r  n  z  t  o
s  s  w  r  r  o  a  r  i  n  g  w  a  t  e  r  s
t  a  d  k  n  y  p  l  m  u  t  f  h  d  s  o  t
r  e  f  u  g  e  p  b  t  g  h  d  e  a  c  u  g
e  p  l  o  h  e  r  r  f  e  t  c  h  o  o  b  l
n  l  e  d  d  s  e  v  e  x  r  g  s  o  a  l  c
g  u  f  f  y  m  a  n  d  s  a  c  n  u  r  e  z
t  u  n  e  b  a  n  t  s  p  e  h  i  g  h  b  i
h  k  a  l  e  r  e  b  e  c  c  n  a  m  o  n  i
w  i  e  v  e  r  s  e  a  s  l  a  t  m  a  e  s
f  n  o  k  c  h  r  i  s  f  u  n  n  h  u  g  s
l  m  g  a  l  a  t  i  a  n  s  b  u  r  e  r  n
u  o  m  a  r  s  h  m  a  l  l  o  o  t  s  l  a
f  o  t  r  a  e  f  t  o  n  b  e  m  i  l  k  p
```

Fencing Practice

If you haven't already done so, turn in your Bible to Psalm 46:1-3 and read it. You may underline it and add it to your list of verses in the back of your Bible if you like.

This passage speaks to us of God's loving care for us when everything around us is falling apart. In this passage do you see any promise that God will prevent bad things from happening? _____
This passage speaks of the reality of living in a sin-cursed world. Bad things will happen. We will suffer. The very foundations of our world may be shaken and turned upside down. Yet God is a God of love. Rather than preventing bad and tragic things from happening, in His love God promises something else. Because he loves you, what does He promise to you when your world is turned upside down? _____

Thrust and Parry

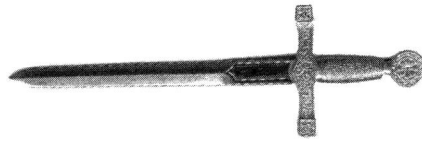

Define 'refuge': _____

Define 'strength': _____

This is what God promises to us in our trials. He doesn't promise us an easy life, but He promises to hide and shield us in our troubles. He doesn't promise to remove our trouble. In this passage He doesn't even promise to make you strong through your trials. He promises *to be your strength*! You don't have to generate strength to face a bad day. Just take refuge in Him and let Him be your strength when you are weak!

Think of something that is a trial to you, that you find difficult or impossible to face. It can be a foundation-shaker (like the death of a loved one) or relatively minor (like giving a public speech or asking forgiveness from someone you've hurt). Write it here: _____

When you face this trial and are in the midst of it, where will you find security? _____ Where is your strength? _____

Memory work: Copy Romans 8:*38*-39 here (the entire passage): _____

_____

_____

_____

_____

_____

_____

_____

_____

Prayer suggestion: It takes faith to find refuge and strength in God, to *not* fear when facing trials. Ask God to increase your faith and to see His goodness even when things are crumbling around you.

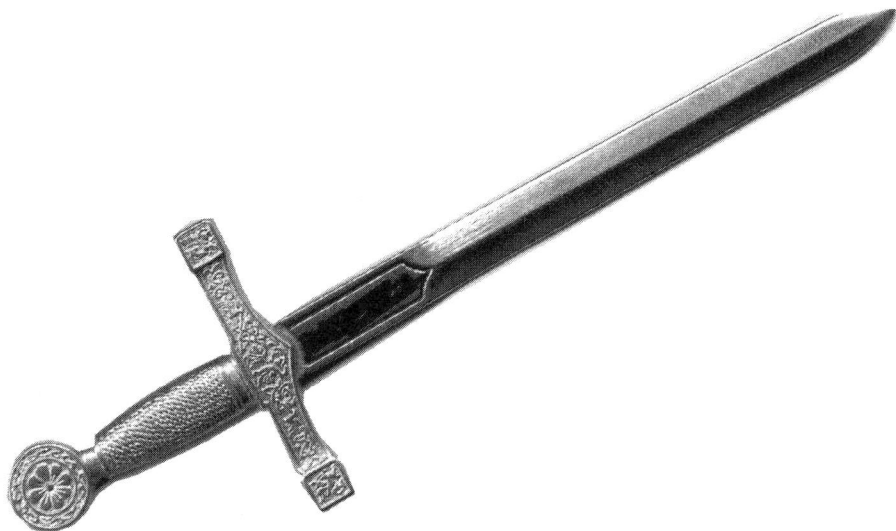

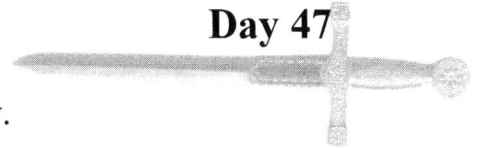

Begin with prayer. Ask God to be your strength today.

Sword Drill

   M_ _ _ _ _ speaks to distressed people who struggle with doubts. It is the last book of the O_ _ T_ _ _ _ _ _ _ _ .   List the last four minor prophets here:
Z_ _ _ _ _ _ _ _, H_ _ _ _ _, Z_ _ _ _ _ _ _ _, M_ _ _ _ _ _ .

Sword Play

The answers to the crossword puzzle on the next page are found in 1 John 4:7-10. Fill in the blanks below, then use those words to complete the puzzle.

Across

2. Verse 9 explains that God sent Jesus into the _ _ _ _ _ to bring life.

4. According to verse 7, loving others is *the* sign that we are _ _ _ _ of God.

5. The word which explains how Jesus, the Son, came (in verses 9 and 10): because God _ _ _ _ Him.

7. A word in verse 10 that means a sacrifice meant to take away the enmity brought by sin: _ _ _ _ _ _ _ _ _ _ _ _ _ .

9. Jesus is God's only _ _ _ .

Down

1. According to verse 8, if you don't love one another, then you don't really know God, because _ _ _ _ _ _ _ _ _ .

3. God sent His Son to be a propitiation for our _ _ _ _ (plural). (Verse 10)

4. What does John call *you* at the beginning of verse 7? _ _ _ _ _ _ _ _ .

6. A word meaning *to reveal the purpose of; to make obvious*. The love of God was made _ _ _ _ _ _ _ _ (verse 9).

8. To have knowledge. If you love, that indicates you are born of God and you _ _ _ _ God. (verse 7)

Fencing Practice

If you haven't already done so, turn to 1 John 4:7-10 in your Bible and read it. If you like, you can underline these verses and add them to your "God is love" list in the back of your Bible.

If you remember one thing about this passage, remember the final statement of verse 8: "God is love." Think about that statement for a moment. God isn't *just* loving (although He IS). He doesn't just *act* loving (although He does). Love isn't *just* a characteristic of God's personality (though it IS). That is what can – and should – be said about *us*: You *are* loving. You *act* loving. You have a *loving personality.*

But, with God it's different. Love isn't just an extension of His personality. God IS love. Love is embodied. Love lives and is active, animated, and functioning with supreme energy…and has a name. ***God is love.*** Here's another thing: LOVE cannot act contrary to its nature. Can LOVE be cruel? _____. Can LOVE be indifferent? _____.

Can LOVE be mean or hurtful? _____. Of course not!...or it wouldn't be love anymore!

There are two lessons to learn from this passage:

1. When difficult or horrible things happen, remember that God IS love. We will probably not ever understand while we live on earth why life can hurt so much...but God IS love. This takes faith. But I will tell you this: It. Is. True. I've seen horrible things happen to the best of people, yet God IS with them – and He IS good.

2. If you are God's child, you will exhibit His love. You will love others. *Their* good and *their* joy will be your goal (verse 7).

Thrust and Parry

This exercise might stretch you a bit, but I think it will help you to really capture this important truth. Look at and emphasize each word in the statement, and explain what each means to you:

GOD is love: _____

_____

God **IS** love: _____

_____

God is **LOVE**: _____

_____

Since this scripture clearly explains that God's children will also love others, think about your own life.

1. Do you love your parents? Do you value their care, protection, and nurturing of you? _____

2. Do you love your sibling(s)? Is *their* joy and *their* good a goal for you? _____

3. Do you love your friends? Do you strengthen them in the Lord and encourage them? _____

4. Do you love your enemies? Do you pray for them and are you kind to them? _____

If your answers to those four questions show a lack of love, don't despair! Take it to your heavenly Father – who IS love – and tell Him about it. Plead with Him to make you willing to love others. Ask Him to love others through you. Make it your goal, by God's grace, to grow in this area.

Memory work: Copy Romans 8:*38*-39 here: _____

_____

_____

_____

_____

_____

_____

_____

_____

Prayer suggestion: Think of a person that is difficult for you to love. Pray for that person…but also pray that God will help you to love that person. Pray that God will *make you willing* to love that person.

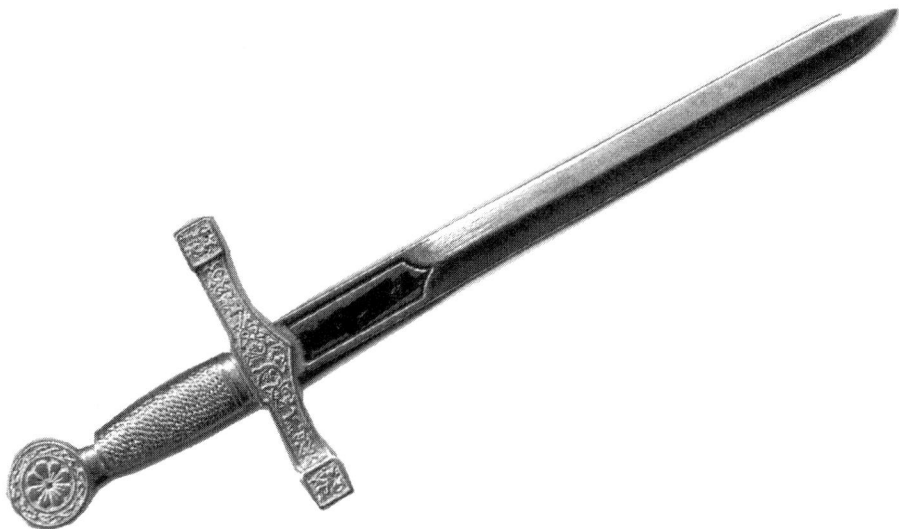

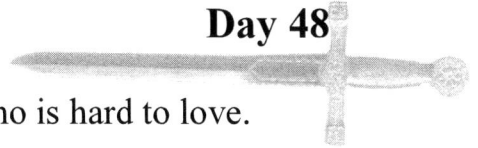

Begin with prayer. Pray for that person in your life who is hard to love.

Sword Drill

Matthew, the first of the four gospels, demonstrates how Jesus fulfills Old Testament prophecies. List the gospels – the first four books of the New Testament – here: *M* _ _ _ _ _ _, *M* _ _ _, *L* _ _ _, and *J* _ _ _

Sword Play

For the next several days, you will be studying God's justice, holiness, and purity. The answers to this true/false quiz are found in Psalm 5:4-6. Circle T for true or F for false.

T or F – Our God does not delight or take pleasure in wickedness.

T or F – Evil is not allowed to dwell with God.

T or F – Proud foolish people will not be able to stand before God.

T or F – God hates all evildoers.

T or F – God destroys liars.

T or F – God hates cruel, bloodthirsty people.

T or F – God hates deceivers.

T or F – God is love.

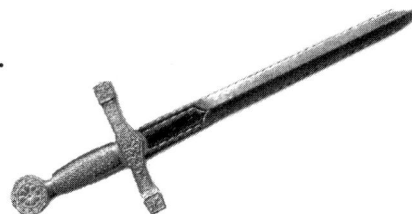

Fencing Practice

Turn in your Bible to Psalm 5:4-6 if you haven't already done so and read it. If you are anything like me, you found this passage to be sobering, uncomfortable, and even scary. This passage reveals to us the perfect holiness of God.

Picture 'holiness' to be like light. What happens to darkness when you turn on light? _____

_____ Is it even remotely possible for darkness to exist in the *presence* of light? _____ Can even a little darkness exist where light directly shines? _____ What happens even to shadows when you shine light on them? _____

The same thing happens to sin in the presence of our holy God. It is simply obliterated. It ceases to exist. It cannot survive in the light of God's holiness.

Thrust and Parry

This passage, Psalms 5:4-6, speaks very bluntly of our dilemma, doesn't it. Let's make it personal.

In these verses we read the truth that God takes no pleasure, no delight, in wickedness. Have you ever done anything wicked? _____

We learn that wickedness and evil will not live with God. If *this* was the end of the story, would you be allowed to live with God? _____

We also find that proud and foolish people won't be able to stand before God. Have you ever been proud? _____ Have you ever been foolish? _____

We are also taught that God destroys anyone who speaks lies. Have you ever told a lie? _____

Finally, we learn that God hates people who deceive. Have you ever deceived your parents, perhaps to avoid punishment? _____

Our God is a holy God, and we would be obliterated in His presence because of our sin (as you've discovered)...*IF* that was the end of the story. However, *here* is the end of the story, found in the very next verse of this passage (in three translations):

"But as for me, I will come into your house in the multitude of thy mercy..." Psalms 5:7a KJV

"and I in vastness of kindness of you I shall enter house of you..." Psalm 5:7a (Direct Hebrew-to-English translation of Authorised Version)[7]

*"But I, **through the abundance of your steadfast love**, will enter your house..."* Psalm 5:7a ESV[8]

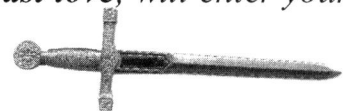

Memory work: Copy Psalm 145:17 here: _____
_____
_____
_____

End with prayer: Recognize your helpless state in the presence of God's holiness, and thank Him for His amazing mercy and love.

---

[7] PDF Files © 2008 by Scripture4all Foundation. Translation: Authorised Version
www.scripture4all.org/onlineinterlinear/otpdf/psa5.pdf.
[8] The Holy Bible, English Standard Version Copyright © 2001 by Crossway Bibles, a division of Good News Publishers.

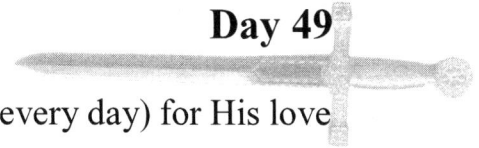

Begin with prayer. Thank God once again (today and every day) for His love and amazing mercy.

Sword Drill

M_ _ _ _ _ _, the first of the four gospels, demonstrates how Jesus fulfills Old Testament prophecies. *Mark*, the second gospel, was written to gentiles (non-Jews), so it contains explanations of Jewish customs. List the gospels – the first four books of the New Testament – here:
M_ _ _ _ _ _, *M_ _ _*, *L_ _ _*, and *J_ _ _*

Sword Play

Leviticus 20:26 tells us that God is holy and that we are to be holy. The acrostic below will give you the definition of *holy*. Use the key to fill in the missing letters.

<u>O</u> <u>U</u> <u>R</u>   <u>G</u> <u>O</u> <u>D</u>   <u>I</u> <u>S</u>   <u>T</u> <u>H</u> <u>E</u>   <u>H</u> <u>O</u> <u>L</u> <u>Y</u>   <u>O</u> <u>N</u> <u>E</u>.
1 2 3   4 5 6   7 8   9 10 11   12 13 14 15   16 17 18

O _ _ _ _ _ _ _ _ _ _ _.
  2 3 4 16 6 7 8 12 1 14 15

U _ _ q _ _.
  17 7 2 18

R _ va_ _, _ _ _ _a_ _ _ _ _.
  7 14 8 12 18 12 8 17 1 17 18

G _ _ _ _ _ a _ _ wa_ _.
  1 13 6 7 17 14 14 15 8

Ov_ _ a_ _.
  11 3 14 14

D _ _ _ _ _ c _.
  7 8 9 7 17 9

I _ m_ _a_ _ _ p_ _ _.
  8 1 3 14 14 15 2 3 18

S _ pa _ a _ _.
  11 3 9 11

Hav $\underline{}$ $\underline{}$ $\underline{}$ $\underline{}$ $\underline{}$ $\underline{}$ $\underline{}$ $\underline{}$.
7 17 4   17 16   8 7 17

O $\underline{}$ $\underline{}$ **a** $\underline{}$ $\underline{}$ $\underline{}$ $\underline{}$ $\underline{}$ $\underline{}$.
17 11   17 6   1 17 14 15

L $\underline{}$ **v** $\underline{}$ $\underline{}$ **a** $\underline{}$ **wa** $\underline{}$ $\underline{}$.
1 18 8   14 15 8

Y $\underline{}$ $\underline{}$ $\underline{}$ $\underline{}$ $\underline{}$ **m** $\underline{}$ $\underline{}$ $\underline{}$ **b** $\underline{}$ $\underline{}$ $\underline{}$ $\underline{}$ $\underline{}$.
16 2   9 13 5   2 8 9   11   12 1 14 15

Fencing Practice

Turn in your Bible to Leviticus 20:26 if you haven't already done so, and read it.

When you solved your *Sword Play* acrostic, you discovered the definition of **holy**. **Holy** is a word we hear a lot in church, and we sing about it. Holy means:

'*to be distinct, separate, in a class by oneself; unique; having no rivals or competition; to be morally pure.*'

In science class you might have learned Newton's Third Law of Motion: for every action there is an equal and opposite reaction. We can see this law even in the spiritual realm:

God is H_ _ _. This is the 'action.' *Because* God is H_ _ _, and *because* He wants a people to be His, then He has *separated us* and called us to be H_ _ _ as well. This is the equal-and-opposite 'reaction.'

Thrust and Parry

Did you notice the work of God in Leviticus 20:26? *He* separated you.

Did you notice the reason why? *He* wants you for His very own.
Did you notice the proclamation? *He* proclaims that you shall be holy.

God's holiness is one of the things that separates Him from all the other so-called gods out there. Fill in the blanks below with words from the acrostic on pages 141-142.

My God is H_ _ _.

My God is u_ _ _ _ _.

My God has no r_ _ _ _ _.

My God is g_ _ _.

My God is p_ _ _.

My God has no s_ _.

My God l_ _ _ _.

Memory work: Copy Psalm 145:17 here: _____

_____

_____

_____

End with prayer: Thank God for His holiness…for His uniqueness, goodness, purity, sinlessness, and love.

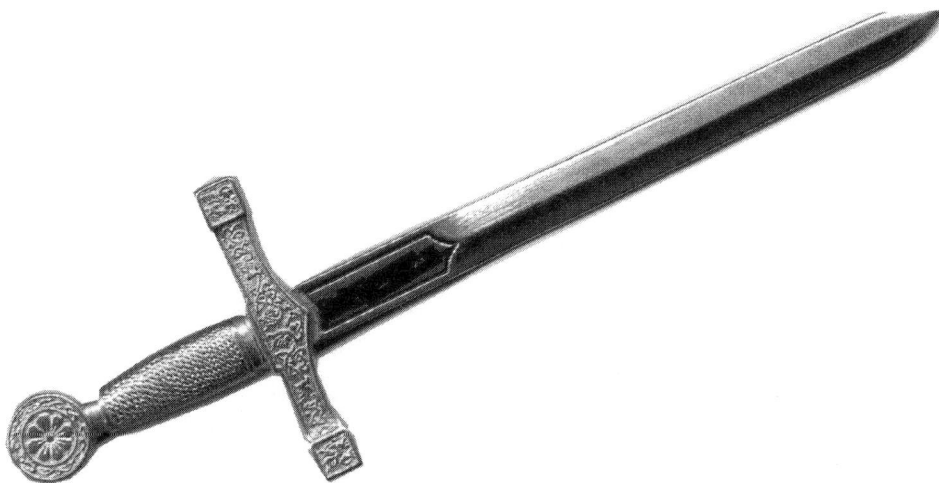

Day 50

Begin with prayer: Thank God for making you His very own because He loves you so much!

M_ _ _, the second gospel, was written to gentiles (non-Jews), so it contains explanations of Jewish customs. *Luke* was written by a doctor, so it has details of sick people being healed. List the gospels – the first four books of the New Testament – here:
M _ _ _ _ _ _, M _ _ _, L _ _ _, and J _ _ _

Sword Play

Below you will find a paraphrase of 1 Peter 1:15-16; however, many of the words are missing. Fill in the missing words to complete the paraphrase. Clues are in the brackets.

Someone has c_ _ _ _ _ [summoned] you .
That Someone is G_ _. [Creator of the universe]
God is h_ _ _. [set apart, separate]
That means you must be h_ _ _ [set apart], too, in everything you do.
That means you must be s_ _ _ _ _ _ _ [set apart from], u_ _ _ _ _
[different than; a one-and-only], g_ _ _ [opposite of bad], p_ _ _
[opposite of contaminated], and l_ _ _ _ _ [opposite of hating] in your
a_ _ _ _ _ _ [the things you do; rhymes with 'fractions'], s_ _ _ _ _
[what you say; rhymes with 'teach'], and t_ _ _ _ _ _ [what you think;
rhymes with 'caught']. Similar to Newton's Third Law of Motion,
where for every a_ _ _ _ _ [what you do], there is an e_ _ _ _ [a math
symbol meaning 'is the same as'] and opposite r_ _ _ _ _ _ _
[consequence], you are called to be h_ _ _ [set apart] *because* God is
holy…and you b_ _ _ _ _ to Him [owned by; rhymes with 'song'].

Fencing Practice

Turn in your Bible to 1 Peter 1:15-16 and read it if you haven't already done so. This passage puts an incredible claim on your life. In the simplest terms, it's this: since our holy God called you, your identity is essentially tied to Him. That being the case, you also shall be h_ _ _. And notice that holiness isn't just a vague concept. Does going to church on Sunday mean you are holy – if you continue to live like the world the rest of the week? _ _ _ _ _ _

Peter tells us that holiness should affect all your manner, conversation, and conduct. Wow! What does 'all your manner, conversation, and conduct' mean? _____

_____

_____

_____

Thrust and Parry

Let's go ahead and really personalize this passage. **But** as you do, I want you to remember that apart from Christ, this would be impossible. *In Christ* you **can** do this. Not only is it possible, it will be your delight. *Trust Him.* Ready? (Please answer honestly rather than as you think you *should.*)

Because I am His and am called to holiness…

    …I am *unique.*

        Am I like the world? ____
        Do I look like the world? ___
        Do I talk like the world? ___
        Do I think like the world? ___
        Is this uniqueness something to be embarrassed about?__

    …I am *good.*

        Do I act kindly? ___
        Do I listen attentively? ___
        Do I honor and obey? ___
        Am I helpful and self-less? ___

    …I am *pure.*

        Do I avoid sinful programs and movies? ___
        Do I avoid sinful books? ___
        Do I avoid sinful music? ___
        Do I avoid sinful acquaintances? ___
        Do I avoid sinful games? ___
        Do I dress modestly? ___

    …I *love.*

        Do I put my friends' wants and needs before my own? __
        Do I serve my siblings cheerfully? ___
        Do I honor and obey my parents joyfully? ___

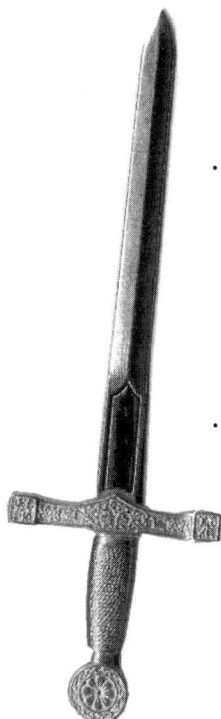

Do I initiate opportunities to serve? ___
Do I pray for others? ___
Am I quick to allow others to choose first, go first, have the biggest and the best? ___
Am I quick to forgive? ___
Do I seek after and pursue peace? ___

Memory work: Copy Psalm 145:17 here: _____

_____

_____

_____

End with prayer: Look over your list of holiness that you just completed. Ask God to help you in one or two specific areas where holiness is a struggle for you.

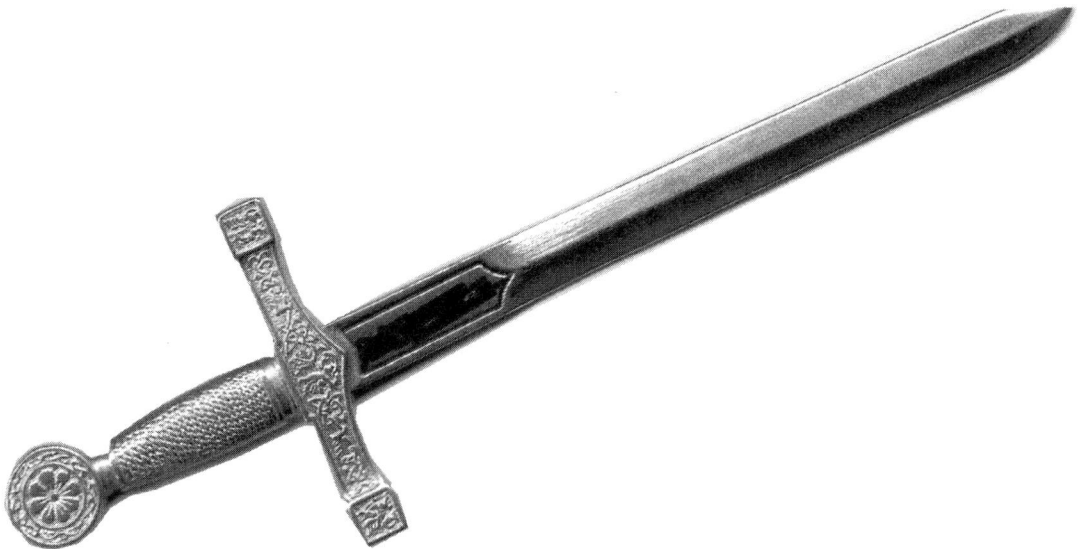

Day 51

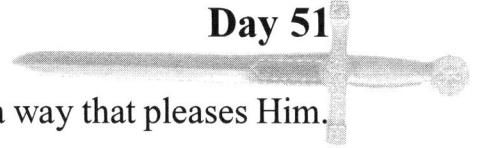

Begin with prayer. Ask God to help you talk today in a way that pleases Him.

Sword Drill

L _ _ _ was written by a doctor, so it has details of sick people being healed. *John,* the 4th gospel, was written to persuade people to believe in Jesus. List the gospels – the first four books of the New Testament – here: *M _ _ _ _ _ _, M _ _ _, L _ _ _,* and *J _ _ _*

Sword Play

The answers to the multiple choice questions below can be found in Isaiah 6:2-7.

1. What creatures are proclaiming God's holiness in verse 3? (Look back at verse 2.)
    a. Humans
    b. All created things
    c. Seraphim
    d. God's chosen people

2. They not only proclaim that He is holy in verse 3, but also that His glory fills…
    a. The whole earth
    b. Human hearts
    c. His Word
    d. The temple

3. According to verse 4, what two things happened at the sound of His voice?
    a. People worshipped and fell at His feet
    b. The sacrifice burned up and sins were forgiven
    c. An earthquake and smoke
    d. The stone rolled away and resurrection

4. What did Isaiah say first in verse 5 when this happened?
    a. "Praise the Lord!"
    b. "Woe is me!"
    c. "Our God reigns!"
    d. "Save me, O Lord!"

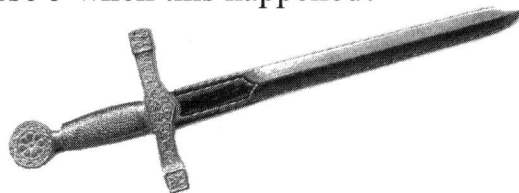

5. Why did Isaiah say this according to verse 5?
    a. Because of the angels and God's majesty
    b. Because he had unclean lips and saw God
    c. Because God rules nations and people
    d. Because his sin separated him from God

6. What did the seraphim do to Isaiah in verses 6-7?
    a. They said, "Fear not"
    b. They carried him before God's throne
    c. They wrapped a pure white robe around him
    d. They touched his lips with a burning coal

7. What did the seraphim tell Isaiah in verse 7?
    a. "You cannot enter God's presence because of your sin"
    b. "God's holiness will consume your unholiness"
    c. "Welcome to God's presence, faithful child"
    d. "Your iniquity is taken away and your sin is atoned for"

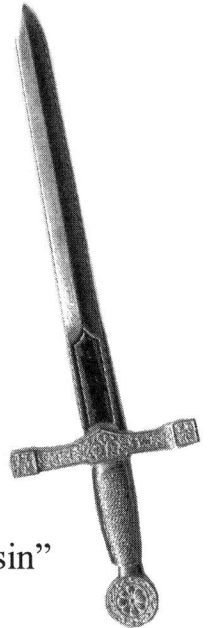

Fencing Practice

If you haven't already done so, turn in your Bible to Isaiah 6:2-7 and read it. Here we have a fascinating glimpse at what happens when a human comes into the presence of God.

But Let's talk about Isaiah for a moment.

Was Isaiah one of God's chosen people? ___

Was Isaiah a believer? ___

Did Isaiah love God? ___

Did he live for God? ___

Knowing Isaiah, wouldn't you assume he would easily be able to enter God's presence without any trouble at all? So, if Isaiah was one of God's chosen people, and he believed in God, loved God, and lived for God, why was he horrified ("O woe is me!") when his eyes saw God? It's because sin separates us from God. Even the smallest sins of the kindest, nicest person will keep that person separated from God.

Was Isaiah himself (without God) able to do anything about his sin and uncleanness? ___. Isaiah had already done his personal best. He loved God and lived for Him. He was one of God's chosen people. Was that enough to allow him to enter God's presence? ___. Something had to be done to him and for him before he could enter God's holy presence.

Thrust and Parry

Something *has* been done for you and to you so that you can enter God's presence. Does this passage prove how intolerant and unaccepting God is? Absolutely not! Rather, Isaiah 6:2-7 demonstrates how loving He is and how passionate He is about you.

Think about your very best-behavior day. On a day when you are at your very best and holiest…

- How much Bible would you read? _____
- How long would you pray? _____
- How would you do chores and school work?

  _____

- How would you treat your siblings?

  _____

- How would you treat your parents?

  _____

- What would fill your thoughts? _____

If you managed to pull off a perfect-behavior day like this, would it entitle you to enter the holy presence of God? _____

Thank God we have a savior who took away *all* our iniquity and atoned for *all* our sin!

Memory work: Copy Psalm 145:18 here (notice this is the next verse in the passage you are memorizing): _____

_____

_____

_____

End with prayer: Acknowledge, like Isaiah, that you are undone before God without the atoning blood of Jesus. Thank Him for His blood.

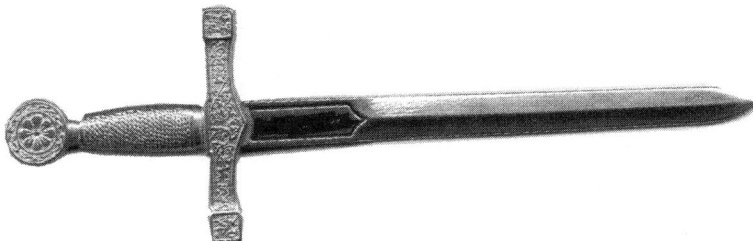

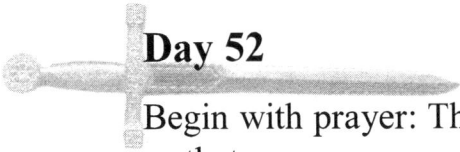

Day 52

Begin with prayer: Thank God for giving His Son as a sacrifice for your sin so that now you can enjoy God's holy presence.

J _ _ _, the 4th gospel, was written to persuade people to believe in Jesus. List the gospels – the first four books of the New Testament – here:
M _ _ _ _ _ _, M _ _ _, L _ _ _, and J _ _ _

Sword Play

Below is a paraphrase of Numbers 23:19. However, it is very messed up. In order to fix it, you will have to fill in the blanks with the antonyms (opposites) of the underlined words. See the word bank below for help.

God is not [woman] _ _ _, that He would tell a [truth] _ _ _, or a [daughter] _ _ _ of man, that He should [stay the same] _ _ _ _ _ _ His mind. He has [written] _ _ _ _ _ _ it, so obviously He will [fail to do] _ _ _ _ _ _ _ _ _ _ it.

Accomplish	Man	Change
Son	Lie	Spoken

Fencing Practice

If you haven't already done so, turn in your Bible to Numbers 23:19 and read it. I love this verse because it teaches us two things about God – two things that are hard for us to grasp because we are the opposite of God. This verse tells us that:

1. God doesn't lie. Whatever He says is rock-solid truth. It's so rock-solid, you can stake your future, your hopes, your dreams, and your life on what He says. But, what about you?
   - Have you ever lied? _ _ _ _
   - Have you promised to do something, then failed to keep that promise (even if it was by accident)? _ _ _
   - Have you ever exaggerated? _ _ _
   - Have you ever told only part of the truth so you wouldn't get in trouble? _ _ _

But, God isn't like us. He never lies.

2. God doesn't change His mind. When He proclaims something, it is truth. Truth, by its very nature, can't change. If you loved someone yesterday, but changed your mind and decided you didn't love that person today, then which was true? You loved?...or you don't love? Since only one can be true, then the other was a lie. True love doesn't change. That's just one example. When you learn that God doesn't change His mind, you can be sure He doesn't change His mind about anything. But, what about you?

- Have you ever changed your mind about something? _____
- Have you ever had a friend who is no longer a friend? _____
- Have you ever started something (like a Bible-reading plan, a diet, an exercise program, a money-saving plan), then changed your mind and failed to reach your goal? _____

But God isn't like us. He never changes His mind.

Thrust and Parry

Since God never lies and doesn't change, let's look at just a few promises God has for those of us who belong to Him. You will need to look these up. You may underline them in your Bible if you'd like. (It would be a great idea! You can even start a new list, "Promises," in the back of your Bible!)

1. In Jeremiah 29:11 God promises you He has a plan for your life. Not only that, but He promises you that they are good plans. He promises you a future and He promises you hope. Since God doesn't lie and He doesn't change His mind, what can you know for sure about your future?

_____

_____

2. In Isaiah 40:29-31 God promises to give you power and strength when you are tired or powerless. He promises that you will soar! Since God doesn't lie or change His mind, what can you know for sure about those awful, low periods of life when you have no strength left? _____

_____

_____

3. In Philippians 4:19 God promises He will provide all your needs. Since God never lies or changes His mind, what can you know for sure about those times in your life where you have little? _____

_____

_____

4. In Romans 8:37-39 God promises that nothing – absolutely nothing – can separate you from God's love. Since God never lies or changes His mind, what can you know for sure about those times in life when God seems very far away? _____

_____

5. In Romans 6:23 God promises you the free gift of eternal life through Jesus. Since God never lies or changes His mind, what can you know for sure about what will happen when you die? _____

_____

If you find these promises encouraging, let me give you a few more you can read, underline, and add to your 'Promises' list: Matthew 11:28-29, John 14:27, Romans 10:9, 1 Corinthians 10:13, Romans 8:28, Psalm 32:8, Lamentations 3:21-23, Ephesians 3:20. Take time to look them up, soak them in, and enjoy your inheritance as **His** child.

Memory work: Copy Psalm 145:18 here (notice this is the next verse in the passage you are memorizing): _____

_____

_____

_____

End with prayer: Choose one of the promises you read today and thank God that *that* promise is true.

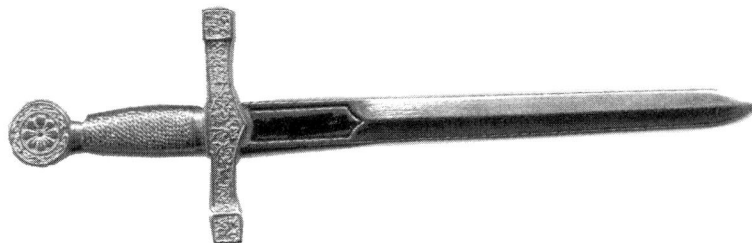

Begin with prayer. Thank God for all His promises. Tell Him that you believe what He says and that you trust Him.

Sword Drill

Acts, written by Dr. Luke, tells the story of the early church. Write the next six books of the New Testament here: *A_ _ _, R_ _ _ _ _,*
I & II C_ _ _ _ _ _ _ _ _ _, G_ _ _ _ _ _ _ _, E_ _ _ _ _ _ _ _.

Sword Play

The following statements are paraphrased from Psalm 145:17-19. (These should sound familiar to you because you've been memorizing them.) Match the first part of each statement with its correct ending.

The Lord is righteous...	*...to all who call on Him.*
The Lord is holy and kind...	*...in all His ways.*
The Lord is near...	*...your cry.*
To those who call in truth...	*...the Lord is near.*
The Lord fulfills the desires...	*...in all His works.*
The Lord hears...	*...those who fear and cry to Him.*
The Lord saves...	*...of those who fear Him*

Fencing Practice

If you haven't already done so, turn in your Bible to Psalm 145:17-19 and read it. This is another beautiful passage! Feel free to underline it in your Bible and add it to your 'God is love' list and your 'promises' list.

These verses show us that our God is *just*. *Just* means:
1. Fair
2. Honorable
3. Righteous
4. Upright
5. Good
6. Impartial
7. Reasonable

The word **righteous** in verse 17 (*"The Lord is **righteous**..."*) can also be translated *just*.

Since our God is just, righteous, holy, and kind in **all** His ways, you can be confident of His actions toward you. Fill in the seven synonyms for the word *just* from the list above in the blanks below. Because God is righteous and just, you can confidently say:

"I know that toward me God will always be 1._____,

2. _____, 3. _____, 4. _____, 5. _____,

6. _____, and 7. _____.

Thrust and Parry

Because our God is righteous and just, holy and kind, you can rest in the *fact* that He will always act in a way that is consistent with His nature. Psalm 145:17-19 reassures us of this *fact*. Mark all true answers by checking the circle next to them. Put a line through all wrong answers. Some statements may have more than one right or wrong answer. The answers are all found in today's passage.

A. When you call out to Him in truth, you can know that you know that you know that…:
- o The Lord is near to you.
- o The Lord hears you.
- o The Lord will help you *if* He has time.
- o The Lord might ignore you if He's too busy.

B. If you fear the Lord – reverently stand in awe of Him – then you can be absolutely sure that…:
- o He loves watching you be scared. It humors Him.
- o He will save you.
- o He will fulfill your desires.
- o He will cause you to fall on your knees before Him.
- o He will hear your cries.

Of course these truths often come wrapped in horrible trials and tragedies, and it's terribly difficult to make sense of it. But you can *still* KNOW that God IS just, righteous, holy, and kind. That is actually what true faith in God looks like. You *will* face trials in this life AND God *is* always good. Rest in *this* truth.

Memory work: Copy Psalm 145:18 here: _____
_____
_____
_____

End with prayer: If you are in the midst of a trial right now, can you – in faith – thank God for His kindness toward you even though you don't understand why you must face this trial. If you don't have this faith, ask God to give you this kind of faith.

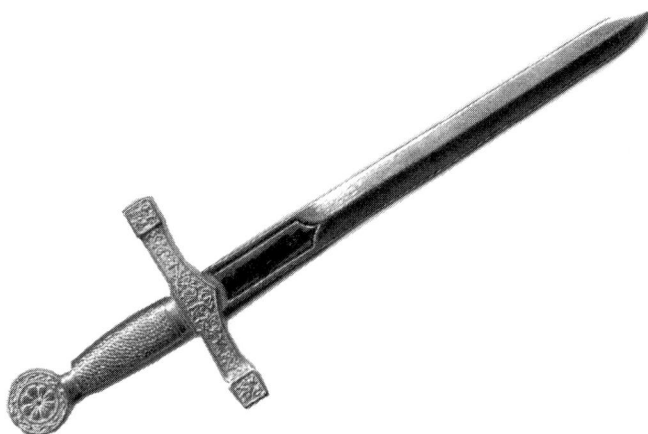

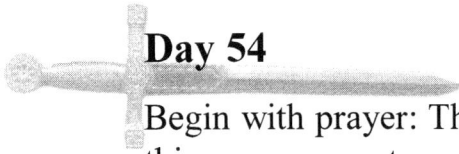

Day 54

Begin with prayer: Thank God that He hears your prayers and is near to you this very moment.

Sword Drill

A_ _ _, written by Dr. Luke, tells the story of the early church. *Romans* was written by Paul to logically present the case for Christianity. Write the next six books of the New Testament here: *A_ _ _, R_ _ _ _ _, I & II C_ _ _ _ _ _ _ _ _ _, G_ _ _ _ _ _ _ _, E_ _ _ _ _ _ _.*

Sword Play

To complete these puzzles, you will need to read James 1:13-14. This passage gives us some truths about the pure and holy God we serve…and some truth about ourselves. Complete the clues below, then use those words to fill in the mini-puzzles.

1. If you've ever been tempted to do something wrong, you can't say, "I was _ _ _ _ _ _ _ by _ _ _.

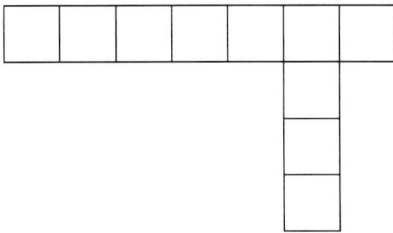

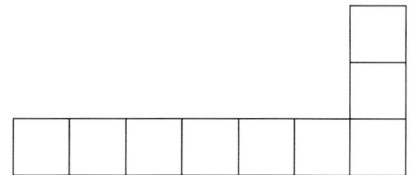

2. James 1:13 tells us that God cannot be _ _ _ _ _ _ _ with _ _ _ _.

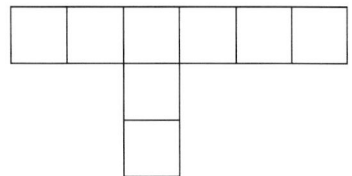

3. James 1:13 also tells us that God _ _ _ _ _ _ no woman or _ _ _.

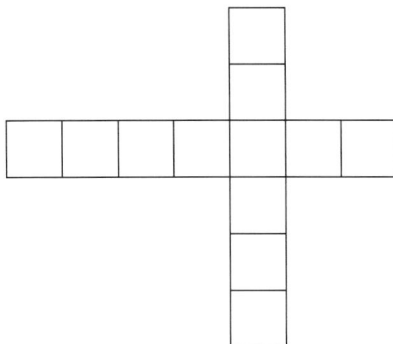

4. If God doesn't tempt us, then how are we tempted? James 1:14 tells us that when we are _ _ _ _ _ _ _, it is our own lusts/desires that _ _ _ _ _ _ us and lure us.

Fencing Practice

If you haven't already done so, turn in your Bible to James 1:13-14 and read it.

Have you ever heard the phrase, "the devil made me do it"? _____ After reading James 1:13-14, how well would you say that phrase aligns with God's Word? _____

James 1:13-14 reveals to us the complete purity of God…and how impure we are. We learn that God is so pure, He can't be tempted by evil. Can you imagine never being tempted to get back at someone who hurt you, never being tempted to sit around lazily while Mom does the work, never being tempted to grumble or complain, or never being tempted to lie to keep from getting in trouble?

We also learn that God never tempts us. Scripture *does* tell us that God tests us…but He never tempts us. What is the difference between a test and a temptation? _____

_____

The last thing we learn in this passage is where those temptations come from. Where do temptations come from according to James 1:13-14? _____

Thrust and Parry

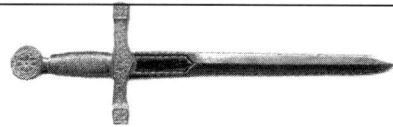

Let's personalize this.

Have you ever been *tempted* to lie to cover up something?...Perhaps because you were afraid you'd get in trouble? _____ Did you give in to the temptation and actually lie? _____ According to James 1:13-14, where did that temptation come from? _____

Have you ever been hurt or insulted by a sibling or a friend? _____
If you were, were you *tempted* to get back at that person, yell at them, tattle on them to get them in trouble, snub them, or hurt their feelings? _____
Did you give in to that temptation and actually do something mean back at that person who hurt you? _____ According to James 1:13-14, where did that temptation come from? _____

Have you ever seen your mom or dad trying to rush around to get everything done, cook, clean, and so on…and you were *tempted* to sit lazily without offering to help, or you went off to play or do your own thing without offering to help? _____ Did you actually give in to the temptation to do your own thing rather than to clean up after yourself and serve your family? _____ According to James 1:13-14, where did that temptation to be lazy or selfish come from? _____

It can be discouraging when we realize just how impure we are! When I got to the point where I realized sin and impurity contaminated every part of my heart and life, I was absolutely undone! But, it was also at that point that I realized how awesome my savior is and how amazing His grace is.

Memory work: Copy Psalm 145:19 (the next verse in the passage) here: _____

_____

_____

_____

_____

_____

End with prayer: Thank God for His purity and that, through Christ, He has imputed His purity to you.

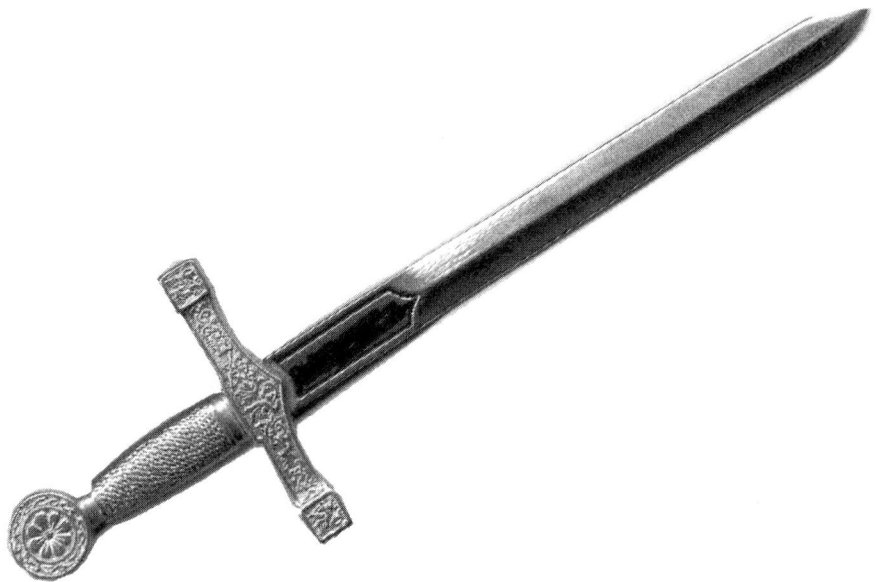

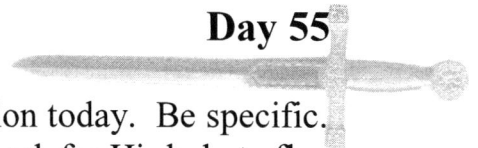

Begin with prayer. Ask God to help you flee temptation today. Be specific. If you're tempted to fight your siblings or be lazy, then ask for His help to flee that temptation.

Sword Drill

    R _ _ _ _ was written by Paul to logically present the case for Christianity. *I Corinthians* was written by Paul to address big problems in the church in Corinth. Write the next six books (after the gospels) of the New Testament here: *A_ _ _*, *R_ _ _ _ _*, *I & II C_ _ _ _ _ _ _ _ _ _*, *G_ _ _ _ _ _ _ _*, *E_ _ _ _ _ _ _ _*.

Sword Play

    This word search contains many words that describe what it means to be perfect, because in Matthew 5:48 we are told to be perfect. The ten words are listed in the word box below the puzzle. Words can be forward or backward, horizontal, vertical, or diagonal.

```
E  X  C  E  L  L  E  N  T  N  U  J
F  P  O  K  N  H  R  F  D  S  N  D
L  B  V  G  F  T  U  H  O  P  D  E
A  Y  W  O  B  T  P  B  E  E  I  H
W  L  A  C  C  U  R  A  T  E  L  S
L  M  C  A  Z  Q  U  U  D  U  I
E  S  X  K  O  P  L  T  L  G  T  M
S  E  A  E  R  I  T  S  O  W  E  E
S  N  J  F  D  W  W  I  S  A  D  L
X  Y  O  U  R  E  A  P  B  T  A  B
K  S  S  E  L  T  L  U  A  F  H  N
H  E  A  R  D  E  R  R  A  M  N  U
```

Absolute	Flawless
Accurate	Pure
Exact	Unblemished
Excellent	Undiluted
Faultless	Unmarred

Fencing Practice

If you haven't already done so, turn in your Bible to Matthew 5:48 and read it. Personally I think this could be one of the most discouraging verses in the Bible. In one sentence we are shown just how different God is from us and how impossible our situation is. According to this verse, the God we love and serve is p _ _ _ _ _ _, so we are commanded to be p _ _ _ _ _ _ also. After all, it is impossible for imperfection or impurity to exist in the presence of God.

I read that verse and just *knew* it was impossible! Surely there had to be a loophole or a catch. I decided to look up the definition of 'perfect.' Below is a list of synonyms for 'perfect.' Put a checkmark next to the ones that describe God.

The word 'perfect' means:
- Lacking nothing ___
- Without defect ___
- Complete ___
- Pure; undiluted ___
- Excellent; delightful ___
- Faultless; flawless ___
- Unblemished; absolute ___
- Accurate; exact ___
- Unmarred ___
- Whole and intact ___

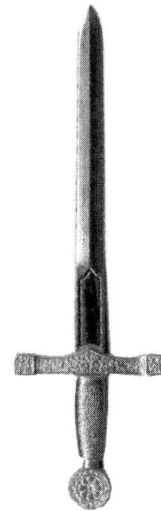

Now remember, God is *all* those things at *all* times. And, that certainly doesn't describe me! I'm some of those things some of the time, but not all of those things all the time! And, *that* means I'm in terrible trouble. I'm **not** perfect...but God commands me to be perfect! How about you? Are you in the same situation? ___

One last question for you: Would a loving God command something (like 'perfection') that was totally impossible for you, knowing you could never comply? The answer is yes!

Thrust and Parry

God does indeed command impossible things of us...and He *is* a loving God. We already established His perfection. Let's establish our imperfection. Rate yourself on a scale of 1-10 (1 being 'not at all me' and 10 being 'that's definitely me') on each of the following synonyms for 'perfect.' Picture yourself on an average school day, your attitudes and performance...

- I lack absolutely nothing. ____
- I have no defects at all. ____
- I am complete, needing nothing. ____
- I am morally pure. ____
- I am excellent and delightful. ____
- I am faultless and flawless. ____
- I have no blemishes. ____
- I am completely accurate and exact. ____
- I am unmarred and unscarred. ____
- I am whole and intact. ____

Total: _____

The truth is that if you scored anything less than 100, then you aren't perfect and have broken this clear command of God.

You know, however, that God *is* love. Since you and I can't keep this commandment, He became sin for us, so that in Him we might become the righteousness of God! (2 Corinthians 5:21)

Memory work: Copy Psalm 145:19 here: _____

_____

_____

_____

_____

_____

End with prayer. Thank God for His love that causes *Him* to fulfill all His commandments for you!

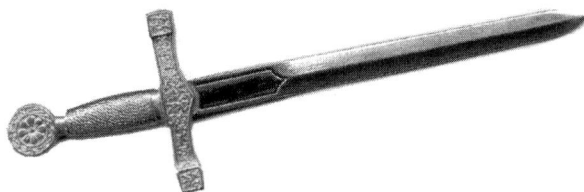

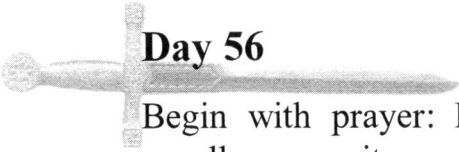

Day 56

Begin with prayer: Praise Him for His perfection - His delightfulness, excellence, purity, completeness, and flawlessness.

Sword Drill

I C_ _ _ _ _ _ _ _ _ _ was written by Paul to address big problems in the church in Corinth. *II Corinthians* was Paul's thank you to the church in Corinth for their obedience. Write the next six books of the New Testament here: *A_ _ _*, *R_ _ _ _ _*, *I & II C_ _ _ _ _ _ _ _ _ _*, *G_ _ _ _ _ _ _ _*, and *E_ _ _ _ _ _ _*.

Sword Play

All the words in the puzzle below are taken from Isaiah 64:6. Fill in the puzzle (you can use the word bank below to help) by counting the letters in each word and using those words to fill in the blanks with the same number. For example, the top line has four blanks, so you need to find a word with four letters. There are three words with four letters in the word bank, but only one that begins with an r. Obviously, then, the four-letter word that begins with an r goes in the top line. The acrostic down the center tells us something we *don't* have apart from Christ.

Become	Leaf
Deeds	Polluted
Fades	Rags
Filthy	Taken Away
Garment	Unclean
Iniquities	Wind
Isaiah	

What is the thing we are required to have, but no matter how hard we try, we don't have? _ _ _ _ _ _ _ _ _ _ _ _ _ _

Fencing Practice

If you haven't already done so, turn in your Bible to Isaiah 64:6 and read it. In the last lesson you read Matthew 5:48, and I had mentioned that in my opinion, it was a discouraging verse. Well, today's verse is equally depressing!

This verse grants that we do indeed manage to do good, righteous deeds. But guess what! Our righteous deeds don't impress our perfect, holy God! In fact, according to Isaiah 64:6, our righteous deeds are like

_____.

The God of the universe is *not* impressed with the good things we do. He describes the *good* things we do as *filthy* or *polluted*! Ouch! Just when you thought you were doing pretty good…and BAM! If the *good* things we do are filthy and polluted in God's sight, how might He view the bad attitudes or mean things we do?!

Thrust and Parry

It may seem like *Fencing Lessons* are really beating you up and revealing you as a horrible person. There really is an important reason for you to 'own' your helpless and hopeless situation. When you 'get it,' you'll realize how desperately you need a Savior and how amazing God is to love you and provide a Savior for you!

List (below) six good things you've done. It might be something 'big' (like going on a mission trip) or 'small' (like reading the Bible or doing a chore cheerfully).

- _____
- _____
- _____
- _____
- _____
- _____

To really bring home this truth, pick the two most impressive things on your list and rewrite them in the blanks below, completing each sentence so it makes sense. For example, I could say:

"When I read the Bible in a year, that righteous deed is like a *filthy rag* to God." Now it's your turn:

- When I _____, that righteous deed is like a *polluted garment* to God.

- When I _____, that righteous
  deed is like a *filthy rag* to God.

Please understand that your righteous deeds are good. You *should* be
practicing such things. You *should* be *increasing* in practicing good works,
deeds, and attitudes! *But,* there is a very important distinction we must make.
If you are doing good things to gain God's favor, *or* if you think your good
deeds make you righteous, *or* if you think your righteous deeds make you
better than your siblings or your friends, *then* you are wrong. Your righteous
deeds do not bring you closer to God, nor do they set you above others.
However, if you are doing righteous deeds simply because of your love for
God and for those around you, because you want to glorify God and bless
others with your life, *then* you are on the right track. *That* kind of work is what
you were created for.

Pick two more things from your 'good deeds' list and complete the
sentences below (see my sample) using the same deed **twice** in each sentence,
like this:

"When I *wash dishes without being asked*, I pray God will be glorified
and others will be blessed. Thank you, Father, for helping me to *wash dishes
without being asked.*"

- When I _____, I pray
  God will be glorified and others will be blessed. Thank you, Father,
  for helping me to _____.
- When I _____, I pray God
  will help me to be more like Him. Thank you, Father, for helping
  me to serve you when I _____.

Memory work: Copy Psalm 145:19 here: _____

_____

_____

_____

_____

_____

End with prayer. Thank God for His love that causes Him to fulfill all His
commandments for you!

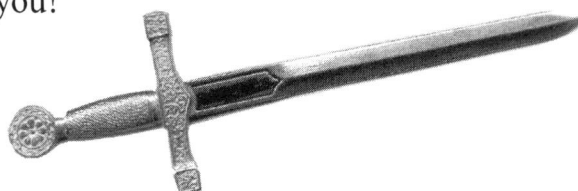

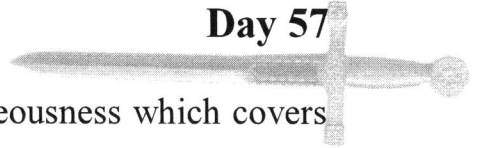

Begin with prayer. Thank God for His robe of righteousness which covers you today.

Sword Drill

II C_ _ _ _ _ _ _ _ _ was Paul's thank you to the church in Corinth for their obedience. *Galatians* is Paul's letter to the church in Galatia to remind them that their works won't save them. Write the next six books of the New Testament here: *A_ _ _*, *R_ _ _ _ _*, *I & II C_ _ _ _ _ _ _ _ _*, *G_ _ _ _ _ _ _ _*, *E_ _ _ _ _ _ _ _*.

Sword Play

The answers to the following riddles are words found in Isaiah 61:10.

I am a verb (an action word).
You do this to yourself every day.
This is how you cover your nakedness and shame.
What am I?
To _ _ _ _ _ _

I am a verb.
I am commanded in 1 Thessalonians 5:16 to do this always.
I "take joy" ever more.
In Isaiah 61:10 I do this in the Lord.
What am I?
To _ _ _ _ _ _ _

I am beautiful.
White, for purity, is my color.
It's not good for man to be alone, so God made me.
What am I?
A _ _ _ _ _

These are put on.
But you can't put me on by your own effort.
You can't stand before God without me.
What am I?

_ _

I am a garment.
I am something you cannot make for yourself.
You may have tried, but the result is filthy and polluted.
I am a gift.
What am I?

_ _ _ _   _ _   _ _ _ _ _ _ _ _ _ _ _ _ _

I am beautiful.
Formed by heat and pressure.
Cut and polished by the Master.
Set into something lovely and useful and very rich.
What am I?

_ _ _ _ _ _

Fencing Practice

If you haven't already done so, turn to Isaiah 61:10 and read it. You may want to underline it and add it to your lists. After the last two lessons, as you became more aware of how hopeless your situation is, you should have no trouble understanding Isaiah's excitement.

Do you remember the command you were given in Matthew 5:48? Jesus says you must be _____. Have you been able to keep this command? _____

Do you remember how God describes your righteous deeds in Isaiah 64:6? He says your righteous deeds are like _____. Are you able to improve those deeds to the point that they cover you and are clean? _____

And *that* is why today's passage is so encouraging! Our loving God doesn't just leave you in your pitiful, imperfect, filthy, ragged state! No! He did something about it – as *only* He can. And not only does He *provide* the garments you need, but He even does the work of dressing you!

According to this passage, what two things does God put on you?

- _____

- _____

When a ragged beggar comes to the door, most people would rummage through their closets for old clothing to pass on to those less fortunate. But that's *not* what God did for you. He dressed you in His finest and best…then went above and beyond, and gave you garments so rich and gorgeous, it is like they are covered with jewels!

No wonder Isaiah was so relieved! According to Isaiah 61:10, how did Isaiah react to his new 'wardrobe' of salvation and righteousness?

_____

Thrust and Parry

Let's compare the two passages we've most recently studied.

According to Isaiah 64:6, even with my best efforts at being good and righteous, the best I can cover myself with is like _____.

According to Isaiah 61:10, God clothes me (despite all my failings and weaknesses) with rich and lavish _____

_____.

What does this mean? It means that doing this Bible study, though it's a good thing, doesn't cover you enough to enter God's presence. According to Isaiah 64:6, the merit of doing this Bible study is like _____

_____ in His presence. I can do a million Bible studies and it wouldn't be enough to earn me a place in heaven.

It means that going on that mission trip to Haiti or sponsoring that starving child, though they are very righteous deeds, won't cover me enough to enter God's presence. According to Isaiah 64:6, the merit of mission trips and sponsoring homeless orphans is like _____ in his presence and is not able to cover the enormity of my sin. I could pour my life out on the mission field and sponsor a million orphans, and it wouldn't be enough.

_Praise God! His righteousness, His garments of salvation, covers all my sin and adorns me like a _____._

Memory work: Copy the _entire_ passage of Psalm 145:17-19 here: _____

_____

_____

_____

_____

_____

_____

_____

End with prayer: Rejoice in the amazing love God has shown in providing for you a wardrobe fit for a king.

Day 58

Begin with prayer: Take a few minutes to praise God for saving you and clothing you in *His* righteousness.

Sword Drill

G _ _ _ _ _ _ _ _ is Paul's letter to the church in Galatia to remind them that their works won't save them. *Ephesians* is Paul's letter about God's amazing grace for you and for the church. Write the next six books of the New Testament here: *A* _ _ _, *R* _ _ _ _ _, *I & II C* _ _ _ _ _ _ _ _ _ _, *G* _ _ _ _ _ _ _, *E* _ _ _ _ _ _ _.

Sword Play

Complete the clues below and on the next page to complete the crossword puzzle below. These words are taken from 1 Corinthians 1:30-31. (You may use the word bank on the next page for help.)

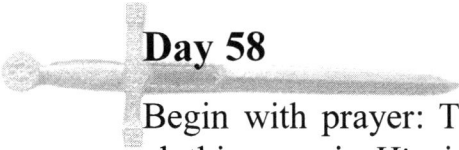

Across

5. The phrase in verse 31 meaning 'it is recorded.' _____

7. A past tense word meaning 'to transform' or 'to change into.' _____

8. One of the 4 things Jesus became for us. _____

9. Another word for 'to glory in' or 'to brag about.' _____

Became	Glory	Righteousness
Boast	It is written	Sanctification
Christ Jesus	Redemption	Wisdom

<u>Down</u>

1. One of the 4 things Jesus became for us. _____

2. Another word for 'to boast in': to _____ in.

3. One of the 4 things Jesus became for us. _____

4. One of the 4 things Jesus became for us. _____

6. Where you are, or Who you are in. You are in _____ _____.

Fencing Practice

If you haven't already done so, please turn in your Bible to 1 Corinthians 1:30-31, and read it. This passage promises so much good toward us! What four things has Christ become to us? _____, _____, _____, _____ The promise, though, also implies that these are four things we lack. Let's define each of these words.

Wisdom: The ability to *act* based on discernment, knowledge, experience, understanding, insight, and common sense. Wisdom isn't so much an *intellectual* quality that only 'smart' people enjoy. It is a moral quality, a character quality.

The Bible tells of two kinds of wisdom: worldly wisdom and the wisdom of God. One leads to death; the other leads to life. In 1 Corinthians 1:30, which kind of wisdom do we have in Christ? _____.

Righteousness: Conformity to a right standard *and* right conduct in relation to others. Righteousness is holiness in action. If righteousness is conforming to a right standard, Who decides what that standard is? _____.

Sanctification: Being made holy, purified, set right in relationship to God and His law. There is 'action' to sanctification as well. It is 'being set apart for' and 'dedicated to' God and His purposes. Sanctification is the process of becoming like Him, for Him. Can a 'set apart' (sanctified) person serve two masters (Matthew 6:24)? _____

Redemption: Being set free, ransomed, bought back by paying the set price. When something or someone is redeemed, the ownership transfers from the original owner to the one who paid the price. What was the price for your redemption? _____ Who paid it? _____

Thrust and Parry

To fully understand the precious truth and amazing promise, we first need to understand just how 'broken' we are and just how much we need to be 'fixed.' Let's look at the four things Christ became to us in 1 Corinthians 1:30-31 and evaluate ourselves.

- Do you always know what to do in every situation? _____
- Is it possible for you to know what to do in every situation if you tried hard enough? _____
- Do you always know what to say in every situation? _____
- Is it possible for you to know what to say in every situation if you thought hard enough about it? _____
- Could you truthfully say, "I've never acted shamefully?" _____
- Is it possible for you to act in a way that is never shameful? _____
- Do you conform to God's standard at all times? _____
- Is it possible for you to conform to God's standard at all times? _____
- Do you follow all 10 commandments at all times? _____
- Is it possible for you to never again ever break a commandment? _____
- Is every moment of your time dedicated to God's purposes? _____
- Is it possible for you to live every moment of your life to God rather than for yourself? _____
- Since the price for our redemption is a *perfect* sacrifice, based on your above answers, can you redeem yourself? _____
- If you could, from this moment onward, live a perfect life (changing all your answers to 'yes'), would that be enough to redeem yourself? _____

Praise God that *in Christ* we have *all* these things! *In Christ, all* your answers become yeses!...Not because you suddenly *can* do all the things I listed, but because *He* did it for you. *He* is your wisdom. *He* is your righteousness. *He* is your sanctification. *He* is your redemption.

Memory work: Copy the *entire* passage of Psalm 145:17-19 here: _____

_____
_____
_____
_____
_____
_____
_____

End with prayer: Rejoice in the amazing love God has shown in providing for you a wardrobe fit for a king.

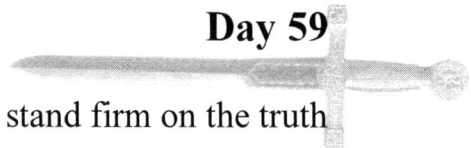

Begin with prayer. Ask God to help you to rest in and stand firm on the truth of Christ's *finished* work on your behalf.

Sword Drill

    E _ _ _ _ _ _ _ _ is Paul's letter about God's amazing grace for you and for the church. Write the next six books of the New Testament here:
*A*_ _ _, *R*_ _ _ _ _, *I & II C*_ _ _ _ _ _ _ _ _ _ _, *G*_ _ _ _ _ _ _ _,
*E*_ _ _ _ _ _ _.

Sword Play

    The following truths come from Joshua 21:45. Use the key to solve the secret code below. Then transfer the boxed letters in order on the lines at the bottom of this page for a wonderful truth about God.

a	e	i	o	c	d	f	g	h	l	m	n	p	r	s	t	v	y
1	2	3	4	5	6	7	8	9	10	11	12	13	14	15	16	17	18

□□_   _ _□_   _ _□_   _ _ _ _ _□_.
8 4 6   11 1 6 2   11 1 12 18   13 14 4 11 3 15 2 15

_ _ _   _ _ _   _ _ _   _ _ _ _ _ _.
12 4 16   4 12 2   9 1 15   7 1 3 10 2 6

_□□□_   _ _ _ _□_   _ _ _ _□_ _
2 17 2 14 18   15 3 12 8 10 2   13 14 4 11 3 15 2

_ _ _   _ _ _□   _ _   _ _□_.
9 1 15   5 4 11 2   16 4   13 1 15 15

What do you absolutely know to be true about God?

_ _ _   _ _ _ _ _   _ _ _ _!

Fencing Practice

    If you haven't already done so, turn in your Bible to Joshua 21:45 and read it. I love this verse! It's, like, the promise of all promises! God makes promises (lots of them). His promises never fail. They always come to pass. That's a promise! If you would like to underline this one in your Bible, or add it to your list in the back of your Bible, feel free to do so. Just think for a moment and list a few things you *know* God has promised in His Word. (Do this just from the top of your head. No need to research.)

- _____
- _____
- _____

Just in the last few lessons you learned about these promises, which you can underline or add to your 'promise' list in the back of your Bible:

- Isaiah 61:10 – You are clothed with garments of _____ and a robe of _____.
- 1 Corinthians 1:30-31 – In Him, Jesus became _____, _____, and _____ for you.

Look at the memory passage for this section (Psalm 145:17-19). What are some of the promises listed in there? _____
_____
_____

Does *God* make these promises to *you*? _____
Will any of them fail? _____

Thrust and Parry
There are so many promises God makes to His children. Here are just a few. Look up each promise, then answer the questions. (You can underline these in your Bible and add them to your list of promises in the back of your Bible if you want.)

- Read Psalm 23:6. What is promised? _____
  Will God keep this promise to you? _____
- Read Hebrews 13:5. What is promised? _____
  Will God keep this promise to you? _____
- Read Isaiah 26:3. What is promised? _____
  Will God keep this promise to you? _____
- Read Matthew 11:28. What is promised? _____
  Will God keep this promise to you? _____
- Read Isaiah 43:2. What is promised? _____
  Will God keep this promise to you? _____
- Read Lamentations 3:22. What is promised? _____
  Will God keep this promise to you? _____

- Read Romans 8:38-39. What is promised? _____
  Will God keep this promise to you? _____
- Read Psalm 91:11. What is promised? _____
  Will God keep this promise to you? _____

How do you know God will keep all these promises toward you? (Remember today's scripture – Joshua 21:45.) _____

Memory work: Copy the *entire* passage of Psalm 145:17-19 here: _____
_____
_____
_____
_____
_____
_____
_____
_____

End with prayer: Choose one of the promises in today's lesson and pray it. Ask God to bring that promise alive in your life.

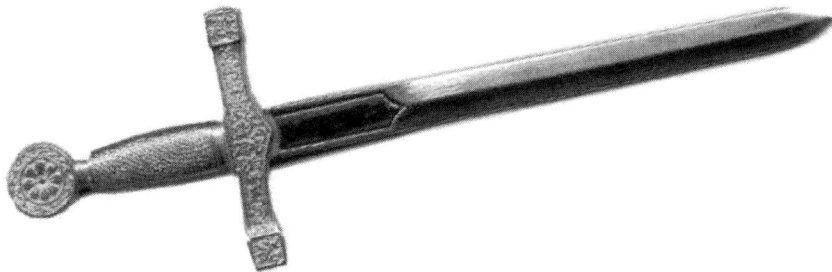

Day 60

Begin with prayer: Ask God to give you the kind of faith that trusts Him even when it doesn't look like His promises are true in your life. Proclaim in faith that you *know* His promises are true!

Sword Drill

The next eight books of the Bible are epistles written by Paul. *Philippians* is a book about joy. Write the next epistles (letters) here:
P _ _ _ _ _ _ _ _ _, *C* _ _ _ _ _ _ _ _ _, *I & II T* _ _ _ _ _ _ _ _ _ _ _,
I & II T _ _ _ _ _ _, *T* _ _ _ _, and *P* _ _ _ _ _ _ _.

Sword Play

The answers to the following True-False quiz can be found by reading Romans 3:23. Circle T for true and F for false.

- T or F   Adam sinned.
- T or F   Abraham never did anything wrong.
- T or F   Rebekah was a perfect woman.
- T or F   Joseph was always good.
- T or F   Moses broke several of the commandments.
- T or F   David really messed up morally.
- T or F   Esther was perfect in every way.
- T or F   Isaiah was the ideal man.
- T or F   Mary sinned and needed a savior.
- T or F   Paul never sinned.
- T or F   Your parents never sinned.
- T or F   You have sinned.

Fencing Practice

If you haven't already done so, turn in your Bible to Romans 3:23 and read it. For the next eleven lessons, we'll be learning about the *Roman Road*.

The *Roman Road* is a name given to a series of scriptures from the book of Romans that explain the entire gospel, start to finish. We will be covering it in *Fencing Lessons* for two reasons:

1. To lead you through the gospel for your own salvation. If you are already saved, this will strengthen your foundations.
2. To give you a tool to lead others to Christ.

I would suggest to you that in the back of your Bible you start a section labeled *Roman Road.* You can add the scriptures from these lessons to that new list and reference it whenever you struggle with doubt or you want to share the gospel with a friend.

Romans 3:23 tells us something about every person you know, including you. What truth does Romans 3:23 tell us about you and all your friends and family? _____.

Thrust and Parry

In your life you probably know people who seem perfect. They never do anything wrong. They're the 'goody two shoes,' always perfect. You probably also know people who just can't seem to be good. They annoy everyone, always hurting those around them. Romans 3:23 reminds us the truth about all of these people in your life.

It's obvious that the consistently 'bad' ones demonstrate the truth of Romans 3:23. As it says in Romans 3:23, these 'bad' people in your life have _____. But, remember all those 'good' people in your life are in the exact same situation – according to God – as the 'bad people. As it says in Romans 3:23, they also have _____. I don't know whether you consider yourself to be a 'bad' person or a 'good' person, but in God's eyes you are a sinner in need of a savior.

Memory work: Copy Romans 3:23 here: _____
_____
_____
_____

End with prayer: Acknowledge before God that you are a sinner. Thank Him for sending a savior.

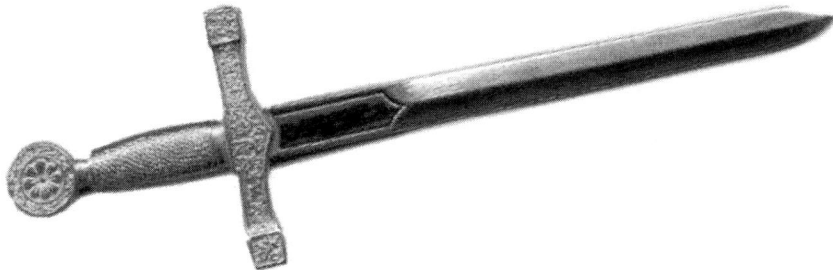

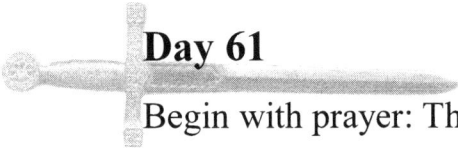

Day 61

Begin with prayer: Thank God for saving you.

Sword Drill

The next eight books of the Bible are epistles written by Paul. The book of *P_ _ _ _ _ _ _ _ _ _* is a book about joy. *Colossians* is an epistle that teaches against legalism and for holiness. Write the next eight epistles here:

P_ _ _ _ _ _ _ _ _ _, *C_ _ _ _ _ _ _ _ _*, *I & II T_ _ _ _ _ _ _ _ _ _ _ _*, *I & II T_ _ _ _ _ _*, *T_ _ _ _*, *P_ _ _ _ _ _ _*.

Sword Play

The answers to the following fill-in-the-blank questions are taken from Romans 3:10-18.

- According to verse 10, no one is _____, not three people, not two, not even _____.
- According to verse 11, how many people understand? _____ How many actually seek God? _____
- According to verse 12, how many have turned aside out of THE way? _____ How many people do good? _____
- According to verses 12-13, how many have throats like open graves? _____
- How many have venomous/poisonous lips? _____
- According to this passage (verses 12, 15-17), how many are quick to shed innocent blood? _____
- How many know the way of peace? _____
- According to this passage (verses 12, 18), how many are there who fear God? _____

Fencing Practice

If you haven't already done so, turn in your Bible to Romans 3:10-18 and read it. As you can see, this passage further emphasizes the completely "lost" state of every human being apart from divine intervention.

Take a moment to add Romans 3:10-18 to your *Roman Road* list in the back of your Bible.

List some of the harsh, hopeless statements made in this passage about every person on the next page. This passage states ideas such as:

No one…

- _____

- _____

- _____

Everyone…

- _____

- _____

- _____

Tip: You will have to rephrase some of these to turn them into "no one" statements and "everyone" statements.

One problem that all mankind tends to share (besides our obvious depravity) is our tendency to believe we aren't all THAT bad, especially when we compare ourselves to other people. God wants us to know the truth about ourselves. The truth, according to this passage, is: _____ _____ .

Thrust and Parry

Perhaps you never thought about these statements from Romans 3:10-18 as God's judgment on you, your friends, and your family apart from Christ. But allow yourself to think about it. It IS frightening and unsettling…but it is the foundation of His amazing grace. If this wasn't truth, then grace wouldn't be so amazing! So, think about it. Do the statements in this passage, *apart from the saving work of Jesus Christ*, apply to…

- Good people? _____
- Your grandmother? _____
- Kids raised in Christian homes? _____
- Your family members? _____
- Cops? _____
- Pastors? _____
- Nurses? _____
- Homeschoolers? _____
- You? _____

To really "own" these truths, you are going to recopy the statements from your fencing practice at the top of this page onto the lines on the next page. Insert your name where indicated on the line on the next page to replace the phrase "no one," then *rephrase the statements* from the top of this page so they make sense and write them on the blanks on the next page. The first one is done for you.

Apart from Christ _____ [write your name]:

-     __*is not righteous*__
- _____
- _____ **AND...**

Insert your name to replace the word "everyone," then rephrase the '*everyone*' statements from page 177 so they make sense and rewrite them on the lines below.

Apart from Christ _____ [write your name]:

- _____
- _____
- _____

    This passage leaves us in a tragic place, indeed. Please, though, don't be afraid to embrace these scriptural truths about yourself. It is these very truths that teach us about God's amazing G __ __ __ __. And, it IS amazing!

Memory work: Copy Romans 3:23 here: _____
_____
_____
_____

End with prayer: Dwell again on God's amazing grace in light of the fact of your tragic spiritual circumstances. Let it fill you with worship!

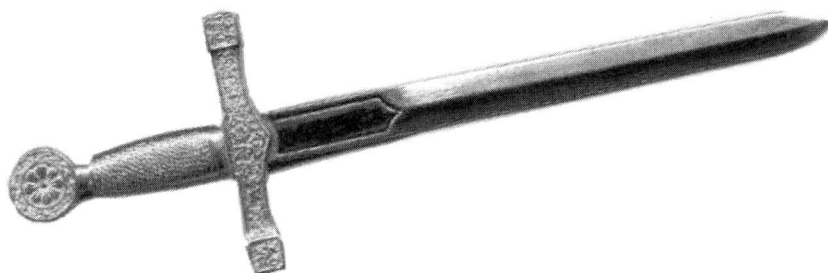

Begin with prayer. Ask God to help you understand the depth of your boundless sin and the immensity of His boundless grace.

Sword Drill

The next eight books of the Bible are epistles written by Paul. The book of *C_ _ _ _ _ _ _ _ _ _* is a book that teaches about legalism and holiness. *I & II Thessalonians* are epistles that teach about the second coming of Jesus. Write the next eight epistles (letters) here: *P_ _ _ _ _ _ _ _ _*, *C_ _ _ _ _ _ _*, *I & II T_ _ _ _ _ _ _ _ _ _ _*, *I & II T_ _ _ _ _ _*, *T_ _ _*, and *P_ _ _ _ _ _ _*.

Sword Play

All the words in the puzzle below are taken from Romans 5:12. Fill in the puzzle (you can use the word bank below to help) by counting the letters in each word and using that word to fill in the blank with the same number. For example, the top line has six blanks, so you need to find a word in the word bank with six letters. Since there are two words with six letters, you'll have to wait until more of the puzzle is filled in before you can figure out which 6-letter word goes in the top line. The acrostic down the center tells us *how many* people have sinned.

		L			
		N		
		E		

All men	Death	Entered
Into	Man	One
Passed	Sin spread	World

How many people have sinned? (Take your answer from the center acrostic.)

_ _ _   _ _ _ _ _ _

Fencing Practice

If you haven't already done so, turn in your Bible to Romans 5:12 and read it. Here is another verse that shows how 'lost' we are. Take a moment to add Romans 5:12 to your *Romans Road* list in the back of your Bible. (You're really turning your bible into a true "sword," a weapon you can use throughout your life!)

Sin *entered* the world through the choice of how many men according to this verse? _____ As a result, something else entered the world because of that one man's action. What was it? _____ Death then spread to how many people? _____

Our world is a scary place. Have you ever heard of the bubonic plague? It's a terrible disease - caught from a simple flea bite - that strikes its victims, killing them in a matter of days. If you were to catch the plague, first you would feel like you had the flu. But, then your lymph nodes would swell into hard knots. Your toes, fingers, lips, and nose would turn black (which is why some people call this the Black Death), because your extremities begin to rot.

During the Middle Ages, some estimate that 60% of Europeans died of plague. During the 1300's the plague killed 75 million people. From 1855 to the 1950's, twelve million people died. Even as recently as 2012, a teenager in the U.S. died of plague! Some scientists believe the plague is still around, hiding dormant in fleas and rodents; and someday another epidemic may sweep the earth. Thankfully we now have antibiotics to cure bubonic plague!

As horrific and scary as these facts are, a worse, more deadly plague swept through the earth at the beginning of time. It was also spread through a single bite, a bite by one man of forbidden fruit. One hundred percent of all people die from it – a spiritual death.

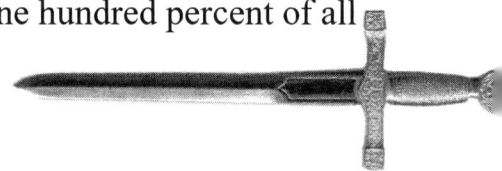

Bubonic Plague	**Sin**
• Caused by the bite of one _____	• Caused by the disobedience of one _____
• Disease spread to many.	• Sin spread to all _____
• 60% of Europeans died from it.	• _____% of mankind die from it.
• Death is *physical*.	• Death is _____.

Thrust and Parry

In our study of the *Roman Road*, it is important to remember how completely we need a savior. We study verses like Romans 5:12 in the light of history so that we really understand how amazing God's grace is and how blessed we are.

The plague was finally conquered when the first true antibiotics were discovered in 1928. If you caught bubonic plague, and you refused antibiotics because you didn't believe in them, what would happen to you? _____ _____ What if you believed in them but didn't feel like going to the doctor to get antibiotics. What would happen to you? _____ _____ What if your parents took the antibiotic, and you decided, "Hey, my parents took them, so that makes me safe," what would happen to you? _____ What if you thought, "I live in the U.S.A., which is a medically advanced nation, so I'm safe," what would happen to you? _____ Exactly! YOU have to actually take the cure to be cured, right?

The same is true concerning the worldwide plague of sin and death. There is a perfect cure. The cure is the blood of Jesus shed for you, and His resurrection. This is how he conquered sin and death.

If anyone refuses this cure because they don't believe in it, what will happen to him/her? _____

If anyone believes, but doesn't feel like doing anything about it, waiting until they're older or more ready, what will happen to him/her? _____

If someone's parents are believers, and their children claim, "I was raised in a Christian family," but don't accept the cure themselves, what will happen? _____

If anyone claims, "I live in a Christian nation, one nation under God and all that stuff," but doesn't accept the cure themselves, what will happen?

_____ Sin causes death 100% of the time. Romans 5:12 says *all* have sinned and *all* die. Thank God we have a cure that is 100% effective! We'll talk about that in future lessons.

Memory work: Copy Romans 3:23 here: _____

_____

_____

_____

End with prayer: Thank God for His perfect cure for our horrible disease of sin.

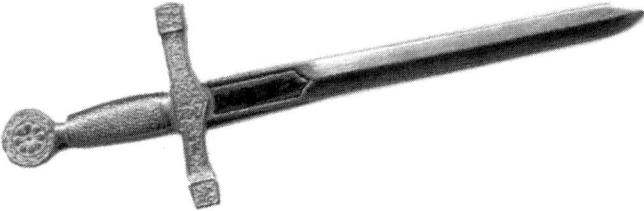

Day 63

Begin with prayer: Pray for someone who needs salvation, God's perfect cure for sin and death

Sword Drill

*I & II T*_ _ _ _ _ _ _ _ _ _ _ teach about the Second Coming of Jesus. *I & II Timothy* were written to young Timothy to teach him about the church and about sound doctrine. Write the next eight epistles (letters) here:

*P*_ _ _ _ _ _ _ _ _ _, *C*_ _ _ _ _ _ _ _ _, *I & II T*_ _ _ _ _ _ _ _ _ _ _ _,
*I & II T*_ _ _ _ _ _, *T*_ _ _ _, and *P* _ _ _ _ _ _ _.

Sword Play

The answers to the multiple choice questions below are based on Romans 6:23.

1. A 'wage' is…
    a. An allowance; money you receive just for being part of a family.
    b. A fixed payment you receive in exchange for work or service rendered according to a contract.
    c. A punishment you have to pay; a fine.

2. Our wage is death according to the Bible. What earns us death?
    a. Big sins that affect people, like stealing, bullying, molesting.
    b. 'Acceptable sins' like lying, arguing, selfishness, prideful showing off, cheating, gossiping.
    c. All of the above.

3. Eternal life can be earned by…
    a. Being good, kind, generous, loving.
    b. Going to church, reading the bible, praying.
    c. It can't be earned.

4. How do we get eternal life?
    a. It is a gift.
    b. By trying hard to follow what the Bible says.
    c. By getting baptized and joining the church.

5. Can eternal life come through any religion?
    a. No, only through Jesus Christ.
    b. Yes, as long as you're sincere, all religions provide a way to eternal life.
    c. No, only some religions that worship an all-powerful God: Islam, Christianity, Judaism.

Fencing Practice

If you haven't already done so, turn in your Bible to Romans 6:23 and add it to your *Romans Road* list in the back of your Bible.

Romans 6:23 tells us something important. It tells us that we are earning a wage. A wage is what you get paid in exchange for something you do. A wage is usually agreed on ahead of time: "If you babysit my kids (feed them dinner, change them, tuck them in), I'll pay you $10 an hour." If you babysat for me – feeding my kids, changing their diapers, reading them a story and tucking them in – for three hours, what would I owe you? _____

We are all 'in a contract' with God. He told the first man, "Don't eat the fruit from this tree or you will die." (Genesis 2:17) Adam *did* eat it, and he died spiritually and, eventually, physically (Genesis 3; 5:5). The 'contract' we have with God didn't end with Adam's death. It extends to every person, including you. In your last lesson you learned that sin and death entered the world *through Adam* and spread to us all (Romans 5:12). *We* also sin and thus earn our promised wage. What is that wage we earn? _____

Now, God wouldn't be just or holy if He overlooked our sin. Let's say I hired you to babysit my kids, asked you to feed them dinner, change their diapers, tuck them in, for $10 an hour. I come home after three hours and ask for a report on the evening. You explain, "I fed them jelly beans for dinner (they're fruit, you know). I didn't change them into pajamas, and I don't do diapers. They fell asleep on the couch and I didn't want to disturb them, so I left them there." Did you fulfill our contract and earn your wage? _____ Would it be *just* if I said, "No problem! I'll feed them, change them, and put them to bed. Here's $30." _____

Because God is *just*, the earned wage *must be paid.* Death must happen. *Your* death must happen because you're the wage-earner. A death *did* happen, but not *your* death. Who got your death wage? _____ And, what unearned, absolutely free gift did you receive instead? _____

Thrust & Parry

Most youth earn money, either through doing chores, a part time job, a home business, or working for a family business. How do *you* earn money?

_____

Have you ever *not* fulfilled a contract (like not doing your chores or not showing up for work)? _____ If yes, what was the result? _____

_____

Have you ever sinned? _____ What 'wage' did you earn according to Romans 6:23? _____

Jesus accepted *your* wage and gave you a free gift instead. What gift did you receive in exchange for your wage of death? _____

Imagine if you and your best friend agree to each mow a lawn. You each will earn a ticket to Disney World as your wage. Failure to mow earns the punishment of mowing *both* lawns alone while everyone else is enjoying a Disney vacation. On mowing day you choose to sleep in, but your friend mows his lawn. Pay day comes and your boss turns to you and says, "Here are the keys to the lawnmower. Both lawns better be mowed by the time we get back from vacation or you're fired." Then he turns to your friend and says, "Well done! Here is your plane ticket, your ticket to Disney, your hotel reservation, and $500 spending money. Enjoy!"

Imagine your friend turning to you in that moment, taking the mower keys from your hand and pressing the tickets and cash into your hand. This is the great exchange: what you earn and deserve in exchange for what your friend earned and deserved. According to Romans 6:23 you are privileged to be part of a greater exchange.

What did you earn? _____

What did you receive instead? _____

Memory work: Copy Romans 5:8 (new verse) here: _____

_____

_____

_____

_____

End with prayer: Thank God for the great exchange: your sin and death for His righteousness and life.

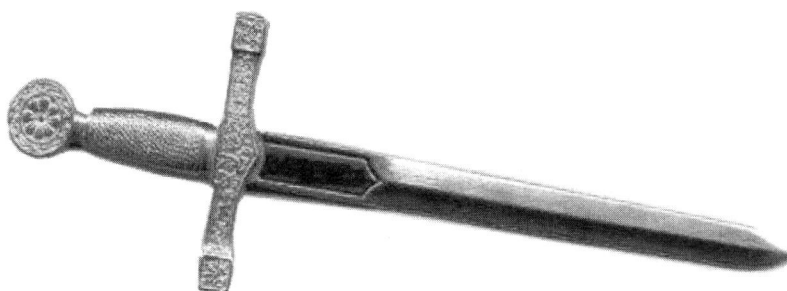

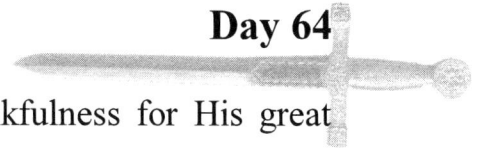

Begin with prayer. Ask God to increase your thankfulness for His great exchange – death for life.

Sword Drill

I & II T_ _ _ _ _ _ were written to young Timothy to teach him about the church and about sound doctrine. *Titus* also teaches about the church and sound doctrine. Write the next eight epistles (letters) here:
P_ _ _ _ _ _ _ _ _ _, *C_ _ _ _ _ _ _ _ _ _*, *I & II T_ _ _ _ _ _ _ _ _ _ _ _*,
I & II T_ _ _ _ _ _, *T_ _ _ _*, and *P_ _ _ _ _ _ _*.

Sword Play

Cross off the first two words in the paragraph below, then circle the third word. Continue this pattern, crossing off two words and circling the third, to the end of the paragraph. Write the circled words in order on the lines below, revealing a crazy-amazing truth based on Romans 5:8.

Allah Buddha God sometimes occasionally demonstrates their hers his awesome crazy amazing hate joy love about over for boys girls you. Who Where How? Mary Moses He handed kept sent Paul Timothy Jesus with for to live walk die out over in my his your house job place, yes maybe not which where when me he you went can't were brothers sisters friends, nor and but who how when we when you was are were rivals competitors enemies.

____ ____ ____ ____ ____ ____ ____
____. ____? ____ ____ ____ ____ ____ __
____ ____, ____ ____ __ ____ ____,
____ ____ ____ ____ ____.

Fencing Practice

If you haven't already done so, turn in your Bible to Romans 5:8 and read it. Take a moment to add Romans 5:8 to your *Romans Road* list in the back of your Bible.

I used a phrase in your **Sword Play** to describe God's love: crazy-amazing. From a human point of view, these adjectives perfectly describe God's love. What adjectives would *you* use to describe the kind of love that targets *enemies* with such extravagant generous kindness and relationship?

Write some adjectives (describing words) that describe God's love here. His love is _____.

Don't forget, God *targeted* you with this scandalous display of crazy love. *But* He didn't do this when you were doing pretty good pulling your life together. According to Romans 5:8 He targeted you with His amazing-crazy love when? _____

Thrust & Parry

Let's examine how "amazing-crazy" is this love with which God has encircled you.

Think of a person you really, really dislike. Don't mention names, but take a moment to describe how this person angers you. *Why* do you dislike this person? How has he/she treated you or hurt you? _____

_____

Now think back to the last few ***Fencing Lessons*** and the scriptures you've studied in light of those truths: You **were** a sinner, sinful through and through, in complete opposition to God. Then, think of your disliked person and why you dislike him/her. The important lesson you must own is that *you were like that dislikeable person* to God. We all snub God, choosing to disregard Him in favor of other pleasures. We know our sin nailed Jesus to the cross, but we also ungratefully snub His death on the cross as we continue to lie and argue and disobey and live selfishly.

Look back at what you wrote about the person you dislike. Try to imagine amazing-crazy loving *that* person the same way God loves you. Answer honestly.

- Will you love that person even *while* they're sinning against you? _____

- Will you keep loving that person even if they *continue* to sin against you? _____
- Will you joyfully lavish generous gifts on that person? _____
- Will you joyfully share your inheritance with that person? _____
- Will you pursue that person and give that person a place of honor in your life? _____
- Will you spend your life doing *all* the work of building a relationship, alone, with nothing in return, to win that person? _____

- Will you joyfully, willingly exchange your *most loved* person in order to spend eternity with your disliked person? _____
- Will you lay down your life, in tortured agony, for that person? _____

But, according to Romans 5:8, that is *exactly* how God loves you. And, *that* is amazing-crazy love, isn't it!

Memory work: Copy Romans 5:8 here: _____
_____
_____
_____
_____

End with prayer: Spend a few moments worshipping God for His amazing-crazy love.

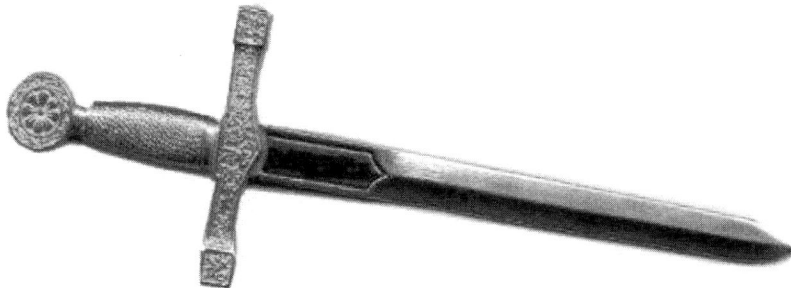

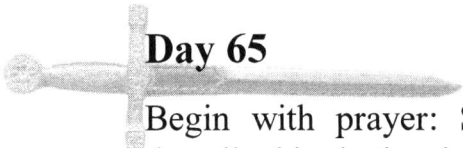

Day 65

Begin with prayer: Spend time praying for the dislikeable person you described in the last lesson. Ask God to help you love him/her with amazing-crazy love.

Sword Drill

In *T _ _ _ _* Paul teaches about the church and sound doctrine. ***Philemon*** is a letter to a slave owner urging him to accept back his runaway slave as an equal brother in Christ. Write the next eight epistles (letters) here:
P _ _ _ _ _ _ _ _ _, *C _ _ _ _ _ _ _ _ _*, *I & II T _ _ _ _ _ _ _ _ _ _ _ _*,
I & II T _ _ _ _ _ _, *T _ _ _ _*, and *P _ _ _ _ _ _ _*.

Sword Play

Match the phrase in the first column with a phrase in the center column and one from the last column to complete truths based on Romans 10:9-10

…If you confess…	…heart that God…	…is justified.
…And you believe in your…	…with your mouth that…	…saved
…You will…	…believes and…	…and is saved.
…With the heart one…	…one confesses…	… raised Him from the dead
…With the mouth…	…be…	…Jesus is Lord,

Fencing Practice

If you haven't already done so, turn in your Bible to Romans 10:9-10 and read it. Take a moment to add Romans 10:9-10 to your *Romans Road* list in the back of your Bible.

In the last two *Fencing Lessons* you learned about the great exchange of eternal life for your sin and death, and the amazing-crazy love God has for you that accomplished this exchange. *How* does this exchange take place? You already know part of the answer. How much will it cost to receive eternal life according to your memory verse (Romans 5:8)? _____

But, surely there's *something* we must do to win such a lavish gift and to be targeted by such amazing-crazy love, right? Write a 'yes' or 'no' next to the items on the list below that you must do (according to Romans 10:9-10) to enjoy the great exchange of Christ's righteousness and life for your sin and death:

- Read your Bible. _____
- Love your enemy. _____
- Confess 'Jesus is Lord.' _____
- Pray at least once a day. _____
- Obey your parents. _____
- Don't argue with your siblings. _____
- Go to church. _____
- Be homeschooled. _____
- Believe in your heart that He is risen. _____
- Stop lying. _____
- Do your chores without complaining. _____
- Go on a missions trip. _____
- Only listen to worship music. _____
- Witness to a lost soul. _____
- Be baptized. _____
- Feed the homeless. _____
- Put all your money in the offering. _____
- Sponsor an orphan. _____
- Stop gossiping. _____

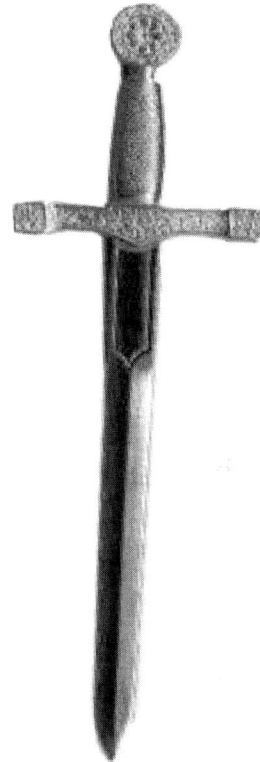

According to Romans 10:9-10, how many items on the list are needed in order for you to be saved? _____

Thrust and Parry

Confessing and *believing* are the necessary requirements for making the great exchange. According to Romans 10:9-10…

- What part of you must make confession? _____
- What exactly must you confess? _____
- What happens when your mouth confesses that? _____
- What part of you has to do the believing? _____
- What exactly must you believe? _____
- What happens when your heart believes in the risen savior? _____

_____

I'd like to encourage you to make that confession, with your mouth, out loud to someone. Explain to him/her why you are confessing that Jesus is Lord. Share with him/her about the astounding free gift and the great exchange of your sin and death for Christ's sinlessness and eternal life. Did you confess with your mouth? _____

Memory work: Copy Romans 5:8 here: _____

_____

_____

_____

_____

End with prayer: Pray that God will make your mouth-confession effective, so that you can share with others the amazing-crazy thing God has done for you.

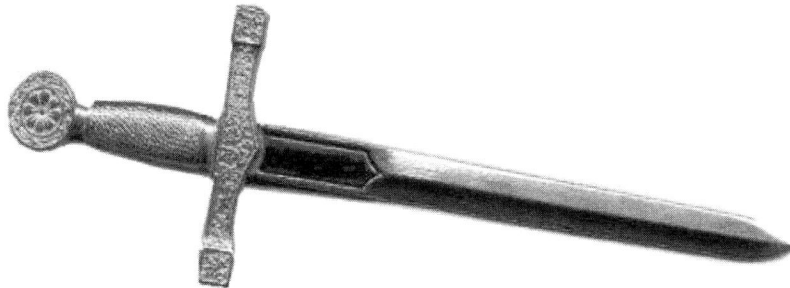

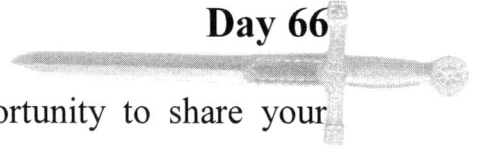

Begin with prayer. Ask God to give you an opportunity to share your testimony with someone today.

Sword Drill

P _ _ _ _ _ _ is a letter to a slave owner urging him to accept back his runaway slave as an equal brother in Christ. Write the next eight epistles (letters) here:
P _ _ _ _ _ _ _ _ _, *C _ _ _ _ _ _ _ _ _*, *I & II T _ _ _ _ _ _ _ _ _ _ _*,
I & II T _ _ _ _ _, *T _ _ _ _*, and *P _ _ _ _ _ _ _*.

Sword Play

This antonym puzzle is based on Romans 10:13. For each bold word in the following sentence, write the *opposite* in the matching blanks below. Use your Bible to figure out which antonym you need.

'**No one**' who **whispers off** the **pseudonym** of the **devil won't** be **condemned.**

_____ who _____ _____ the _____

of the _____ _____ be _____.

Fencing Practice

If you haven't already done so, turn in your Bible to Romans 10:13 and read it. Take a moment to add Romans 10:13 to your *Romans Road* list in the back of your Bible.

In this verse we see another aspect of God's amazing-crazy love and the great exchange of Christ's sinless life for your sin and death. According to this verse, what must you do to be saved? _____

That's it?? Surely we have to do something more than just call, right? The answer is no. In the last *Fencing Lesson* you learned you had to confess He is Lord and believe He is risen. Romans 10:13 shows us that *confessing* and *believing* can be demonstrated by *calling on the name of the Lord.* Let's put these two lessons together.

- What are you supposed to call on according to Romans 10:13? _____

- If you confess "Jesus is Lord," is *Jesus* the name of the Lord? _____

- If you believe in your heart that He conquered death and is risen, wouldn't you be believing He is awesomely powerful? _____

- If you believe He is a powerful death-conquering Lord, loving you so much that He exchanged His sinless life for your sin and death, would you trust Him? _____

- If you trust Him, wouldn't you call on Him? _____

- Would you call on His name if you *didn't* trust Him? _____

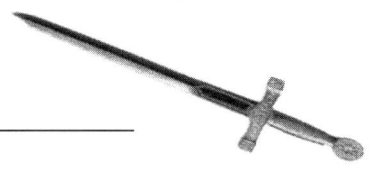

Thrust and Parry

God has made His spectacular gift of eternal life with His amazing-crazy love absolutely, utterly free. And, now you *get* to call on Him in complete trust any time, all the time! Which of the following people do we tend to trust, and why?

- Mom and Dad. Why? _____

- Doctors. Why? _____

- Teachers. Why? _____

- Policeman. Why? _____

- Soldiers. Why? _____

- Best friend. Why? _____

- Pastor. Why? _____

- Spouse. Why? _____

You would call on any of these people *because* you trust them and believe they have your best interest at heart. You demonstrate your belief in their trustworthiness by calling on them. If you call on the Lord, what is His promised response according to Romans 10:13? _____

_____

Memory work: Copy Romans 10:13 (new verse) here: _____

_____

_____

_____

_____

End with prayer: Call on the Lord in prayer. Tell Him you trust Him, the conqueror of death and giver of eternal life, to make all that is wrong in your life completely right.

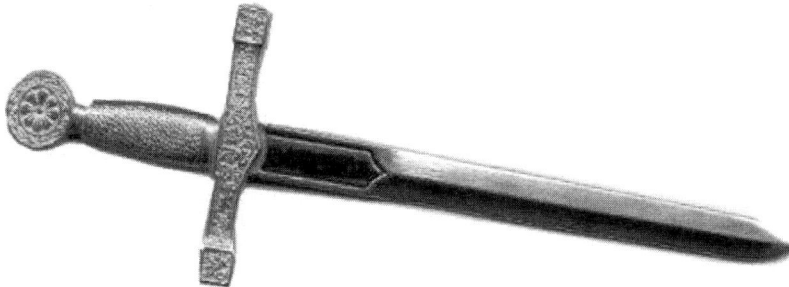

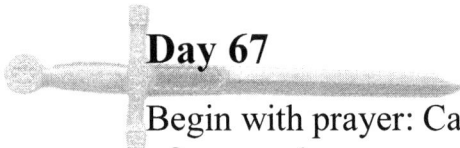

Day 67

Begin with prayer: Call on the name of the Lord to *be* Lord over every minute of your today.

Sword Drill

Hebrews teaches us about the perfect priesthood of Jesus. Write the next four epistles (letters) here: *H* _ _ _ _ _ , *J* _ _ _ _ , and *I & II P* _ _ _ _ .

Sword Play

These mini-puzzles are based on Romans 10:17. Complete the puzzles with words from Romans 10:17 by counting letters and spaces. Then use the same words to fill in the blanks below to complete the sentence.

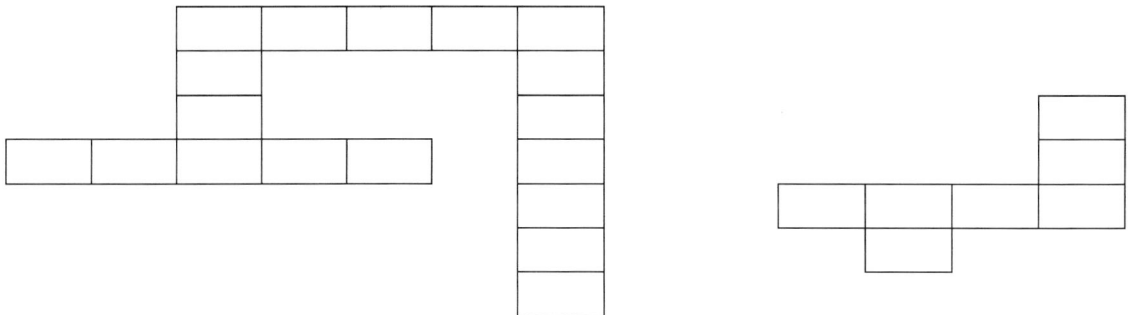

F _ _ _ _   c _ _ _ _   f _ _ _   h _ _ _ _ _ _   the

W _ _ _   o _   G _ _ .

Fencing Practice

If you haven't already done so, turn in your Bible to Romans 10:17 and read it. Take a moment to add Romans 10:17 to your *Romans Road* list in the back of your Bible.

There are three simple but important components of this verse:

- The message being spoken.
- What happens to that message.
- What it produces.

Let's start with the last component first. According to Romans 10:17, what comes through hearing the Word of God, specifically from hearing the Word of Jesus Christ? _____ Look up Hebrews 11:6. Why is faith necessary according to this verse? _____

The second component in Romans 10:17 tells us that faith comes by
_____. *Something* must be *heard*, and that *something* brings
faith. According to Romans 10:17, what is the *something* that must be heard?
_____.

There are a few important things to remember from Romans 10:17:

- Can *you* work up enough faith if you try hard enough? Can you *self-produce* faith? _____
- Can you get faith by hearing what a wonderful person you are and by building your self-esteem and loving yourself enough? _____
- Does faith come by being born into a Christian family? _____

How does faith come? _____

Thrust and Parry

Stepping back a moment, Romans 10:17 shows us not only how
important *hearing* the Word of Christ is (because through it comes _____),
but also how important it is for us to *speak* the Word to others! Paul actually
says this in Romans 10:14. After all, you can't believe in something you've
never even heard of.

As a faith-filled believer, you have the *privilege* of *being* a living,
walking, breathing gospel letter from Christ for the world to see and read (see
2 Corinthians 3:3). Your *faith* in God (which came from hearing the Word of
Christ) causes you *to be* and *to act* differently than the world:

- A family member is annoyed and speaks harshly to you. Your flesh wants to react in anger, but can your *faith in God's unconditional love* cause you to be kind, gentle, forgiving, turning the other cheek? _____
- You are stuck with extra chores while everyone else gets to finish up early. Your flesh wants to grumble and complain. Can your *faith in God's eternal rewards* cause you to do those chores cheerfully? _____
- You believe your parents are treating you unfairly and your flesh wants to disobey. Can your *faith in God's perfect plan for your life* cause you to walk in obedience, even when it's hard? _____
- Can *faith in God's justice* cause you to rest in peace even when injustice is happening to you? _____
- Can *faith in God's provision* cause you to be joyfully content in the midst of poverty? _____

- Can *faith in God's sanctifying power* cause you to lovingly pursue broken believers in your church or your family? _____
- Can *faith in God* cause you to respond differently than an unbeliever would in every disappointment, every hurt, every struggle, every heartache in your life this side of heaven? _____

The answer to all these questions is absolutely yes! With *faith* your **life** *is* a powerful message of hope, love, and power in a lost and dying world. Boldly live your faith!

Memory work: Copy Romans 10:13 here: _____

_____

_____

_____

_____

End with prayer: Thank God that you've heard the faith-giving message of Christ's Word.

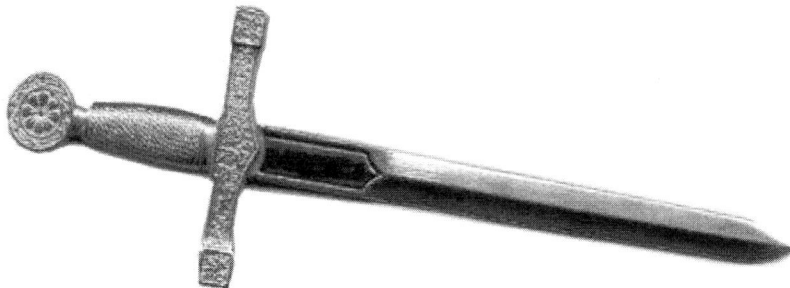

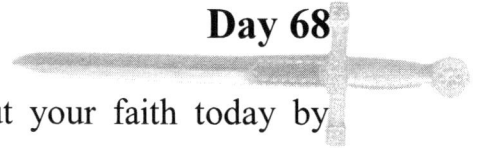

Begin with prayer. Ask God to help you walk out your faith today by responding in every circumstance as a child of faith.

Sword Drill

H _ _ _ _ _ teaches us about the perfect priesthood of Jesus. *James*, the brother of Jesus, wrote this wisdom sermon for the church. Write the next four epistles (letters) here: *H _ _ _ _ _ _*, *J _ _ _*, and *I & II P _ _ _ _* .

Sword Play

The words in the following word search puzzle are all taken from Romans 5:1. They can be vertical, horizontal, diagonal, forward, or backward.

Christ	Jesus	Peace
Faith	Justified	Romans
God	Lord	Therefore

```
P T R B N S U S E J
Z E V C I L O R D U
K F A I T H O A O S
W E B C A F L I N T
O U C H E N J P I I
X T E R O M A N S F
A R E I S D K L H I
W H O S E P E A R E
T R O T B I G G O D
```

Fencing Practice

If you haven't already done so, turn in your Bible to Romans 5:1 and read it. Take a moment to add Romans 5:1 to your *Romans Road* list in the back of your Bible if you would like to do so.

I love the amazing puzzle-perfect fit of God's perfect Word. Every piece fits exactly in place. In your last *Fencing Lesson* you learned that _____ comes by hearing the Word of Christ (Romans 10:17). In Romans 5:1 you see that faith does what? _____ .

That, in turn, gives us _____ through our Lord Jesus Christ. It's a beautiful circle of truth. Fill in the circle with words from Romans 10:17 and Romans 5:1 (see box).

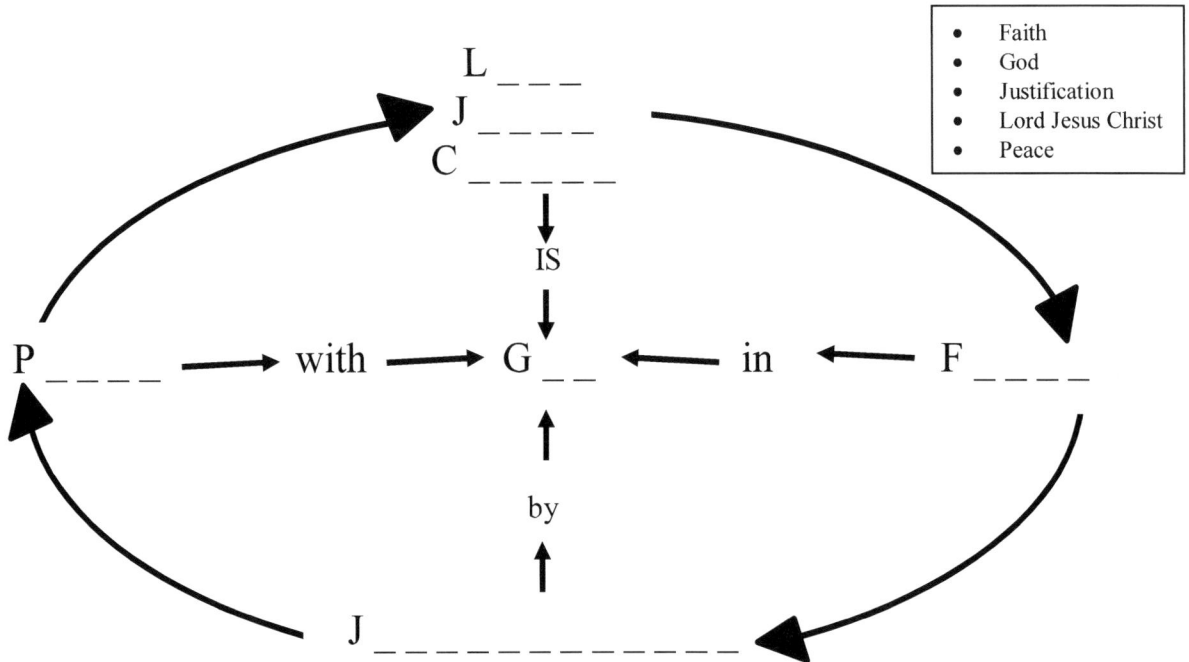

• Faith
• God
• Justification
• Lord Jesus Christ
• Peace

L _ _ _
J _ _ _ _
C _ _ _ _ _

IS

P _ _ _ _ → with → G _ _ ← in ← F _ _ _ _

by

J _ _ _ _ _ _ _ _ _ _

Thrust and Parry

Peace with God. What a remarkable truth and a precious treasure. Peace with God. *Peace.* Our world, our nation, our families, our lives are often marked with strife, but faith which comes from hearing brings justification, which gives __ __ __ __ __.

Think about your week. Yes or no: Have you experienced strife, arguments, disagreements, anxiety, disappointments in any of these areas this week?

With a family member? _____
With more than one family member? _____
With a neighbor? _____
Concerning school? _____
Concerning church? _____
Concerning work? _____
With a friend? _____
In your town? _____

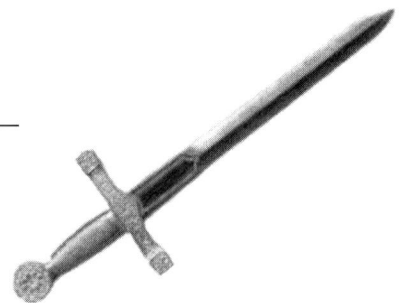

But, if your week *has* been marked by strife, anxiety, or disappointments, then *live* in this truth: You have **P __ __ __ __** with God, and HE is sovereign ruler of the universe, Lord of all, and your future home is with Him. HE gives you **F __ __ __ __** to respond with joy to stressful disappointments. His **P __ __ __ __** is real and powerful. It is *yours* in Christ.

Memory work: Copy Romans 10:13 here: _____
_____
_____
_____
_____

End with prayer: Ask God that you would be marked by His peace in every circumstance this day.

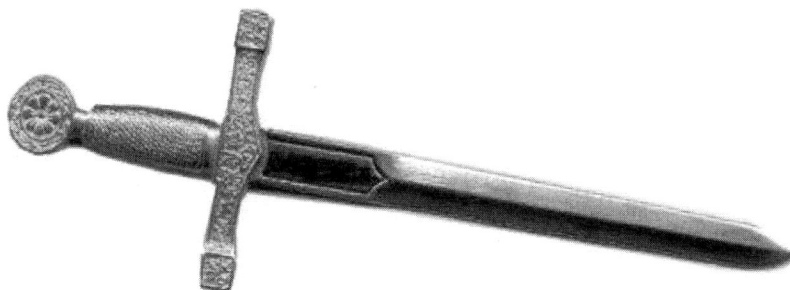

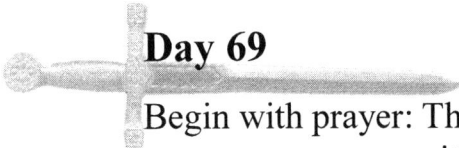

Day 69

Begin with prayer: Thank God for His peace today. As much as it depends on you, pursue peace with everyone (Romans 12:18). Pray God will help you.

Sword Drill

J _ _ _ _, the brother of Jesus, wrote this wisdom sermon for the church. *I Peter* was written to strengthen persecuted believers. Write the next four epistles (letters) here: *H_ _ _ _ _ _*, *J_ _ _ _*, and *I & II P_ _ _ _* .

Sword Play

The following hidden message is based on Romans 8:1. Replace the numbers below each blank with the appropriate letter. Here is the key:

A	B	C	D	E	F	H	I	J	L	M	N	O	P	R	S	T	U	W	Y
1	2	3	4	5	6	7	8	9	10	11	12	13	14	15	16	17	18	19	20

‾‾ ‾‾‾‾ ‾‾‾‾‾ ‾‾‾‾‾‾‾‾‾‾‾‾‾‾‾‾‾. ‾‾‾‾‾‾
 8   1 11 12 13 17 3 13 12 4 5 11 12 5 4 1 10 10

‾‾‾‾ ‾‾‾‾‾ (‾‾‾‾‾, ‾‾‾‾‾‾‾‾‾‾, ‾‾‾‾‾
11 20 16 8 12 14 1 16 17 14 15 5 16 5 12 17 1 12 4

‾‾‾‾‾‾‾‾) ‾‾‾‾‾ ‾‾‾‾‾‾‾‾ ‾‾‾‾‾ ‾‾‾‾
6 18 17 18 15 5 19 1 16 1 17 13 12 5 4 6 13 15 8 12

‾‾‾‾‾‾‾‾. ‾‾ ‾‾‾‾ ‾‾‾‾‾ ‾‾‾‾‾‾‾‾‾‾‾‾‾‾‾‾‾,
9 5 16 18 16 8 1 11 12 13 17 3 13 12 4 5 11 12 5 4

‾‾‾‾‾‾‾‾‾‾‾‾‾. ‾‾‾‾ ‾‾‾‾‾.
2 5 3 1 18 16 5 7 5 19 1 16

Fencing Practice

If you haven't already done so, turn in your Bible to Romans 8:1 and read it. Take a moment to add Romans 8:1 to your *Romans Road* list in the back of your Bible.

Romans 8:1 is one of the best loved verses in the Bible. It says that if you are in Jesus, you are not _____. Let's talk about what it means to be condemned. Condemnation comes at the end of a trial. The allegedly guilty person stands publicly before a judge and jury. During the trial the suspect's entire life is examined in detail, discussed, and made public. Witnesses are called to repeat conversations and events. Motives are uncovered. Finally, a judgment is pronounced. If the suspect is found guilty, he is then condemned. He must bear his guilt and shame and pay the price for his guilt.

We already know from previous *Fencing Lessons* that we are already found guilty. We already know what the price is for our sin/guilt. The price is _____ (Romans 6:23). We also know from our study in Romans that we are justified through faith in _____ and we have _____ with God (Romans 5:1).

Does this mean that God overlooks our sin, like an indulgent parent might overlook a naughty child's misbehavior? Is God on His throne patting us on our heads, saying, "Now, now, I love you. Stop throwing a fit. Here's a lollipop…"? Did He just wink at your sin, pretend it's not there while we go on our spoiled way? Is He intent on making you feel validated in all your beliefs and quirks and issues? No!!!

Your sin *was* condemned. All *your* public shame and humiliation *was* borne. The price *was* paid. How? _____
God did *not* wink at your sin or mine. He did not turn a blind eye like an over-indulgent parent to a spoiled child. Your blame and mine was placed squarely on His Son Jesus Christ. And now, you can say with confidence (as it says in Romans 8:1), "I am not _____."

Thrust and Parry

Our sin, shame, humiliation, and condemnation are very real, and carry a very real, very high price which was paid by Jesus. What was the price Jesus paid for your sin? Yes or no: was Jesus…

- Shamed? _____
- Humiliated? _____
- Beaten? _____
- Mocked? _____
- Stripped? _____
- Scorned? _____

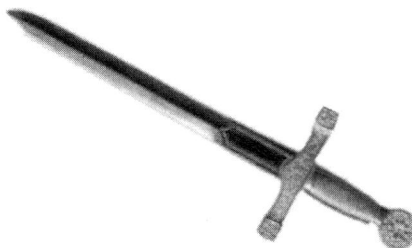

- Abandoned? _____
- Devalued? _____
- Forsaken? _____
- Tortured? _____
- Killed? _____

Was this punishment just? Yes, because it was done in substitution *for* you. The wages of sin *is* death (Romans 6:23). If you are *in Jesus*, then *all* your sin was completely paid for. In Jesus, do you still have to bear condemnation? _____! Are there consequences for our daily choices? _____. But, is our standing before God as His precious child impacted if we are truly *in* Christ Jesus? _____. If you are *in Christ* how much condemnation must you bear if you mess up and sin? _____

Memory work: Copy Romans 10:13 here: _____

_____

_____

_____

_____

End with prayer: Worship Jesus for taking *all* your sin and shame and condemnation on Himself.

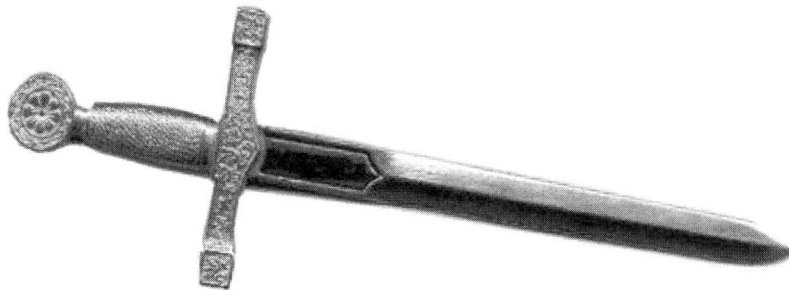

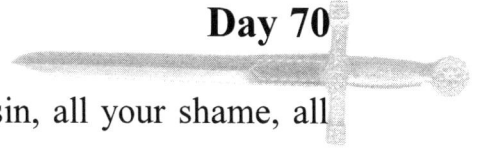

Begin with prayer. Thank Jesus for taking all your sin, all your shame, all your condemnation on Himself.

Sword Drill

I P _ _ _ _ was written to strengthen persecuted believers. *II Peter* warns believers against false teaching. Write the next four epistles (letters) here: *H_ _ _ _ _ _*, *J_ _ _ _*, and *I & II P_ _ _ _* .

Sword Play

The answers to the following mini-puzzles are taken from Romans 8:38-39 (see bulleted list below). Each mini-puzzle shows us the extremes of what *cannot* separate us from God. Fill in the blanks by counting the letters in the word list below, and writing them in the matching spaces. Some letters are already filled in as clues.

- All creation
- Angels
- Anything in
- Death
- Depth
- Height
- Life
- Present
- Rulers
- Things
- To come

Fencing Practice

If you haven't already done so, turn in your Bible to Romans 8:38-39 and read it. Take a moment to add this final scripture to your *Romans Road* list in the back of your Bible.

If there is one truth, one foundation, one fact that has not, is not, and will not change, it's God's love for you. If you are in Christ, you are His. He looks at you and sees Christ. You are adopted. You are His. Forever. According to Romans 8:38-39 what can separate you from the love of Christ?

_____

From previous *Fencing Lessons* you know your sin separated you from God. But you also know that you have been justified by f_ _ _ _ (Romans 5:1) when you called on the n_ _ _ of the L_ _ _ (Romans 10:13). You know Christ d_ _ _ for you while you were still a s_ _ _ _ _ (Romans 5:8) and so now there is no c_ _ _ _ _ _ _ _ _ _ _ in Christ Jesus (Romans 8:1).

This absolute reality means that nothing will separate you from the love of God. Think about it.

- *He had already set His love on you while you were a sinner, and He proved it!*
- *He made provision for your sin/separation, demonstrating His love, by giving His Son to die for you!*
- *You are His forever!*

Fill in each blank below with the word 'love:'

- God is _ _ _ _.
- God _ _ _ _s you.
- He _ _ _ _d you while you were still a sinner.
- He demonstrated His _ _ _ _ by dying for you.
- You are now His be_ _ _ _d child.
- Nothing can separate you from His _ _ _ _.

Thrust and Parry

What a powerful, all-conquering force is God's love! You are the target of His unending love if you are His child. He promises that goodness will follow you (Psalm 23:6) all your life. He promises you new mercies daily; every day is a new clean-slate day (Lamentations 3:22-23). He promises that you *will* make it safely through every storm, every trial, victoriously (Isaiah 43:1-3). He promises to remake, recycle, redeem every trial and tragedy into a benefit and a blessing for you (Romans 8:28). Do you believe He is who He says He is and that He will do what He says He will do? _____

You can trust Him to keep all these promises *because* you are His beloved child and *nothing* can remove you from the target of His love…and God's love *always* hits the bullseye. Yes or no:

- Can your death separate you from His love? _____
- Can your life? _____
- Can demonic warriors fighting over your soul remove you from His love? _____
- Can presidential orders, laws, and cultural shift create a barrier between you and God's love? _____
- Can current events in your life cause His love to grow cold? _____
- Can future struggles convince Him to turn His back on you? _____
- Can the authorities in your life (parents, teachers, governments) cancel His love? _____
- Can you travel so far, so high, so low, that you can travel further than His love can reach? _____
- Can anyone, anything, any circumstance or event in your life prove to conquer God's love for you? _____
- If God IS love (1 John 4:8), can He BE contrary to who He is? If He IS love, then is it possible for Him to NOT love you? _____
- Are you forever safe? _____!!!

Memory work: Copy Romans 10:13 here: _____

_____

_____

_____

_____

End with prayer: In prayer, list some things in your life that make you feel separated from God's love. Thank Him that His love consumes, voids, conquers, and pays for those things.

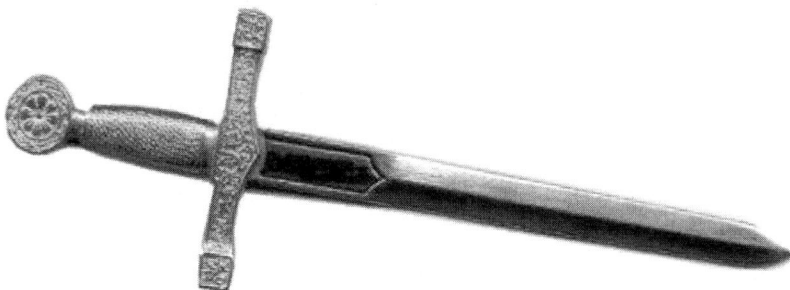

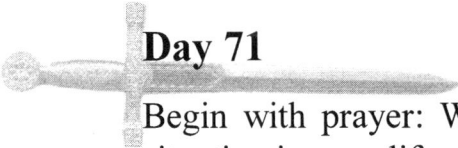

Day 71

Begin with prayer: Worship God for loving you and for redeeming every situation in your life and remaking it for your good.

Sword Drill

II P _ _ _ _ warns believers against false teaching. Write the next four epistles (letters) here: *H* _ _ _ _ _ _, *J* _ _ _ _, and *I & II P* _ _ _ _ .

Sword Play

The answers to the following four riddles are words found in Matthew 22:36-39.

I am to be kept.
Don't keep me and you'll die.
I am ten summed up in two.
What am I? I am a…

_ _ _ _ _ _ _ _ _ _

I am like a pump.
I am feeling, emotion, affection.
I circulate, love, beat, break.
What am I? I am a…

_ _ _ _ _

I am in your head.
I am where YOU takes place:
your thoughts, intentions,
Opinions, motivations.
Learning, believing…
What am I? I am your…

_ _ _ _

I am the kid in the seat next to yours.
I am the person in the pew behind you.
I am the guy next door, the teammate,
The fellow employee, the cashier.
Who am I? I am your…

_ _ _ _ _ _ _ _

Fencing Practice

If you haven't already done so, turn in your Bible to Matthew 22:36-39 and read it. We are going to start a new study on Christian living.

In this passage you read about the two greatest commandments. These two are a summary of the Ten Commandments. Turn in your Bible to Exodus 20:3-17, and summarize the ten here:

1. _____ (verse 3)
2. _____ (verse 4)
3. _____ (verse 7)
4. _____ (verse 8)
5. _____ (verse 12)
6. _____ (verse 13)
7. _____ (verse 14)
8. _____ (verse 15)
9. _____ (verse 16)
10. _____ (verse 17)

Circle the numbers of the commandments (above) that deal specifically with your relationship *with God*. There are four of them. Put a square around the numbers of the commandments that deal specifically with your relationship *with others*. There are six of them.

In Matthew 22:37 Jesus said the greatest commandment is to _____ _____. If you love God the way Jesus says (with all your heart, soul, and mind), would you purposefully break any of the first four? _____ If you loved 'your neighbor' the way Jesus says – as you love yourself – would you break any of the last six commandments? _____

It's easy to see the connection. If you could love God and your fellow humans with your entire being, you wouldn't break any commandments! So, what are the two greatest commandments?

1. _____ (Matthew 22:37)
2. _____ (Matthew 22:39)

However, this is a lot easier said than done!

Thrust and Parry

Training and practice help make a person 'an expert.' How can we train ourselves to obey the greatest commandment? Put a check next to each idea that would help you to love God with all your heart, soul, and mind:

☐ Read the Bible.
☐ Listen to the Bible on your phone or iPod.

- ☐ Listen to world and local news.
- ☐ Go to Sunday School.
- ☐ Attend a Bible study.
- ☐ Memorize scripture.
- ☐ Go to church.
- ☐ Avoid movies that take God's name in vain.
- ☐ Listen to worship music.
- ☐ Try other religions: Buddhism, Islam, etc.
- ☐ Pray.
- ☐ Hang out with Christian friends who are living for God.

How can we train ourselves to obey the second greatest commandment (to love our neighbor)? Put a check next to each idea that would help you to love your neighbor as you love yourself:

- ☐ Obey your parents.
- ☐ Honor your parents even behind their backs.
- ☐ Privately tell your friends of all your parents' inconsistencies.
- ☐ Thank your parents for caring for you.
- ☐ Never use the word 'hate' when referring to a person.
- ☐ Play video games that contain lots of violence.
- ☐ Turn the other cheek.
- ☐ Pray for your enemies.
- ☐ When someone is mean to you, do something kind for them.
- ☐ Avoid dating around; rather, pray for your future spouse.
- ☐ Read romance novels.
- ☐ Talk with your friends about who's 'hot.'
- ☐ Flirt.
- ☐ Dress modestly.
- ☐ Pursue godly friendships.
- ☐ Thank God for what you do have.
- ☐ Be content.
- ☐ Don't consider yourself entitled.
- ☐ Work hard to earn an allowance or income.
- ☐ Serve others joyfully.
- ☐ Always ask before borrowing anything, even from your siblings or parents.
- ☐ Tell the truth, even when it hurts.
- ☐ Exaggeration is okay.

- ☐ You don't want to share? Just say, "Uhhh, sorry, it's gone," then hide it so you won't have to share it.
- ☐ What you post in social media should be with the same integrity as you would in person or in front of your parents.
- ☐ Share only posts on social media that you'd never be ashamed for your parents or God to see.
- ☐ Determine that everything you post glorifies God or uplifts and encourages.
- ☐ On social media, since only friends see it, it's okay to be rude, crude, or immodest, as long as you glorify God in real life.
- ☐ Rejoice with your friends over their successes.
- ☐ Always view your friends as God sees them – as children who are worth so much to Him that He was willing to die for them.

I'm sure you can come up with dozens more ideas to train yourself to think kindly of others and to worship God alone. What is one idea (from the lists here or from your own ideas) that you can work on to practice and train yourself to obey the two greatest commandments? Make this your homework assignment or your challenge to grow in that area. Write it here:

_____

_____

Memory work: Copy Philippians 2:5 (new verse) here: _____

_____

_____

_____

_____

End with prayer: Ask God to help you to obey the two greatest commandments. Specifically ask Him to help you carry out the idea you wrote above.

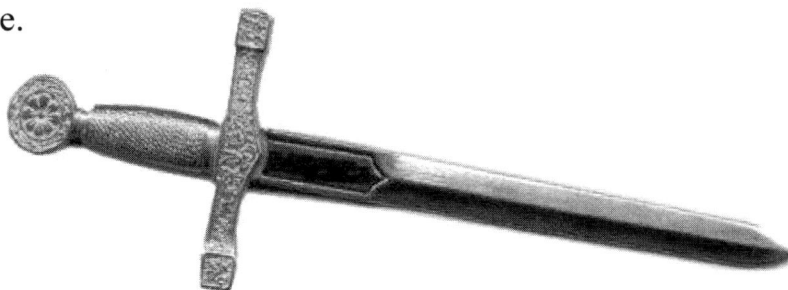

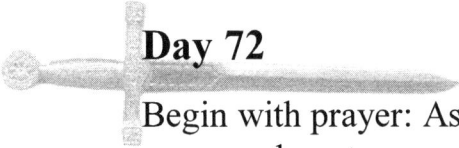

Day 72

Begin with prayer: Ask God to help you continue to practice the two greatest commandments.

Sword Drill

The epistle of *I John* teaches about love in action. Write the last 5 books of the Bible here: *I J_ _ _, II J_ _ _, III J_ _ _, J_ _ _,* and *R_ _ _ _ _ _ _ _ _.*

Sword Play

The following words describe our minds before they are transformed and renewed. Count the letters in each word or phrase in the word bank and place them into the appropriate-length blanks in the puzzle on the next page. There is only one 6-lettered word and one 13-lettered word. Fill those in first and continue to count spaces and fill in words until the puzzle is complete.

4 Letters
Dull
Evil

6 Letters
Futile

7 Letters
Blinded
Corrupt
Defiled
Far Away

8 Letters
Darkened
Depraved
Hardened
Ignorant
Puffed up
Sensuous

9 Letters
Alienated
Reprobate

13 Letters
Without reason

16 Letters
Says there is no God
Separated from God

Fencing Practice

In your last lesson you studied the two greatest commandments. The greatest commandment is to love God with all your heart, soul, and m_ _ _. We're going to study "the mind" in our next two lessons. But first, it's important to know what God tells us about our minds if we aren't born again. It is essentially impossible to know God or to love Him with all our minds if we aren't born again. Look up the following verses and write next to each reference an adjective or phrase describing an unregenerate mind. Without Christ, our minds…

    Romans 1:28   …are _____
    2 Corinthians 3:14   …are _____

2 Corinthians 4:4   ...are _____

Ephesians 4:17-18   ...are _____

_____

_____

Colossians 1:21   ...are _____

_____

2 Timothy 3:8   ...are _____

Titus 1:15   ...are _____

Wow! Just look over that list! It explains why unbelievers cannot understand the most logical of arguments. It demonstrates what a true miracle it is that you *are* born again. If God hadn't intervened in your life, trapped as you were in darkness, where would you be? _____

Thrust and Parry

You may have been raised in a Christian home…or maybe not. But regardless of how sheltered you were or weren't, these truths were true about you. Let's personalize it. Pick six of the adjectives you wrote in your *Fencing Practice* (above) and rewrite them here to complete the following:

Before I was born again, it is true that my mind was…

_____, _____, _____, _____, _____, *and* _____.

If you are not yet born again, then **this** is the truth about *your* mind. It is also the truth about your unsaved friends and relatives. They *can't* understand or reason their way to the knowledge of salvation. You can't teach them into salvation. But you can pray for them, that their minds would be opened. And, you can testify of God's love, knowing God can open their blinded eyes. List two unsaved friends or relatives here: _____ and _____.

Memory work: Copy Philippians 2:5 here: _____
_____
_____
_____

End with prayer: Pray for the two people you listed. Ask God to touch their minds and save their souls.

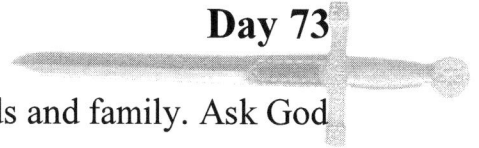

Begin with prayer. Pray again for your unsaved friends and family. Ask God to open their blind eyes and to renew their minds.

Sword Drill

The epistle of *I J_ _ _* teaches about love in action. *II John* warns against false teaching. Write the last 5 books of the Bible here: *I J_ _ _*, *II J_ _ _*, *III J_ _ _*, *J_ _ _*, and *R_ _ _ _ _ _ _ _ _*.

Sword Play

The answers to the true/false quiz below are found in Philippians 2:5-7.

- True or false: *In Christ Jesus* you have a mind like His. _____
- True or false: This "mindset" is to be shared among other believers. _____
- True or false: Jesus was in the form of God. _____
- True or false: Jesus, because He was in the form of God, fought hard to be equal with God. _____
- True or false: Jesus emptied Himself of all claims to greatness or royalty. _____
- True or false: Jesus became someone important, taking the form of well-to-do world-renown Jewish craftsman/carpenter. _____
- True or false: Jesus took on the form and characteristics of a servant, humbly and joyfully serving those around Him. _____
- True or false: Since you already *have* this same mindset, you should *let* this mindset rule you. _____

Fencing Practice

If you haven't already done so, turn in your Bible to Philippians 2:5-7 and read it. In our last lesson we learned how completely corrupt our minds are apart from Christ. This lesson, however, serves as the promise, the hope, the great "but Jesus…"

While you have your Bible open to Philippians 2, read verse 4. Also read verse 21. These two verses both speak about the same topic: selfishness, or self-centered living. What is the problem we need to avoid according to these two verses? _____

When you think back to our last lesson, avoiding self-centered thinking and self-centered living might seem impossible…except for one astounding and powerful reality. In Christ Jesus, you've been given a *new mind*! This new mind is the opposite of your old mind. (Complete the following statements by filling in the opposites.)

This means that instead of….

- …being blind, your new mind can _____.
- …being darkened, your new mind is full of _____.
- …being hardened and unteachable, your new mind is _____ _____ and _____.
- …being ignorant, your new mind is _____.
- …being without reason, your new mind is full of _____.
- …being far from God, your new mind is _____.
- …being evil, your new mind is _____.
- …being puffed up, self-centered, wanting to be served, your new mind is _____.

Does this surprise you? Does it match up with your personal experience of life? _____

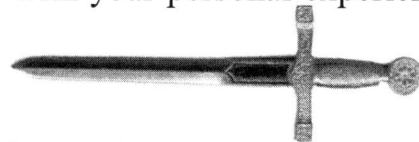

Thrust and Parry

This passage contains a world-changing truth that would be absolutely *dynamite* if we actually *lived* this truth!

Self-centered thinking is a common problem that makes Christians resemble just about everyone else in the world. Christians are supposed to *act* differently, *react* differently, *talk* differently, and *think* differently than everyone else. For example…

- When 'the world' whines and complains about everything, we should (1 Thessalonians 5:18) _____
- When 'the world' gets angry at those who wrong them, we are to…
  - Matthew 5:39 _____
  - Luke 6:28 _____
  - Luke 6:35 _____
  - Romans 12:20 _____
- 'The world' strives to be first, pushing and shoving to be before others, but we are to (Matthew 20:16) _____
- 'The world' struggles to be the greatest, the best, the prettiest, the most popular, the fastest, the strongest, the richest, the smartest; but we are to (Luke 22:25-26) _____

- 'The world' mouths off with rude comments, sarcasm, sass, filthy speech, impure jokes, insults, curse words, and tearing each other down; but we are to (Ephesians 4:29) _____

This list could go on and on, but you get the idea. We are to have the same mind as Jesus – to empty ourselves of 'our rights' and to make ourselves *nothing,* to *be* a servant. Look at the list above of some of the actions/reactions of a Christian. What *should* you do as a child of God?

- When things aren't going as you like, are you going to whine and complain like 'the world,' or are you going to empty yourself and give thanks? _____
- When your sibling or friend teases or hurts you, are you going to get angry and lash back, or are you going to 'turn the other cheek,' do something kind for him/her, and pray for him/her? _____
- When Mom says, "Who wants cookies?!," are you going to shove everyone out of the way to go first, or are you going to allow everyone else to go before you and choose joyfully to go last? _____
- Are you going to post selfies all over social media, demonstrating how attractive/smart/awesome you are, or are you going to use social media redemptively to build up others? _____
- Are you going to insult your sibling, sass your parents and talk down about that annoying kid in youth group, or are you going to encourage and respect your friends and family? _____

Yes, this is hard! It is SO hard because if you willingly empty yourself and step down from the throne of your little personal kingdom to become a servant, you will be treated like one. People will abuse your kindness, take advantage of your selflessness, and use you. But, hey, that's how Jesus was treated, too! And guess what! *You have this same mind in you!*

If every believer *lived* this radical servant-life, we could radically change the world!

Memory work: Copy Philippians 2:5 here: _____

_____

_____

_____

End with prayer: Pray that God will help you to *live* the truth that you *do* have the mind of Christ.

Day 74

Begin with prayer: Ask God to help you react to your circumstances as Jesus would react.

Sword Drill

II J _ _ _ warns against false teaching. **III John** speaks against jealous rivalry in the church. List the last 5 books of the Bible here: **I J _ _ _**, **II J _ _ _**, **III J _ _ _**, **J _ _ _**, and **R _ _ _ _ _ _ _ _**.

Sword Play

The answers to the following matching quiz can be found in Luke 6:27-30. Draw a line from the first part of the statement (in the first column) to the second part (in the second column).

• Love your…	• …those who curse you.
• Do good…	• …enemies.
• Bless…	• …who hurt you.
• Pray for those…	• …get your possessions back.
• Turn the …	• …to those who hate you.
• Give your coat…	• …everyone who begs.
• Give to…	• …and your cloak.
• Don't demand to…	• …other cheek.

Fencing Practice

In our last two *Fencing Lessons* we learned how our old dead minds have been replaced with a new mind, the mind of Christ. We have to *let* this mind *be* in us by being focused on others like Jesus was. In this last section, we're going to practice more specifics in what this looks like in our daily lives.

Although *Fencing Lessons* may seem like a manual on how to 'fight the good fight,' you have to remember that the way Jesus fought was by becoming a servant. A powerful, unafraid, kind, joyful one. If you haven't already done so, turn in your Bible to Luke 6:27-30 and read it.

As a believer you are now a citizen of another Kingdom. The distinguishing characteristic of all its citizens is *love*. Part of your mission as an ambassador of **The Kingdom of Love** is to accurately represent *Love*; and you do that by focusing on others rather than on yourself and by *reacting* exactly the opposite of the way 'the world' would react. Complete these statements from Luke 6:27-30. Notice the 'opposites' in this passage.

- Instead of hating your enemy, _____ them.

- Rather than doing bad to people who are bad to you, you will do _____ to them.

- Instead of cursing those who curse at you, you will _____ them.

- Rather than hitting someone who hits you, you should _____ _____.

- Instead of fighting to get back what has been taken from you, you should _____ more.

As you can see, you've been called to a truly difficult mission! Are you ready for it? Are you ready to live radically different than everyone around you?! With the help of the Holy Spirit within you, you *can* live and thrive on this lifelong mission.

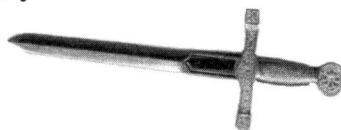

Thrust and Parry

As a citizen of the ***Kingdom of Love*** and as an ambassador from that kingdom, you need to practice this counter-culture mindset. 'Counter-culture' means 'opposite of the today's culture.' It means you must 'put on' this mindset. *Let it be **in** you.* What will this look in *your* life?

Think of the most recent time you got angry at someone. Briefly describe what happened and why you got angry: _____

_____

_____

_____

_____

According to Luke 6:27-30, what *should* your reaction have been? (On the next page, check all that apply.)

- ☐ Love that person.
- ☐ Do good to that person.
- ☐ Bless that person.
- ☐ Pray for that person.
- ☐ "Turn the other cheek."
- ☐ If that person took something, give him/her more.
- ☐ If that person took something, don't demand it back.

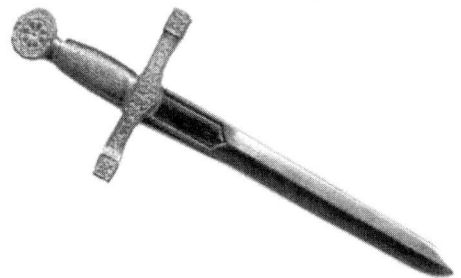

Did you act like a citizen of the **Kingdom**? Yes or no? _____ If you didn't, it's not too late. Purpose *now* to do at least one of the things on the checklist to/for that person. Which one will you do? _____

Think of the most recent time someone hurt your feelings (a different occasion than the first one you described). Briefly describe what happened:

_____

_____

_____

According to Luke 6:27-30, what *should* your reaction have been? (Check all that apply.)

- ☐ Love that person.
- ☐ Do good to that person.
- ☐ Bless that person.
- ☐ Pray for that person.
- ☐ "Turn the other cheek."
- ☐ If that person took something, give him/her more.
- ☐ If that person took something, don't demand it back.

Did you act like a citizen of the **Kingdom**? Yes or no? _____ If you didn't, it's not too late. Purpose *now* to do at least one of the things on the checklist to/for that person. Which one will you do? _____

Memory work: Copy Luke 6:31 (new verse) here: _____

_____

_____

_____

End with prayer: Pray that God will grow love in your life so that you'll have courage to love the way He loves.

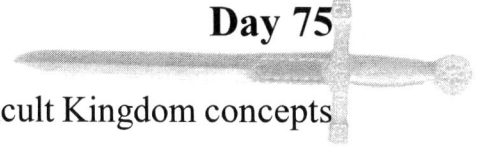

Begin with prayer. Ask God to help you *live* these difficult Kingdom concepts of love and forgiveness today.

Sword Drill

The epistle of ***III J*** _ _ _ speaks against jealous rivalry in the church. ***Jude*** denounces the claim that God's grace gives you free license to sin. List the last 5 books of the Bible here: ***I J*** _ _ _, ***II J*** _ _ _, ***III J*** _ _ _, ***J*** _ _ _, and ***R*** _ _ _ _ _ _ _ _ _.

Sword Play

The following fill-in-the-blank exercise is based on Luke 6:31 as well as on the passage from our last lesson (Luke 6:27-30).

Scripture is clear as to how we should treat others We should treat others the same way that _____.

Instead of taking revenge on my enemies, we should _____ _____.

Instead of cursing those who curse me, we should _____ _____.

Instead of striking back, we should _____ _____.

Instead of refusing to share, we should _____ _____.

If I like being treated kindly, then I should _____ _____.

If I like being helped, then I should _____ _____.

If I like people to be joyful around me, I should _____ _____.

If I don't like show-offs, then I shouldn't be _____ _____.

If I don't like to be ignored, I shouldn't _____ _____.

If I don't like being teased, I shouldn't _____ _____.

Fencing Practice

Remember what you've been learning in the last three *Fencing Lessons*? The way we fight 'the good fight' isn't through a battle of wills, strength, or words, but by becoming a servant. A powerful, unafraid, kind, joyful one like Jesus. If you haven't already done so, turn in your Bible to Luke 6:31 and read it. Keep your Bible open. You'll need it!

I need to remind you, this mission isn't easy! It takes strength and self-control and love. It begins in your heart, then captures your thoughts and your mind. It marches on to shape your emotions, and finally spills over to transform your actions. Today's passage gives you a quick simple self-check to measure yourself. Are you being toward others what you want them to be toward you?

Notice what this verse *doesn't* say. Are you to repeat the same actions to others *after they first do it to you?* Yes or No? _____

Are you to do to others *only if they first* do to you? Yes or No? _____

Look at Luke 6:27-30. Are you to do *back as payback* to others whatever they do to you? Yes or No? _____

Are you to do to others as you want done to you *only to those who treat you right?* Yes or no? _____

Are you to treat others, *but not necessarily family members,* as you want to be treated? Yes or No? _____

Are you to do to others as you want done to you as long as they don't hurt or annoy you, *in which case this command doesn't apply?* Yes or No?

_____

Thrust and Parry

Here's your opportunity to create your very own game plan for life. If you're going to do to others as you want done to you, and if you're going to treat others as you wish to be treated, then it will benefit you to define what that looks like.

Check all that apply. Do you appreciate it when people…
- ☐ …are kind to you?
- ☐ …are kind to you even when you're being not so kind?
- ☐ …encourage you?
- ☐ …point out your mistakes?
- ☐ …criticize you?
- ☐ …are patient toward you?
- ☐ …are patient especially when you're struggling?
- ☐ …are joyful and upbeat toward you?

- ☐ …see the good in you instead of focusing on the bad?
- ☐ …complain about everyone and everything?
- ☐ …lash out at you in anger?
- ☐ …raise their voices and yell at you?
- ☐ …remain calm when talking to you?
- ☐ …assume the worst about you?
- ☐ …talk about you behind your back?
- ☐ …listen to you and really pay attention?
- ☐ …allow you to go first?
- ☐ …share with you?
- ☐ …include you?
- ☐ …smile at you?
- ☐ …ignore you?
- ☐ …are understanding?
- ☐ …are understanding even when you're being grouchy?
- ☐ …are hardworking?
- ☐ …are lazy, so you end up doing all the work?
- ☐ …blame things on you?
- ☐ …are humble?
- ☐ …enjoy your successes rather than being jealous over your success?
- ☐ …are arrogant and show off?
- ☐ …belittle you?
- ☐ …are generous toward you?
- ☐ …want to give you quality time?
- ☐ …laugh with you when you're being goofy?
- ☐ …roll their eyes in disgust when you're being goofy?
- ☐ …are sarcastic toward you?
- ☐ …deliberately humiliate you in front of others?
- ☐ …protect your dignity in front of others?
- ☐ …love you?
- ☐ …love you anyway even when you're not being lovable?

This list could go on and on, but now you have a real game plan of how you are to treat others, based on how you want to be treated.

Does Jesus promise us in this passage that if we treat people this way, then they'll treat us the same way back? _____ This is *NOT* a guarantee of *their* behavior toward YOU. It *IS* an instruction of *your* behavior toward others. However, a promise *is* found in Galatians 6:7-8 that you will eventually reap what you sow. If you consistently sow goodness, kindness, love, joy, patience, and compassion in the lives of others, you *will* reap a harvest in your life of the same!

Take a moment to read through the checked items on your list on the previous two pages. Keep in mind the following by checking all that apply:

- ☐ I am to treat others as I want to be treated.
- ☐ I am to treat others in this way regardless of how they treat me.
- ☐ I am to treat others in this way within my family.
- ☐ I am to treat those who don't even deserve it in this way.
- ☐ I am to treat even my enemies in this way.
- ☐ Living like this makes me look and act differently than the world.
- ☐ In doing this I am being an ambassador for Jesus.

Memory work: Copy Luke 6:31 here: _____

_____

_____

_____

End with prayer: Pray that the Holy Spirit will bring this passage to mind when you're tempted to treat someone in a way that isn't pleasing to God.

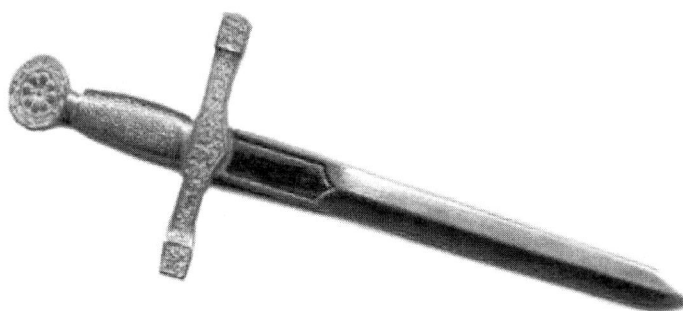

Day 76

Begin with prayer. Ask God to help you treat others the same way you want to be treated.

Sword Drill

J _ _ _ denounces the claim that God's grace gives you free license to sin. *Revelation* reminds us that Jesus has secured the victory through His blood and *will* defeat Satan. List the last five books of the Bible here: *I J_ _ _,* *II J_ _ _, III J_ _ _, J_ _ _,* and *R_ _ _ _ _ _ _ _.*

Sword Play

In the following puzzle taken from Luke 6:32-33, fill in the vowels where indicated below using the code key as a reference, then complete the center acronym with the counter-culture message that Jesus commands us to live.

Code Key

A=1 E=2 I=3 O=4 U=5

D	4	N'	T	J	5	S	T	L	4	V	2	T	H	4	S	2
						W	H	4	L	4	V	2	Y	4	5	.
								2	V	2	N					
			S	3	N	N	2	R	S	D	4	T	H	3	S	.
					3	F	Y	4	5	D	4	G	4	4	D	
4	N	L	Y	T	4	T	H	4	S	2	W	H	4	1	R	2
G	4	4	D	T	4	Y	4	5	,							
		Y	4	5	1	R	2	N	4	T						
		B	2	N	2	F	3	T	T	2	D	.				
		2	V	2	N											
	S	3	N	N	2	R	S	D	4	T	H	2				
		S	1	M	2											
		T	H	3	N	G	S	.								
B	5	T	W	2	1	R	2	T	4	L	4	V	2	4	5	R
	2	N	2	M	3	2	S	.								

Transfer the center acronym here. What is Jesus's counter-culture command to us? _ _ _ _ _ _ _ _ _ _ _ _ _ _ _.

Fencing Practice

If you haven't already done so, turn in your Bible to Luke 6:32-33 and read it. Also review Luke 6:27-31 and yesterday's *Fencing Lesson*.

We've been discussing what it looks like to be a citizen of the **Kingdom of Love**. You and I have been given the challenging mission of representing our **King** here on earth. And, we've been given this command: Be the exact opposite of the world. Love your _____. Instead of being served, we should _____.

What an incredible set of instructions! In today's passage, our concept of life and relationships is turned upside down even more. Let's look more closely at Luke 6:32-33.

Your parents love you. You are a gift from God to them. They care for you, protect you, and provide for you. List three specific ways you benefit by their love for you:

- _____
- _____
- _____

Your friends are good to you. Your friendship is a blessing. Write a friend's name here: _____. Your friends love you, provide companionship, share with you, and understand you. List three specific ways you benefit by the friendship you share with the person you named:

- _____
- _____
- _____

So here's why Jesus's words in Luke 6:32-33 are so disconcerting. Look at the six benefits that you receive from your parents and friends. Jesus is asking, "Does this *really* benefit you?" I want to roll my eyes and say, "Well, yeah. *Obviously*." Jesus, though, is teaching us two important lessons:

- *It's not only the person receiving kindness and love that benefits. The person doing the loving and doing the good deeds benefits even more.*
- ***Reciprocating*** *love and goodness is easy/natural, but loving and doing good to your **enemies** is the way to receive true benefits.*

Wow. Does Jesus *really* mean that those six benefits (and others that you could have listed) aren't *really* benefits? That's exactly right! Of course earthly benefits that you receive are good, and you ought to give thanks for them. But, Jesus is less concerned with your physical comfort and earthly happiness than He is with your eternal good.

We are called to not just *tolerate* our enemies, but to *love* them. We are called to not only avoid lashing out at our enemies, we are called to *actively pursue their good*. And, by doing this, who receives the eternal benefit according to Luke 6:35? _____

Thrust and Parry

What kind of benefit do *you* receive when you love your enemy and do good to someone who is treating you badly? Check all the boxes that indicate benefits you'll definitely receive:

☐ You will get loved back by your enemy.
☐ You will stop being treated badly.
☐ You will get to live in peace and safety on earth.
☐ You will live in comfort and security on earth.
☐ You will grow in character, patience, and humility.
☐ You will be known as a person of integrity.
☐ Someday you will reap what you sowed.
☐ You will demonstrate the gospel by loving like Jesus loved.
☐ You are dying to self and living for Jesus.
☐ No one will hate you anymore on earth.
☐ Everyone will always treat you fairly.
☐ You will be representing the kindness of Jesus to those who don't deserve it.
☐ Your light (the light of Jesus) will shine on the earth.
☐ You will receive your true reward in heaven.

Are you feeling courage rise up within you to *live* this mission? No, it's not easy! It's hard! It's revolutionary! It's counter-culture! We aren't supposed to be concerned about our physical comfort and convenience. Our concern should be the hearts and souls of everyone around us. The Christian walk isn't about doing the easy thing or being comfortable with the nice folks in our lives. It's about doing the hard thing, loving the obnoxious, and being a light in the darkness. Are you ready to take up this challenge? _____
You can start today, right now, with your family and neighbors. *Be* a light!

Memory work: Copy Luke 6:31 here: _____
_____
_____
_____

End with prayer: Ask God to help you love that person who annoys or hurts you. Pray that God will bless that person through you.

Day 77

Begin with prayer: Ask God to help you be patient and kind today, especially if someone is mean to you.

Sword Drill

R _ _ _ _ _ _ _ _ _ reminds us that Jesus has secured the victory through His blood and *will* defeat Satan. List the last five books of the Bible here: *I J* _ _ _, *II J* _ _ _, *III J* _ _ _, *J* _ _ _, and *R* _ _ _ _ _ _ _ _ _.

Sword Play

The answers to the following multiple choice questions can be found in Luke 6:34-36. Circle the correct answer.

According to Luke 6:34-36...

1. You should lend your favorite bike...
    a. ...only to people you trust.
    b. ...only to your best friend.
    c. ...to anyone who asks to borrow it.

2. Lending only to those from whom you'll get something in return...
    a. ...is wise.
    b. ...is of no credit or benefit to you.
    c. ...is what Jesus did.

3. Anyone can lend stuff to people who are careful and generous...
    a. ...so you should only lend to careful/generous people, too!
    b. ...That's easy! Even sinners do this!
    c. ...so don't lend to anyone who mistreats you.

4. Even **sinners** will lend to careful generous people, because *their* motivation is...
    a. ...to receive the same back and to be treated the same way.
    b. ...to be a light.
    c. ...to store up treasure in heaven.

5. You are commanded to...
    a. ...love your enemies.
    b. ...do good to your enemies.
    c. ...expect nothing in return.
    d. ...all of the above.

6. If you follow this command, your reward will be great…
   a. …and you will be a child of the Most High.
   b. …but you'll be miserable here on Earth.
   c. …but your enemies will take advantage of you.

7. Our God is…
   a. …kind to the ungrateful.
   b. …kind to the evil.
   c. …kind to the selfish and self-centered.
   d. …all of the above.

8. We are supposed to be…
   a. …careful about who we are kind to so we're not taken advantage of.
   b. …merciful, just like God, to those who don't deserve it.
   c. …only merciful and kind to those who repent and ask our forgiveness.

Fencing Practice

If you haven't already done so, turn in your Bible to Luke 6:34-36 and read it. Also take a minute to review Luke 6:27-33. Today's passage continues to craft for us a picture of how we are to interact and react to those around us. Specifically, today's passage deals with our 'stuff' and our mindset toward it. Essentially, all your 'stuff' is to be viewed as tools that can be used to bless others, including your enemies.

Jesus is clear about our possessions. Go ahead and lend it! Freely and joyfully let others (including enemies) borrow. And, when you do so, you should lend with a certain mindset.

Should you lend *only* to friends? _____
Should you lend *only* if the favor will be returned? _____
Should you lend *only* if you know you'll get it back? _____
Should you expect at *least* a little back in return? _____
Should you lend reluctantly, putting restrictions on the loan? _____
Should you get angry if it's returned broken or damaged? _____
Should you expect gratitude for your generosity? _____

By viewing our 'stuff' as *His* to be used for *His* Kingdom, no strings attached, you are doing a number of things that benefit *you*. In the following sentences answer the question by underlining the benefits you receive:

- Are you laying up treasure in heaven or on Earth?

- Are you growing in godly character or growing your bank account?
- Are you investing in earthly happiness or eternal reward?
- Are you bound by worry over your stuff or are you free from worrying about stuff?
- Are you a child of the Most High or a citizen of this Earth?
- Is your joy temporary because it's based in 'stuff,' or is it solid because it's based on Jesus?

Thrust and Parry[9]

There are two other things we give (besides 'stuff') when we love like Jesus loves: time and mercy. We often only want to spend time with people who appreciate and encourage us. However, part of our call is to invest in those who are ungrateful. When Jesus served others, He served not only His friends, fun people, and peers. He even cared for people who were ungrateful, disgusting, annoying, embarrassing, creepy, weird, and mean.

Have you ever done a chore or job and received criticism rather than gratitude? _____ If yes, how should you serve if the same opportunity arises again? _____

Have you ever invited a friend over, but they never invite you back? _____ If yes, should you continue to invite your friend over? _____ How many times should you do the inviting before you give up? _____

Have you ever been hurt by a friend? _____ If yes, how merciful should you be toward that friend? Should you wait until (s)he asks forgiveness before reaching out (see Luke 6:28)? _____ What if (s)he does it to you again? How should you treat him/her then? _____

This Christian life, as you can see, is not for the fainthearted! It takes courage and great humility. But, according to Luke 6:35, what is the benefit?

_____

Memory work: Copy 1 Corinthians 13:4-5 (new verses) here: _____

_____

_____

End with prayer: Ask God to help you be kind and merciful when you are being mistreated.

---

[9] Please note that this lesson is referring to typical teenage "stuff," not abuse. If you are being threatened, hurt, harmed, or abused, it is very important that you talk to a trusted adult. Do not be afraid to do so.

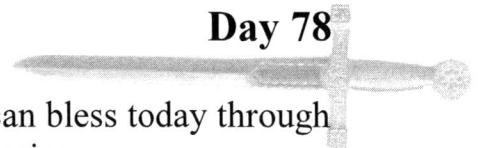

Begin with prayer. Ask God if there's someone you can bless today through kindness. Ask Him to show you how you can be a blessing.

Sword Drill

Review the **Pentateuch.** List the first five books of the Bible here:

G _ _ _ _ _ _, E _ _ _ _ _, L _ _ _ _ _ _ _ _ _, N _ _ _ _ _ _,
D _ _ _ _ _ _ _ _ _

Sword Play

The answers to the following crossword puzzle are found in 1 Corinthians 13:1. Use the word bank for help.

Across	**Down**
2. What *we* speak with.	1. A part of a drum set.
7. The opposite of "have love."	3. Not "of men," but "…."
8. What we do with our tongues.	4. Not quiet.
	5. The sounding of a cymbal.
	6. A large, hanging cymbal.

Clanging	Have not love	Speak
Cymbal	Noisy	Tongues of men
Gong	Of angels	

Fencing Practice

If you haven't already done so, turn in your Bible to 1 Corinthians 13:1 and read it. 1 Corinthians 13 is known as *The Love Chapter*, because the entire chapter teaches us *how* to love.

Think back to our last few *Fencing Lessons,* Days 74-77, (you can take a quick look back at them). In Luke 6, we are instructed – commanded – to l _ _ _ our enemies. We are given all kinds of examples: praying for and blessing someone who badmouths you, turning the other cheek, giving generously, and extending mercy.

Have you noticed that when you consider someone to be an enemy, you don't exactly feel warm friendly feelings toward them! If you're like me, you may struggle with anger toward your enemies. How, then, are we supposed to love our enemies? Is *love* primarily a warm feeling? _____

1 Corinthians 13, *The Love Chapter*, is a manual on what true love really looks like. But before we look at what love *is*, we're going to look at what love is *not.* According to 1 Corinthians 13:1, if you're really good with words, and you are good at speaking or writing, is *this* love? _____

What if your words sound totally angelic? Is *this* love? _____

Our words, even if they're beautiful words *right from the Bible*, if they're not spoken with love (as it is described in the rest of chapter 13), I am nothing but a _____ according to 1 Corinthians 13:1.

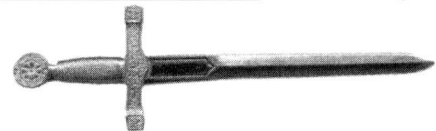

Thrust and Parry

The important thing to remember is that love is more than just mere talk. In future lessons we'll study more closely how our attitudes and actions must back up our words. But, for now, just remember that loving your enemy, or the individuals who annoy or hurt you, is going to require more than just words.

Let's look at some common word scenarios and compare them with the Bible. Circle your answer.

- If you love someone, you'll tell them over and over again that they need to act like Jesus, and *then* they'll be blessed. This is love according to 1 Corinthians 13:1. Yes or no.
- Pointing out another person's faults and mistakes is a loving thing to do as long as you remind them that, "I love you." This is love according to 1 Corinthians 13:1. Yes or no.
- You know you're loved when people quote Scripture at you when you mess up. You can just feel their love as verses pour

from their lips. This is love according to 1 Corinthians 13:1. Yes or no.

- If your "I love you" is followed by patience, kindness, and forgiveness, you are really loving like Jesus loved. This is love according to 1 Corinthians 13:1. Yes or no.
- Your words are full of wisdom and you speak your mind, telling it like it is – the truth, like an angel. People will know you love them if you just "tell it like it is." This is love according to 1 Corinthians 13:1. Yes or no.
- Words, truthful words, wise words, Scripture, lectures full of advice, angelic words: these are just irritating noise that clash on your nerves if they're not offered with love evidenced by actions and attitudes. Yes or no.
- You can look your enemy in the eye and say, "I love you," and still not be in obedience to Scripture if your actions and attitudes don't match your words. Yes or no.

Memory work: Copy 1 Corinthians 13:4-5 here: _____
_____
_____
_____

End with prayer: Ask God to fill your words with love and to help you back up your words with loving actions and attitudes.

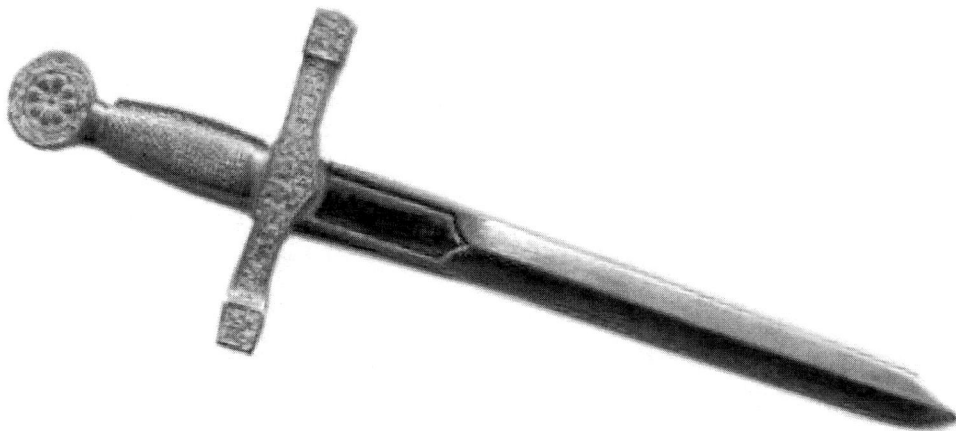

Day 79

Begin with prayer: Ask God to help you be patient and kind today, especially if someone is mean to you.

Sword Drill

Review the five books of history that follow the Pentateuch:
J _ _ _ _ _, J _ _ _ _ _, R _ _ _, I and II S _ _ _ _ _.

Sword Play

The paragraph below, based on 1 Corinthians 13:1-2, contains many words that shouldn't be there. Cross out the wrong words/phrases in each set of brackets, leaving only one correct word/concept in each set of brackets.

Verse 1: If I [walk, think, speak] in the [tongues, land, temple] of men and of [angels, fathers, wisdom], but I don't have [the Bible, love, wisdom] I am a noisy [child, gong, trumpet] or a [roaring, clanging, barking] [cymbal, dog, river].

Verse 2: If I have [prophetic power, Scripture memorized, nothing] and [understand, enjoy, lecture] all [literature, lessons, mysteries] and all [languages, knowledge, pastors], and if I have all [faith, love, power] so as to remove [hearts, mountains, demons], but have not [wisdom, joy, love], I am [something, nothing, loved].

Fencing Practice

If you haven't already done so, turn in your Bible to 1 Corinthians 13:2 and read it. Review verse 1 as well.

This passage reminds us that love is not just words. Only one characteristic establishes who we really are. According to this passage, what "proves" who we really are? Circle or write your answers below:

- Is it spiritual gifts like having prophetic power? Yes or no?
- So, if you hear someone claiming to be a prophet, what characteristic would prove it? _____
- Is it biblical understanding and knowledge that proves you are a Christian? Yes or no?
- If someone who claims to be a Christian is full of knowledge and understanding of the Bible – maybe even has a PhD in biblical studies

– what characteristic would prove him to be a Christian? His PhD in biblical studies: Yes or no? His love: Yes or no?

- Is it mountain-moving faith that proves who you are? Yes or no?
- So, if someone's faith actually moved a mountain or healed someone, what characteristic needs to be evident to prove who they are? _____

Isn't that astounding! Faith, prophetic power, wisdom, knowledge. Does any of this make you *something* according to the Bible? Yes or no? What is the **one** characteristic that is the measure of a Christian? _____

Thrust and Parry

If you're anything like me, it's easy to look at someone's outward accomplishments and assume that that person is an amazing Christian. I can look at a person's life and wish I had his/her faith, knowledge, and talents. Unfortunately, no matter what we do or how hard we try, there are certain things we'll never be talented at or be able to accomplish.

- Have you ever had a school subject that just didn't make sense no matter how hard you try? Yes or no?
- Have you ever prayed for someone's healing and they didn't get healed? Yes or no?
- Did you ever listen to a friend who knows the Bible really well, always knows the verses, and has a lot of verses memorized? Yes or no?

If the only way you could *be* **something** in God's eyes was through your knowledge of doctrine and Bible, or through your mountain-moving faith, or through your prophetic powers, you may be tempted to give up. But according to 1 Corinthians 13:2, these things don't mean anything. The one ingredient necessary according to this passage is _____.

This is really good news, because it's one thing anyone can do.

- Does *love* require any special gifts or talents? Yes or no?
- Does *love* require intelligence or education? Yes or no?
- Does *love* require a certain age or maturity level? Yes or no?
- Does *love* require a certain political party affiliation? Yes or no?
- Does *love* require a degree in theology? Yes or no?
- Does *love* require that you have money? Yes or no?
- Does *love* require that you be in perfect health? Yes or no?
- Does *love* require that you be popular? Yes or no?
- Does *love* require that you be "normal"? Yes or no?
- Does *love* require that you have a whole family? Yes or no?

- Does *love* require you to read a certain Bible version? Yes or no?
- Does *love* require that you be homeschooled? Yes or no?
- Does *love* require that you belong to a certain church? Yes or no?
- Can *anyone* love, any time, in any place? Yes or no?

Don't waste time envying those who are popular, rich, smart, athletic, pretty, spiritually gifted, and theologically profound. Instead, watch those who excel in **love**. Aspire to be like *them*. **They're** the truly successful ones!

Memory work: Copy 1 Corinthians 13:4-5 here: _____

_____

_____

_____

End with prayer: Ask God to show you people who excel in love that would be good examples for you.

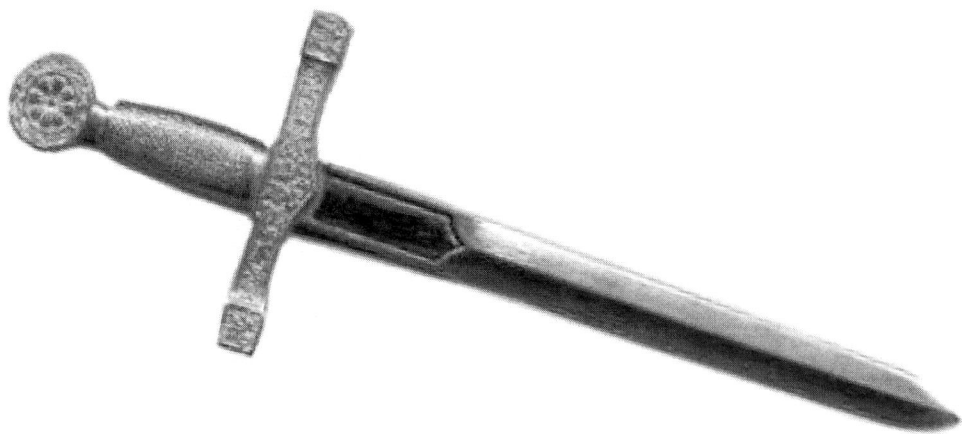

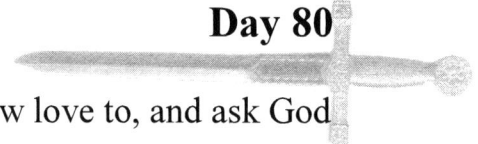

Begin with prayer. Pray for someone you want to show love to, and ask God for ideas on how to love him or her.

Sword Drill

Review the next four *history* books of the Bible:
I K _ _ _ _, *II K* _ _ _ _, *I C* _ _ _ _ _ _ _ _ _, and
II C _ _ _ _ _ _ _ _ _

Sword Play

The following secret code is based on 1 Corinthians 13:3. Use the code key to fill in the letters.

Code Key						
A=1	B=2	C=3	E=4	G=5	H=6	I=7
L=8	M=9	N=10	O=11	P=12	R=13	S=14
T=15	U=16	V=17	W=18	Y=19		

5	7	17	7	10	5		1	18	1	19		1	8	8		7			
11	18	10		11	13		2	4	3	11	9	7	10	5		1			
9	1	13	15	19	13		7	14		9	4	1	10	7	10	5	8	4	14	14
18	7	15	6	11	16	15		8	11	17	4								
	8	11	17	4		7	14		15	6	4								
12	13	7	9	1	13	19		15	6	7	10	5							

Fencing Practice

If you haven't already done so, turn in your Bible to 1 Corinthians 13:3 and read it. Review verses 1-2 as well. The most important thing to learn in this passage is that you can lead a godly life and do all kinds of works for God…and it's all meaningless if you're not doing it out of love. Who is to be the object of this love? God? Or others? What do *you* think? _____

I believe the answer is *both*. As a child of God, your life is to be characterized by love. Do you remember the two greatest commandments? Read Matthew 22:36-39. The two greatest commandments are…

- _____
- _____

It's sobering to think that we could be theologically accurate, with all our doctrine perfect, and do great works for the church, but if we don't *love*, we are _____ (1 Cor. 13:2) and gain _____ (1 Cor. 13:3).

Thrust and Parry

What are some things you do or are involved in that indicate you might be a Christian? List five things:

- _____
- _____
- _____
- _____
- _____

According to 1 Corinthians 13:1-3, those five things are meaningless – *they are nothing* – unless those things are done with love. Let's look at some things that many people believe "prove" that they are Christian. Perhaps some of these appear on your list. Check all the items that you yourself do:

- ☐ Go to church
- ☐ Listen to Christian music
- ☐ Sponsor a child
- ☐ Have given food/clothing/money to the less-fortunate
- ☐ Read the Bible
- ☐ Pray before meals
- ☐ Memorize Scripture
- ☐ Control your tongue; no cursing
- ☐ Refrain from substance abuse (no cigarettes/alcohol/drugs)
- ☐ Are committed to purity
- ☐ Hang out with Christian friends
- ☐ Are homeschooled or go to Christian school
- ☐ Are careful about what you watch on TV or at the movies
- ☐ Are involved in Youth Group, Sunday School, or Bible Study
- ☐ Have been involved in missions or a service project
- ☐ Wear clothing or jewelry with Christian themes/symbols

Obviously these are all good things, and we *should* be doing many of these things if at all possible; but they're meaningless without _ _ _ _. Suppose Jesus knocked on your front door and asked to come in. Suppose He asked you to show proof of your allegiance to Him. Would He consider your checked list (previous page) to be proof enough? _____ What is the one thing He'd look for? _____ . In our next few lessons we're going to study what real love looks like. Surprisingly it doesn't necessarily look like our list from the previous page! Stay tuned!

Memory work: Copy 1 Corinthians 13:4-5 here: _____
_____
_____
_____

End with prayer: Ask God to help you to *do* your Christian disciplines (such as Bible reading, tithing, and church attendance) out of love for God and others.

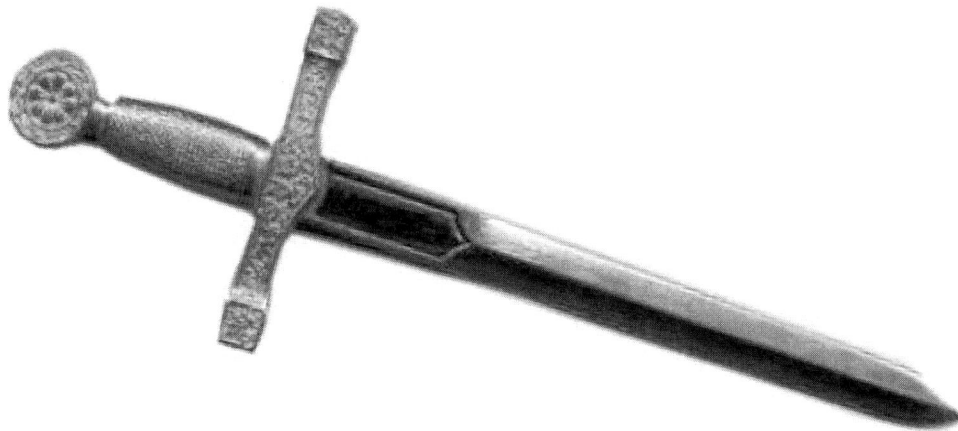

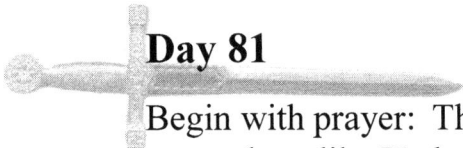

Day 81

Begin with prayer: Thank God for loving you so much...and ask Him to help you to love like He loves.

Sword Drill

List the last four Old Testament history books and the Bible's longest book of poetry:

E _ _ _, N _ _ _ _ _ _ _, E _ _ _ _ _, J _ _, and *P _ _ _ _ _.*

Sword Play

The following word search puzzle contains words from 1 Corinthians 13:1-4. Words can be horizontal, vertical, diagonal, forward or backward.

Word Search Box					
Angels	Burn	Faith	Knowledge	Mysteries	Patient
Arrogant	Cymbal	Gong	Love	Noisy	Prophesy
Boast	Envy	Kind	Mountains	Nothing	Tongues

L	O	V	E	W	R	S	T	O	E	K	M
B	Y	C	N	G	N	I	H	T	O	N	T
M	Y	S	T	E	R	I	E	S	H	O	E
Q	U	I	I	C	F	A	I	T	H	W	K
B	R	O	W	O	N	N	D	O	G	L	J
U	M	P	T	O	N	G	U	E	S	E	E
D	O	V	E	R	T	E	O	H	E	D	T
L	C	Y	M	B	A	L	A	N	A	G	N
P	R	O	P	H	E	S	Y	R	G	E	A
Z	A	S	N	I	A	T	N	U	O	M	G
Y	F	T	O	X	T	H	E	B	Q	U	O
I	C	K	I	N	D	B	R	O	W	E	R
F	O	X	J	E	U	M	P	E	D	O	R
V	E	R	Y	V	N	E	T	H	E	L	A
A	Z	Y	D	M	G	T	S	A	O	B	I

Fencing Practice

If you haven't already done so, turn in your Bible to 1 Corinthians 13:4 and read it. Here's where your theology must get practical. What you *believe* SHOULD impact your life. It SHOULD make you different. If it doesn't, then you *don't* really believe. You merely mentally assent. Mental assent is not the same as true belief. So, let me ask you, does *your* theology change how *you* live? Does your theology cause you to *think* and *act* differently than those around you? Do you try to justify why you act and react just like the world…or do you strive to be the opposite of the world? 1 Corinthians 13:4 is practical Christianity. It impacts the mundane details of your life, and it changes *every* relationship you have. According to 1 Corinthians 13:4 here is what love *really* looks like:

- It is _____
- It is _____
- It does not _____
- It does not _____
- It is not _____

Thrust and Parry

Since today's passage clearly describes what love *is* and *is not*, let's look closely at the character qualities listed in this verse.

First we read that love *is* patient. What is the opposite of patience? _____. So, if you're *impatient*, are you loving? _____. What exactly is patience? It is the quality of bearing kindly with disappointment, trouble, frustration, or delay. It's *not* getting upset when things don't go your way. Think of the last time you were impatient. Did you love as Jesus would have loved in that moment…with patience? _____. If you loved as 1 Corinthians 13:4 requires, how will you act the next time the same thing happens? _____.

We also read that real love is *kind*. What is the opposite of kindness? _____. So, if you're unkind in thought, word, or deed, are you loving? _____. What exactly is kindness? It is the quality of being considerate and affectionate, putting the feelings of others *first*. Think of the last time you were unkind in word or deed. Did you love as Jesus would have loved in that moment, returning evil or disappointment with kindness? _____. If you lived as 1 Corinthians 13:4 requires, what should you do the next time the same thing happens? _____.

We also read that real love doesn't *envy*. What does the opposite of envy look like? _____. So, if you're jealous and envious, are you loving? _____. What exactly is envy? It is a feeling of discontent or resentment when someone else has or gets more than you. More possessions. More friends. More popularity. More attention. More recognition. More anything. Envy essentially says, "God, that person doesn't deserve as much, and I deserve more than I got. It's not fair." Envy blames

God for running the universe unfairly, and it blames others for getting more than you got. Think of the last time you envied someone. Did you love as Jesus would have loved in that moment? _____. If you lived as 1 Corinthians 13:4 requires, what should you do the next time someone else is getting attention or is achieving what you wish you could have? _____.

We also read that real love isn't *boastful*. What does the opposite of boasting look like? _____. So if you're boasting or showing off, are you loving? _____. What exactly does *boastful* mean? It's showing off your self-satisfaction in your achievements, possessions, or your person (your looks or talents)...and using those gifts to make others feel less valuable than you. Think of the last time you were boastful. Did you love as Jesus would have loved in that moment? _____. If you lived as 1 Corinthians 13:4 requires, what should you do the next time you're blessed or you achieve? _____.

And finally we read that real love isn't *arrogant* or *proud*. What is the opposite of arrogance or pride? _____. So, if you're arrogant, are you loving? _____. What exactly does *arrogance* mean? It's exaggerating your importance in your own mind and in your words. It's believing in and acting on the idea that "it's all about you." It's functioning as if everyone in your world is there either to make you feel better or that everything they say and do is designed to annoy you – as if their existence is all about you. Think of the last time you believed or acted as if it was all about you, allowing little things to bother and annoy you greatly...or expecting everyone to notice, esteem, and validate you - as if it was all about you. Did you love as Jesus loved in that moment? _____. If you lived as 1 Corinthians 13:4 requires, what should you do the next time your importance or lack of importance is stirred up? _____.

What do you think? Is Christianity a *crutch* as some people claim? No! It's only for those who are willing to lay down everything: their rights, abilities, plans, hopes, blessings, and importance for the good of others. It's *hard*, but oh so wonderful! And thank you, Jesus, He even helps us to love as He loves! Be encouraged! The Bible tells us that the God who lives *in* you and *through* you (Galatians 2:20) **IS** _ _ _ _ (1 John 4:8).

Memory work: Copy 1 Corinthians 13:6-7 here (new passage): _____
_____
_____
_____

End with prayer: Thank God that LOVE lives *in* you and *through* you.

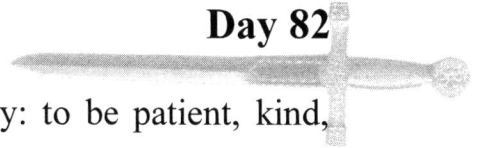

Begin with prayer. Ask God to help you love today: to be patient, kind, supportive, encouraging, and humble.

Sword Drill

Review the three books of poetry and wisdom that follow **Psalms**:

P _ _ _ _ _ _ _ , E _ _ _ _ _ _ _ _ _ _ _ , S _ _ _ of S _ _ _ _ _ _

Sword Play

The answers to the following riddles are words found in 1 Corinthians 13:5-6. Keep in mind that 1 Corinthians 13 is serving as your word bank.

I am an adjective, a describing word.
I am not love.
I am impolite and insulting.
I behave unseemly.
I am disrespectful and tactless.
What am I?
I am **r** _ _ _.

I am a verb, an action word.
I am not love when it's *my* way.
I demand. I won't accept no for an answer.
I seek my own advantage.
I persist, even if I'm annoying.
What do I do?
I **i** _ _ _ _ _.

I am an adjective, a describing word.
I am not love.
I am easily annoyed or provoked.
I am touchy and moody.
I let little things bother me.
What am I?
I am **i** _ _ _ _ _ _ _ _.
I am an adjective, a describing word.

I am not love.
I feel bitter when I am not treated fairly.
I feed that bitterness, dwelling on the unfairness.
I replay the hurt over and over.
I express anger and indignation toward those whom I perceive deserve it.
What am I?
I am **r** _ _ _ _ _ _ _.

I am a verb, an action word.
I am *not* love when the source of me is wrong.
I *am* love when the source of me is right.
I delight.
I show great joy.
I celebrate.
What do I do?
I **r** _ _ _ _ _ _.

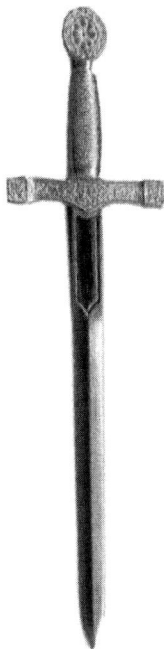

I am a noun, a negative behavior.
Love does not rejoice in me.
I am iniquity.
I am sinfulness, wickedness, vice.
I am corruption and immorality.
What am I?
I am **w** _ _ _ _ - **d** _ _ _ _.

I am a noun, a solid foundation.
Love rejoices in this.
I am sincerity.
I am related to factuality and reality.
I am honest and authentic.
What am I?
I am **t** _ _ _ _.

Fencing Practice

If you haven't already done so, turn in your Bible to 1 Corinthians 13:5-6 and read it. Review verses 1-4 as well. Here is another example of practical theology – a theology that has bearing on even your most mundane moments of interaction with other people. True love centers *first* on God, which makes it possible to love others as *He* does, even when interacting with someone who acts more like an enemy than a loved one.

Lets' look at an example right from the life of Jesus. If you don't remember the story of Jesus at the Last Supper, take a moment to read the following scriptures:

☐ John 13:1-5
☐ Luke 22:17-22
☐ Luke 22:24-27
☐ Luke 22: 31-34

Based on what you read in these passages, let's examine what 1 Corinthians 13:5-6 looks like in action. Fill in the blanks with yes or no.

- Were all 12 disciples present with Jesus at the Last Supper including Judas and Simon Peter? _____
- Did Jesus love all of them to the very end? _____
- Did Judas already have plans to betray Jesus? _____
- Did Jesus know this? _____

What actions did Jesus take toward His betrayer?

- Was Jesus rude to Judas? _____
- Was He irritated that all His kindness toward Judas was wasted? ____
- Like a servant, did He wash His betrayer's feet? _____
- Did He eat dinner, sharing generously with His betrayer? _____
- Did He insist that Judas give up his plans and be nice? _____
- Was He sorrowful that His betrayer would face judgment? _____

Think of Peter's role.

- Did Peter believe himself to be brave, fearless, and loyal to Jesus? ___
- Did Jesus know Peter would deny Him? _____
- Did Peter take part in the argument about who would be greatest? ___
- Did that argument about greatness take place after Jesus, like a servant, washed their feet? _____
- Did that argument take place after He served them communion? ____

What actions did Jesus take toward his unruly followers and the one who denied Him?

- He was rude to them, because they deserved it! _____
- He was provoked that they didn't 'get it' even when He personally demonstrated what love looks like. _____
- He washed their feet. _____
- He ate dinner with them, serving them. _____
- He told them, right in the middle of their arguments, that He would die *for* them. _____

- He resented that they were so ungrateful. _____
- He dwelt on their selfish behavior, replaying it in His mind, and grew bitter. _____
- He loved them to the very end. _____

Thrust and Parry

Real biblical love looks quite different than the way the world loves. Real love doesn't look for revenge or even for fairness. Real love isn't based on how you're treated *by* someone. Real love is based on Jesus Christ. And, because God IS love, we CAN love – *really* love – regardless of how we're treated.

Think of someone who annoys or tends to be hateful toward you and answer the following questions with yes or no.

- Based on past behavior, if given the opportunity, will this person most likely provoke you again? _____
- Like Judas, does this person *intend* to hurt you? _____
- Like Peter, does this person believe in his/her own innocence? _____
- Even so, should you (like Jesus) kindly serve this person? _____
- Will you most likely get gratitude in return? _____
- Should you treat him/her rudely? _____
- Should you get irritated at them? _____
- Should you rejoice over trouble that falls on him/her, or say, "Well, they deserve it!"? _____
- Should you die to self in serving them? _____

This is *hard* stuff! The captivating truth, though, is that we love because *He* loved first (1 John 4:19). We love not like the world loves, but differently. Think about it:

- Did you betray Jesus? _____
- Did you ever argue about going first or having the biggest piece, or about something not being fair? _____
- Did you ever deny Jesus by staying quiet about your faith rather than speaking up? _____
- Did you ever choose to sit and do nothing while others served you? _____
- Did you ever leave a mess for someone else to clean up? Dishes? Toys? Laundry? _____
- Did you gratefully thank that person for loving you by his/her service to you? _____
- Do you expect certain people to wait on you? _____

- Do you look for opportunities to serve? _____
- When doing chores, do you work cheerfully? _____

One way Jesus demonstrated His love was through His kind, patient, humble service. Now, go and do likewise.

Memory work: Copy 1 Corinthians 13:6-7 here: _____

_____

_____

_____

End with prayer: Ask God to help you to serve with kind humility even those who hurt or betray you. Pray for a specific person who hurt you.

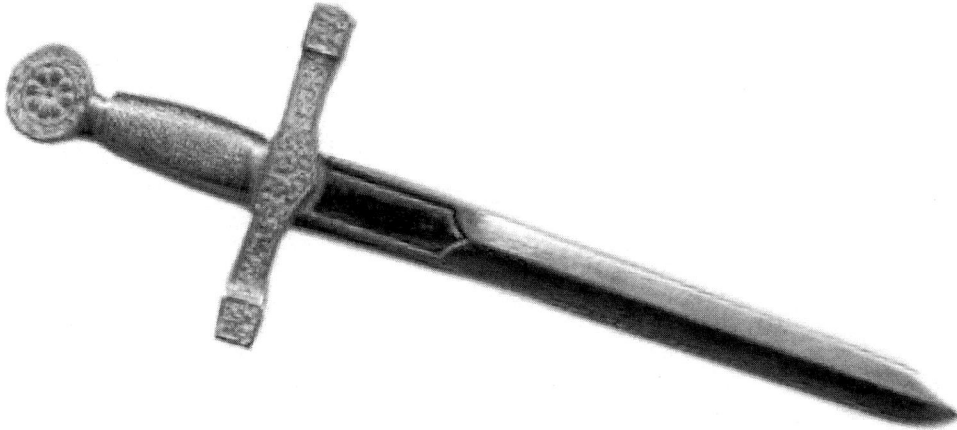

Day 83

Begin with prayer: Pray for the person who irritates you. Ask God to help you love that person in the way that He loves that person.

Sword Drill

Review the first six books of prophecy:

*I*_ _ _ _ _, *J*_ _ _ _ _ _ _, *L*_ _ _ _ _ _ _ _ _ _ _, *E*_ _ _ _ _ _,
*D*_ _ _ _ _, and *H*_ _ _ _.

Sword Play

The following mini puzzles can be completed with four phrases taken from 1 Corinthians 13:7. The phrases are identical with the exception of one word in each phrase. See if you can fill in the blanks. Use the key to get you started.

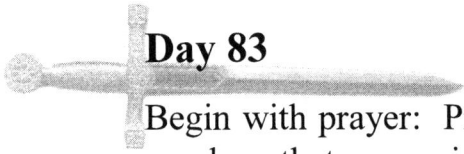

Key: 1=A, 2=B, 3=D, 4=E, 5=H, 6=L, 7=O, 8=S

Fencing Practice

If you haven't already done so, turn in your Bible to 1 Corinthians 13:7 and read it. Take a minute to *really* think about the four descriptors of love in this verse. What four verbs (actions) are *typical* of real biblical love according to this verse?   Love _____, _____, _____, and _____.

If you love as Jesus loves, you'll never give up, but rather *bear* all things. You'll never lose hope, but instead *believe*. Believe what? *Believe* that God is sovereign, and is always at work. No matter how many times that other person fails you, it doesn't matter, because real love is based on Jesus. Real love is based not on circumstances, but on **truth** that God *is* at work. Is real love a matter of *doing and believing* or of *feeling and passion*? _____

_____

If you love as Jesus loves, you'll have *hope* in the rock-solid on-going work of God. You won't view hurtful annoying people through atheistic eyes – without hope of change. Every relationship should be viewed through a lens of hope - a solid hope based on the powerful effective work of Jesus, evidenced by His resurrection. Is that same resurrection power at work in you? ____ Is it at work in the lives of all the true believers in your life? _____

You can say *yes* even if you're dealing with an unbeliever. Everyone, *everyone,* is a pawn in God's hands and *everything* is done for your good and His glory. This is truth.

Finally, if you love biblically, you can *endure* all things. You can *endure* the hurt and irritation. *To endure* means to continue, remain, persist, or to *patiently live through*. If you're patiently living through something, would you...

- Lash out at him/her? _____
- Roll your eyes at him/her? _____
- Ignore him/her? _____
- Cold shoulder him/her? _____
- Be irritable at him/her? _____
- Be courteous and polite toward him/her? _____
- Be kind toward and smile at him/her? _____

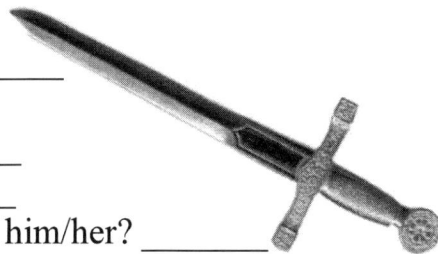

We all *know* what patient endurance looks like. It looks like love. Picture yourself *enduring* patiently and persistently whatever that hateful person dishes out. (**Please Note:** If you are being harmed physically in any way, get help NOW. Real love would not shield a person from the consequences of their actions. Consequences are an important part of repentance and redemption.)

Thrust and Parry

Finally, 1 Corinthians 13:7 tells us something about *how much* these four love actions (bearing, believing, hoping, enduring) apply. We are to bear, believe, hope, endure *all things*. Think for a minute. What does *all things* mean? According to this verse, do the four actions only apply the *first or second* time someone hurts or annoys you? _____

Only up to the hundredth time? _____

Only if it's a little hurt? _____

Only to outsiders? _____

Do these four love actions that we're called to demonstrate in our lives also apply to how we treat our friends? _____

Our enemies? _____

Church members? _____

Family? _____

Do we apply it only to those who treat us well? _____

Do we apply it to those who annoy us? _____

Do we apply it to those who hurt us? _____

Do we bear, believe, hope, endure only *some* things? _____

Does *all things* mean even in the face of insult, false accusation, gossip, and mockery? _____

Does *all things* mean even in the face of ingratitude, injustice, and suffering? _____

Here's the point. Anyone – even sinners – can bear, believe, hope, endure when someone is kind, polite, grateful, and admires you. But *we* are called to love even when it hurts. This is what Jesus did…and we can do it too! Think about the person who hurts or annoys you. Do you believe God can change that person? _____ Do you believe God can even use his/her nastiness to perfect you? _____ Do you believe God can use your biblical love for that person to impact his/her life? _____ This is what it means to bear, believe, hope, endure *all things*.

Memory work: Copy 1 Corinthians 13:6-7 here: _____

_____

_____

_____

End with prayer: Pray that God will help you to see that hateful person in your life through eyes of love and hope rather than through eyes of unbelief.

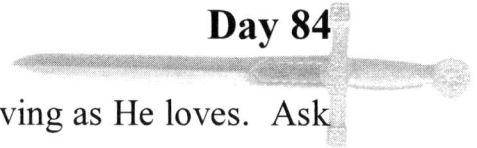

Begin with prayer. Ask God to forgive you for not loving as He loves. Ask Him to love the difficult people in your life.

Sword Drill

Review the next three books of prophecy that follow **Hosea**:

J _ _ _, A _ _ _, O _ _ _ _ _ _.

Sword Play

The answers to the following true/false quiz are found in 1 John 4:7-8. Write *true* or *false* in the blank after each statement.

- Since these verses are addressed to *Beloved*, we know that **we Christians** are the ones that are called to apply these verses. _____

- The call among us as Christians is to love each other – especially our brothers and sisters in Christ. _____

- The source of our love isn't the other person and his/her behavior, it's God. _____

- Loving others, especially other believers, is a sure sign that you know God and have been born of God. _____

- If you don't love other Christians who are being jerks, that's okay. They probably aren't really saved anyway. _____

- According to this passage, we're only required to love those who love and appreciate us. _____

- According to this passage, we're only required to love those who are kind to us. _____

- According to this passage, if I don't love others, I don't know God. Period. _____

- According to this passage, loving others is the same as knowing God. _____

- If I *really* want to know God, then I must love others. _____

- I cannot share Christ with others without loving them. I cannot shame, threaten, or judge others into heaven. Why? Because God isn't shame or humiliation, He is love. _____

- The best way to share Christ with others is through loving them. _____

Fencing Practice

If you haven't already done so, turn in your Bible to 1 John 4:7-8 and read it. I'm sure you can see how these verses tie into what we've been studying in 1 Corinthians 13. 1 Corinthians 13 tells us *how* to live out 1 John 4:7-8. When you read in 1 John 4:7 that you are to love each other, you've already studied how. List some of the ways you are to love others as described in 1 Corinthians 13. (You may look through *Fencing Lessons* 78-83 for help.):

- _____
- _____
- _____
- _____

There's a wonderful lesson in logic here. In 1 Corinthians 13 you've been studying how love is patient and kind, not envious, proud, or rude. In today's passage we see that *God* **IS love.** That means that the one thing (God) *IS equal to* the other thing (love). They are the same. That means we can substitute "God" in place of "love." *God* is patient. _ _ _ is kind. _ _ _ isn't envious, proud, or rude.

This also means we can substitute all of 1 Corinthians 13: 4-7 in place of "love" in 1 John 4:7-8. And, when we do, we have a handy manual on knowing God. We also have clear, concise instruction on recognizing unbelief (or "not knowing").

Thrust and Parry

Let's substitute parts of 1 Corinthians 13:4-7, which describes love, into today's passage to create a clearer picture of our calling. Copy the bold words in order into the blanks on the next page:

1. **Not** be **envious, boastful,** or **rude**
2. Be **patient** and **kind**
3. **Not insist** on **our own way**
4. Not be **irritable** or **resentful**
5. **Love; love; loves**
6. **Patient, kind**
7. Not **envious, boastful, rude**
8. Not **irritable, resentful**
9. Not **insisting** on my **own way**
10. **Born** of God, **knows** God
11. **Love, not know** God
12. **God is love**

Beloved, let us _ _ _ be _ _ _ _ _ _ _ _ , _ _ _ _ _ _ _ _ _ , or _ _ _ _ toward one another. Let us be _ _ _ _ _ _ _ _ and _ _ _ _ toward one another. Let us _ _ _ _ _ _ _ _ _ on _ _ _ _ _ _ _ _ _ with one another.

Let us not be _ _ _ _ _ _ _ _ _ _ with or _ _ _ _ _ _ _ _ _ of one another, because according to 1 Corinthians 13, this is not _ _ _ _ . For _ _ _ _ is from God, and whoever _ _ _ _ _ like this (_ _ _ _ _ _ _ , _ _ _ _ , not _ _ _ _ _ _ _ or _ _ _ _ _ _ _ _ , not _ _ _ _ or _ _ _ _ _ _ _ _ _ , not _ _ _ _ _ _ _ _ nor _ _ _ _ _ _ _ _ _ on my _ _ _ _ _ _) has been _ _ _ _ of God and _ _ _ _ _ God. Anyone who doesn't _ _ _ _ does _ _ _ _ _ _ _ God because _ _ _ is _ _ _ _ .

Now, go back and read the translation you just created of 1 John 4:7-8. We see that love is primarily an action, not a feeling. If you choose to love (be patient, kind, not irritable or demanding), *you will find your feelings submitting to your choices and actions.* Even more importantly, if you choose to love, you are choosing to know God! And ***that*** is the highest goal you can set for yourself.

Memory work: Copy 1 Corinthians 13:6-7 here: _____

_____

_____

_____

End with prayer: Ask God to help you to put love into action.

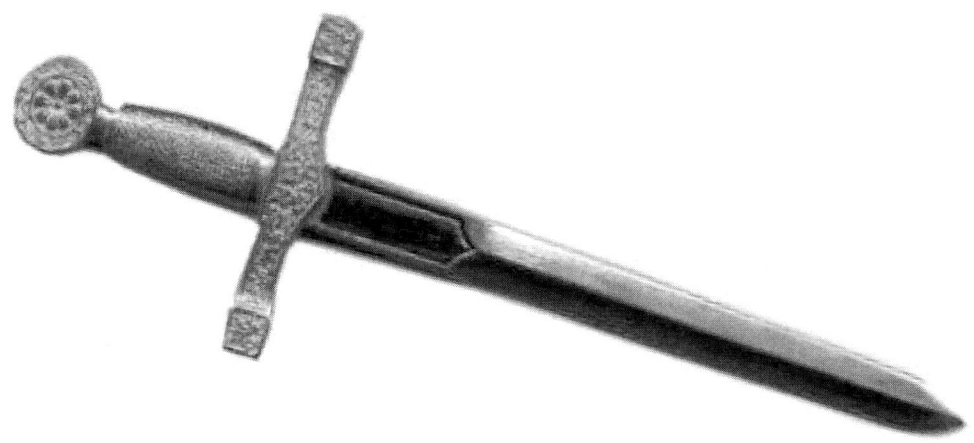

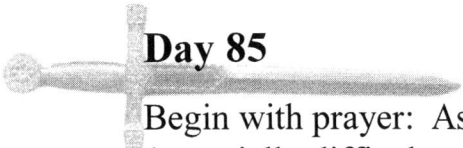

Day 85

Begin with prayer: Ask God to help you to know Him better by loving others (especially difficult people) better.

Sword Drill

Review the next four books of prophecy following **Obadiah**:
J _ _ _ _, **M** _ _ _ _, **N** _ _ _ _, **H** _ _ _ _ _ _ _.

Sword Play

The answers to the following matching quiz can be found in 1 John 4:10-11. Draw a line from the first part of the statement (found in the first column) to its second part (in the second column).

- In this…   …He loved us

- not that…   …propitiation for our sins.

- but that…   …if God so loved us,

- and sent His Son to be the…   …is love,

- Beloved…   …to love one another.

- we also ought…   …we have loved God,

Fencing Practice

If you haven't already done so, turn in your Bible to 1 John 4:10-11 and read it. We've been studying the concept of love for a while because *LOVE* is who God is and *LOVE* is what we're called to do and be. *LOVE* should be what defines us and sets us apart from unbelievers.

In today's passage we see the word *propitiation*. It's an old-fashioned word, but it's so rich in meaning that Christianity has held on to the word. A *propitiation* is an appeasement. It means doing something to win the favor of or to appease God. But, here's the important thing to remember. Is there *anything* you can do to appease God or to win His favor or to pay your debt?

_____

The answer is no. We could never do enough or pay enough to appease Him. So, He did something about it. He sent His perfectly good, perfectly kind, perfectly perfect Son to be the *propitiation* for us. He appeased His righteous anger and fulfilled every bit of righteousness and paid every debt and satisfied every demand *for us*. What is the old fashioned love-soaked word from 1 John 4:10 that embodies this idea? *P*_ _ _ _ _ _ _ _ _ _

Thrust and Parry

In 1 John 4:10-11 we read just how far **LOVE** goes. We've learned love is not primarily a feeling. Put a checkmark next to the concepts that describe real biblical love.

- ☐ You are nice to me and are fun to be with. My heart likes being around you as a result.
- ☐ You aren't very nice to me. Sometimes you're mean to me. But I will be kind to you so you will come to know Jesus.
- ☐ You are popular and gorgeous. My heart does a flip when you smile at me.
- ☐ You have some annoying habits that drive me crazy, but I refuse to get irritated. I'll joyfully reach out to you and include you.
- ☐ I want this, but you want that. I'll joyfully concede to you and not insist on my own way, because *you* are more important to me than *that*.
- ☐ You have betrayed and rejected me, but I will not let your mess define me. I choose to forgive you in hopes you'll come to know Him.
- ☐ You want to go out with me and I really want to be in a relationship with you. It just feels right.
- ☐ Because I want to be like God, I will learn to be a listener, not rude, not demanding that you hear *my* story first, not trying to top your story.
- ☐ I will serve you with joy. Can I get you a drink or help you? You sit and relax and let me serve you.

Memory work: Copy 1 John 3:18 (new verse) here: _____

_____

_____

_____

End with prayer: Ask God to help you *really* love...not just in a feeling, but in word and deed. Pray for a specific person and ask God to help you really love that person.

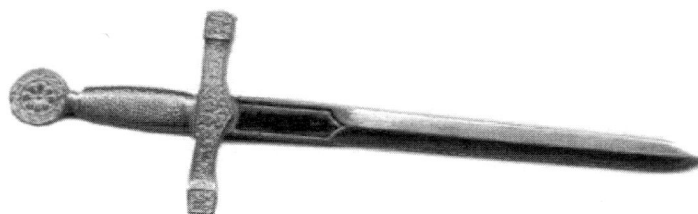

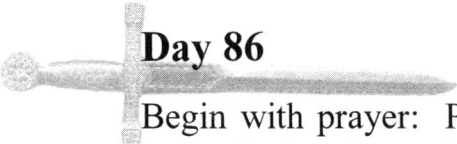

Day 86

Begin with prayer: Pray for a specific person, someone that is difficult to love. Rather than asking God to *just* change that person, ask God to change you to love that person right where he/she is at.

Sword Drill

Review the last four books of the Old Testament:
Z_ _ _ _ _ _ _ _, **H**_ _ _ _ _, **Z**_ _ _ _ _ _ _ _, **M**_ _ _ _ _ _.

Sword Play

The answers to the following fill-in-the-blank exercise can be found in 1 John 4:19-21. Fill in the blanks with the opposite of the words in brackets, then cross off the words in brackets to find a paraphrase of today's passage.

We [hate] _ _ _ _ because He [last] _ _ _ _ _ [hated] _ _ _ _ _ us. If anyone says, "I [hate] _ _ _ _ [the devil] _ _ _," and [loves] _ _ _ _ _ his [sister] _ _ _ _ _ _ _ _, he is a [truth-teller] _ _ _ _; for he who does not [hate] _ _ _ _ his [sister] _ _ _ _ _ _ _ _ whom he has seen cannot [hate] _ _ _ _ [the devil] _ _ _ whom he can't see. And this [suggestion] _ _ _ _ _ _ _ _ _ _ _ _ we have from Him; whoever [hates] _ _ _ _ _ [the devil] _ _ _ must also [hate] _ _ _ _ his [sister] _ _ _ _ _ _ _.

Fencing Practice

If you haven't already done so, turn in your Bible to 1 John 4:19-21 and read it. The epistle of 1 John is a diagnostic tool to help us identify and measure our spiritual pulse by identifying and measuring the quantity and quality of biblical love in our lives.

We've spent many lessons on studying what love really is. In this lesson we want to study hate, because according to 1 John 4:19-21, if we hate, then God's love isn't in us. We're liars if we claim to be Christians and also hate others. We've learned that love isn't primarily a feeling. It's a heart posture that affects behavior. Hatred is also much more than just a feeling. As a believer, you can *feel* discomfort or a lack of compatibility toward someone, yet still love that person in word and deed. You can instruct your heart to think the best, and you can take every hateful critical thought captive. You can choose to serve that person or smile at that person or forgive that person. Just as love is 'contagious' and can spread kindness, joy, and light, hatred is also contagious, spreading gossip, disdain, and bitterness. Let's compare love and hatred. Draw lines from the quality in the *love* column to its opposite in the *hate* column.

Love...	Hate...
Is sacrificial, selfless...	Is insensitive to others...
Is sensitive to others...	Tears down...
Thinks the best of others...	Bears grudges...
Builds others up...	Is typified by Adam's son Cain..
Pursues, identifies with...	Is rude and angry...
Is kind and gentle...	Puts good of self first...
Encourages, focuses on the good...	Is self-centered, selfish...
Puts the good of others first...	Divides...
Unifies...	Is of the devil...
Is life giving...	Is murderous...
Forgives...	Thinks the worst of others...
Is full of compassion...	Avoids, looks down on...
Is of God...	Criticizes, focuses on the bad...
Is typified by God's Son Jesus...	Is full of self-pity...

Thrust and Parry

This is such an important lesson! If you are God's child, then He has given you a new heart and His Spirit dwells in you and empowers you to practice love. Your actions and reactions toward your siblings, parents, and peers should be the opposite of the world's. And, again, God has empowered you to live like this. (Read Galatians 2:20.) But let's take our spiritual pulse to see where the Spirit needs to work in us. Remember, just saying, "I don't hate anyone," isn't enough. If your actions, reactions, and words are hateful, then repent and allow Jesus to free you from the destructive power of hatred.

Think of a person or people who upset or anger you often. Do you have a name in your head? Measure your love or hatred for this person in light of Scripture.

The "I hate" Diagnostic Tool

☐ I will not sacrifice my time, reputation, or emotional energy on this person.

☐ It is helpful if I point out (to them or to others) this person's sin issues and weaknesses and to demonstrate how wrong/obnoxious he/she is.

☐ It's impossible to think/believe the best about him/her. I know him/her too well!

☐ I tear this person down to other people, rarely having good to say *about* him/her or *to* him/her.

☐ I avoid this person. I would never behave like him/her! I'm glad I'm not *that* kind of person.

☐ I tend to be irritable toward this person. I cannot be kind or gentle toward him/her. Believe me, if you knew him/her, you would be irritable too!

☐ I cannot encourage this person. He/she is already **so** puffed up, he/she doesn't need any help from me!

☐ I put my good before this person. I will not let anyone treat me like that. I'm not a doormat!

☐ I am bitter toward this person and relive how he/she hurt me. He she needs a Savior – but until then, I'm staying away!

The "I love" Diagnostic Tool

☐ I willingly sacrifice my time, reputation, or emotional energy for this person.

☐ I try to be sensitive to his/her fears, weaknesses, and shortcomings.

☐ I think the best and believe the best of this person, and I choose to speak only good about him/her.

☐ I pursue friendship with this person and try to identify with his/her issues.

☐ I am kind and gentle, not irritable toward this person.

☐ I try to encourage this person.

☐ I put this person's good before my own good, regardless of how grateful or kind this person is…or isn't.

☐ I forgive this person and seek to ensure that my actions demonstrate this since my Savior has forgiven me so much more.

☐ I demonstrate compassion and affection toward this person regardless of their actions toward me.

☐ I serve this person humbly, just like Jesus served His enemies, whenever the opportunity arises.

Take a moment to reread today's passage slowly and prayerfully, allowing God to minister forgiveness, grace, and freedom to you. Remember that love brings freedom, while hate binds us.

Note: Please understand that there is also a very important reaping/sowing process. If someone is being divisive while claiming to be a believer, true love means going to that person and *talking to him/her first*, as described in Matthew 18:52-20. It is *never* appropriate to be criticizing or gossiping about others behind their backs. If your "normal posture" is to be critical about the believers in your life you are given several options: repent or go to them personally.

Memory work: Copy 1 John 3:18 here: _____

_____

_____

_____

End with prayer: Ask God to help you *really* love...not just in a feeling, but in word and deed. Pray for a specific person and ask God to help you really love that person.

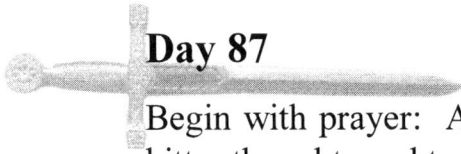

Day 87

Begin with prayer: Ask God to help you take captive any hateful, irritated, bitter thoughts and to help you practice kind loving thoughts.

Sword Drill

Review the four gospels and the history of the early church:
M _ _ _ _ _ _, M _ _ _, L _ _ _, J _ _ _, and *A _ _ _.*

Sword Play

The following acronym is taken from 1 John 3:18, 1 John 4:19-21, and 1 Corinthians 13. The high-lighted center acronym tells us *how* to love. Count the blocks needed to complete a sentence and find a word or phrase in the word bank that would fit *and* would complete the thought.

love my brother,
but I do
, you
. You
be God's
.

Words and are not
.
.

Love is and kind.
Love .
Love isn't .
Love . You
cannot love God and .

Word Bank
4 Letters: RUDE TALK
5 Letters: CHILD
6 Letters: ENOUGH I DO NOT
7 Letters: LOVE GOD PATIENT
8 Letters: ARE A LIAR IF YOU SAY
9 Letters: GOD IS LOVE
10 Letters: HATE OTHERS SACRIFICES
13 Letters: CANNOT HATE AND
15 Letters: PUTS OTHERS FIRST

Fencing Practice

If you haven't already done so, turn in your Bible to 1 John 3:18 and read it. According to this passage, if I just tell you "I love you," have I fulfilled the law of God? _____ If I consistently get irritated at someone and snap at them, but turn around and follow it with, "No offense, I do love you," are those words enough? _____

This passage makes it clear that real love is more than words, more than talk, more than even just a feeling. I think we all already *know* that. We've all been on the receiving end of a meaningless "I love you." That's why today's lesson requires us to examine **our** *delivery* of the "I love you." Are we delivering just empty words or are we loving in deed and in truth?

We've spent many lessons studying the *action* of love and the action of hate. We found that love is more than a fluttery or comfortable-with-you feeling. We found that biblically we are hating others even if we don't actually *feel* dislike but are speaking angry murderous words or putting our desires and comfort before others. Today adds another facet to the concepts of love and hate: truth. According to 1 John 3:18 we are to love in deed and in _ _ _ _ _.

What does it mean to love in truth? Remember, truth frees us (John 8:32, 36) so one of the most loving things we can do is to offer truth. But truth devoid of love is like clanging cymbals (1 Corinthians 13:1). Likewise, love without truth is just a lie, and lies kill, destroy, enslave. While you practice loving your family and friends today in your words and actions, don't neglect offering a kind and gentle truth as well.

Thrust and Parry

See if you can identify how we love. After each statement write "word" if it's an example of loving with words, "deed" if it demonstrates loving with action, "truth" if it shows loving with truth, and "not love" if it isn't loving. Some have more than one answer.

- I look you in the eye, smile, and say, "I love you." _____
- Your little brother has been bratty all morning. You offer to play his favorite game with him (even though he doesn't deserve it) just to cheer him up. _____
- You offer to go last, conceding cheerfully to the I-get-to-go-first selfish team member. _____
- Your friend is afraid of getting in trouble and asks you to cover for him/her. You say, "I'm scared too and that tempts me to lie too…but it's not right. Let's pray about it and face the truth and consequences together." _____

- Your friend is afraid of getting in trouble. Her parents always overreact. So together you come up with a plausible lie to cover. You don't intend to make a habit of lying, but telling the truth is causing too many problems. _____
- That one person in youth group thinks he/she is so great, craving attention and flirting with everyone to get it. At youth group you decide that rather than focusing on his/her attention-grabbing and criticizing it, you are going to offer real encouragement to him/her. You write a note of encouragement, explaining how you see God using him/her to impact others. _____
- You volunteer to do the dishes without being asked so that your mom can enjoy an evening off. _____
- Your sibling keeps taking your stuff without asking. You've had enough! It's *your* stuff and he/she needs to respect that! You march to your parents to complain about this constant annoyance. _____
- You tell your friends, in great detail, all about that awful thing your other 'friend' did and said, emphasizing how much it hurt you. You magnify his/her issues and minimize and justify your sinful reaction to the 'event.' _____
- The conversation on social media chat is so much more interesting than the conversation at the table. Besides, your friends *need* you. They will just die if you don't respond immediately and fix all their problems. So you curl up in a corner with your Ipod and quietly ignore everyone in the room. _____
- All your friends are busy criticizing the pastor, making a big joke about it. You don't want to look superior, but God is convicting you big time. So you say, "I have an idea. Let's share something good about him, how he's blessed us. It's way too easy for me to be critical, and I need your help to practice thinking and believing the best. I need your help."
_____

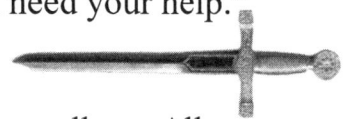

Our list of opportunities to love in word, deed, and truth is endless. Allow God's love to shine through you and set you free!

Memory work: Copy 1 John 3:18 here: _____

_____

_____

_____

End with prayer: Ask God to convict you powerfully whenever you aren't walking in love and to empower you to love like He loves.

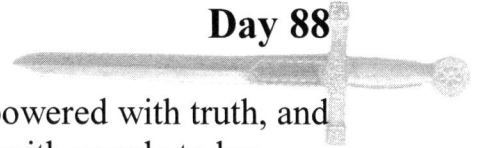

Begin with prayer. Ask God to help your love be empowered with truth, and for that truth to be empowered by love as you interact with people today.

Sword Drill

Review the first seven epistles written by Paul:
R_ _ _ _ _, 1 & II C_ _ _ _ _ _ _ _ _ _, G_ _ _ _ _ _ _,
E_ _ _ _ _ _ _, P_ _ _ _ _ _ _ _ _, C_ _ _ _ _ _ _ _.

Sword Play

The answers to the following multiple choice questions can be found in 1 John 4:18. Put a checkmark next to the correct answer.

- *According to 1 John 4:18* there is no _____ in love.
  - ☐ Fear
  - ☐ Shame
  - ☐ Hatred
  - ☐ Impatience

- *According to 1 John 4:18* there is no fear in _____.
  - ☐ Heaven
  - ☐ Judgment
  - ☐ Church
  - ☐ Love

- *According to 1 John 4:18* what casts out fear?
  - ☐ Jesus
  - ☐ Perfect love
  - ☐ Prayer and supplication
  - ☐ Wisdom

- *According to 1 John 4:18* what does love do?
  - ☐ Saves us from sin
  - ☐ Casts out fear
  - ☐ Strengthens you
  - ☐ Shields you

- *According to 1 John 4:18* what kind of love casts out fear?
  - ☐ Perfect
  - ☐ Godly
  - ☐ Unconditional
  - ☐ Any

- *According to 1 John 4:18* what is fear associated with?
  - ☐ Demons
  - ☐ Nightmares
  - ☐ Judgment and punishment
  - ☐ Sinners

- *According to 1 John 4:18* if you struggle with fear, you haven't been perfected in _____.
  - ☐ His Word
  - ☐ Obeying the greatest commandment
  - ☐ Love
  - ☐ Jesus

- *According to 1 John 4:18* if you struggle with fear, you aren't yet _____ love.
  - ☐ Experiencing
  - ☐ Tasting and seeing
  - ☐ Practicing
  - ☐ Made perfect in

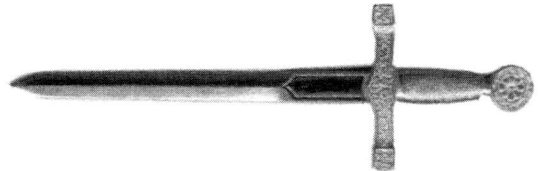

Fencing Practice

If you haven't already done so, turn to 1 John 4:18 and read it. It is one of my favorite scriptures in the Bible. You can it to both your love list and your promise list. It's a good one to underline and memorize. As a teenager I battled crippling fear, and this verse comforted me. It teaches another truth about the awesome power of God's love: it is freeing from fear. It frees us from crippling fear and empowers us to be who He has proclaimed us to be.

Complete these faith statements from 1 John 4:9 and 18.

God IS _ _ _ _.
There is no f_ _ _ in l_ _ _.
Perfect l_ _ _ casts out f_ _ _.

What wonderful truths for us to embrace and live by! It is another identifier that we are His children: fearlessness. But wait! I struggle with fear all the time.

Fear of the future.

Fear of what people think.

Fear of man.

Does that mean I'm *not* His child? No! It means I'm not yet made perfect in love. But I'm getting there. Here's the truth: the more I practice lay-down-my-life love, the less I fear. Love turns my gaze away from me and my image and to those around me and their well-being.

Some fear is actually good and healthy. For example, the Bible tells us that fear of the lord is the beginning of wisdom and knowledge (Psalm 111:10, Proverbs 9:10 and 1:7). When you love someone, a healthy awe and respect (or "fear") keeps you from presumption. Imagine if your future spouse someday said to you, "I knew you wouldn't mind if I went on a date with this attractive person because I know you love me and will forgive me. After all, it's YOU I married." A healthy reverential awe-fear is the beginning of wisdom. Likewise, you would never say to God, "It's okay if I do this sinful thing. God loves me and His grace covers all my sin." That's presumption!

Another healthy fear is one that contributes to safety. It's wise to obey traffic laws, to not play with weapons or fire, to take precautions when dealing with deep water or heights, and to handle animals with respect. These are all healthy fears that are part of wisdom.

But other fears aren't healthy. They are symptoms of spiritual sickness. These fears proclaim: "I don't trust God to be who He says He is or to do what He promises to do. I don't believe His plan for me really is good. I don't believe His blood was sufficient to save me and cleanse me." These are the fears addressed in 1 John 4:18. These are fears having to do with God's sovereignty and goodness and our punishment. Praise God His perfect _ _ _ _ casts out all _ _ _ _!

Thrust and Parry

Read through the following list of fears and write "wisdom" or "cast out" after each to indicate if it's a fear that is healthy or a fear that needs to be cast out by His perfect love.

- I will treat others with love and kindness. I fear that if I keep sinning against them, they'll not want my friendship. I don't want to presume on their love._____

- I will check mirrors and obey the speed limit. I'm afraid to get in an accident! _____

- I'm afraid God won't forgive me if I die today. I just can't get victory over this sin and I deserve judgment._____
- I'm afraid I'm not really a Christian. I don't enjoy reading the Bible. It's hard! Don't real Christians love reading it?_____
- I'm afraid for my future. What if no one falls in love with me and I never get married. I'm afraid God's plan for me might not be a good one. _____
- I'm afraid God isn't really good. My life is so hard! How can God be good and make me go through this?! _____
- I'm taking a hunter's safety course. I'm afraid to shoot a gun without first learning all I can about gun safety. _____
- I'm afraid of what people will think if I testify or try to share the love of Jesus. They'll think I'm intolerant or weird. _____

Now take a moment to list three things that you fear or that scare you.

- _____
- _____
- _____

Let the truth and power of God's love minister to your fear. His love will cast it out! Do you believe His love has that kind of power? …Power to free you from fear? _____

Memory work: Copy 1 John 4:18 (new verse) here: _____
_____
_____
_____

End with prayer: Pray about the three fears you listed and ask God to cast out those fears, making you perfect in His love.

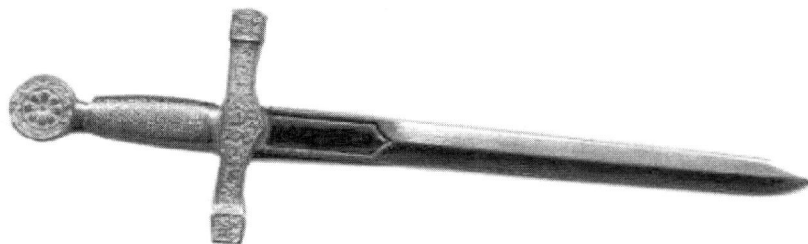

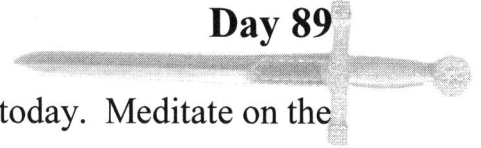

Begin with prayer. Ask God to set you free from fear today. Meditate on the truth that His perfect love casts out fear.

Sword Drill

Review the next six epistles after *Colossians*:
1 & II T _ _ _ _ _ _ _ _ _ _ _ _ _, *1 & II T* _ _ _ _ _ _, *T* _ _ _ _, and
P _ _ _ _ _ _ _.

Sword Play

The answers to the following riddles are words found in Romans 8:15.

I am a verb, an action word.
I obtain.
I get.
I capture.
What do I do?
I **r** _ _ _ _ _ _.

I am a noun, a thing.
You can't see me.
Some say I'm ghostly.
I'm the third person of the trinity.
What am I?
I am **s** _ _ _ _ _.

I am an involuntary condition.
I am bondage.
Politically I ended in America in 1863.
Spiritually I ended when Jesus rose from the dead.
What am I?
I am **s** _ _ _ _ _ _.

I am a noun, a negative ideal.
I have to do with judgment.
I have to do with punishment.
Perfect love casts me out.
What am I?
I am **f**_ _ _.

I am a noun, an institution.
I am a new relationship.
I am a chosen child.
I am a new family.
What am I?
I am **a**_ _ _ _ _ _.

I am a title.
I embody love and protection.
I embody safety and acceptance.
I am a Greek word meaning "daddy."
What am I?
I am **A**_ _ _.

I am a noun, a person.
I lead with strength and godliness.
I guide and train.
I protect and provide for.
I love you.
Who am I?
I am **f**_ _ _ _ _.

Fencing Practice

If you haven't already done so, turn in your Bible to Romans 8:15 and read it. Let this scripture speak to your soul. When you were saved, what did you *not* receive according to this passage? _____
Instead, what *did* you receive? _____.
Think about these two concepts and let's compare.

Is a slave chosen? _____
Is an adopted child chosen? _____

Does a slave belong to the family that chose him/her? _____
Does an adopted child belong to the family that chose him/her? _____

Does a slave have chores and responsibilities that benefit the family? _____
Does an adopted child have chores/responsibilities that benefit the family?

_____

Does a slave suffer consequences for his/her disobedience? _____
Does an adopted child suffer consequences for his/her disobedience?

_____

Does a slave receive food, clothing, and shelter from the family? _____
Does an adopted child receive food, clothing, shelter from the family? _____
*   *   *
Does a slave have freedom? _____
Does an adopted child have freedom? _____

Does a slave normally inherit anything from the family? _____
Does an adopted child normally inherit anything from the family? _____

Is a slave entitled to family's love and appreciation? _____
Is an adopted child entitled to a family's love and appreciation? _____

Is a slave equal in status and privilege to other family members? _____
Is an adopted child equal in status and privilege to other family members?

_____

Does a slave get to call the heads of the family "mom and dad"? _____
Does an adopted child get to call the heads of the family "mom and dad?"

_____

It's interesting when you consider the similarities between a slave and an adopted child. Though the similarities are great, the differences are even greater. Slavery carries the weight of fear and terrible punishment in the face of failure. Adoption carries the confidence of guidance and compassionate help in the face of failure. Slavery is loveless. Adoption is love filled. Slavery is given the family's cast offs and receives no compensation. Adoption is given the family's best and receives an inheritance. Slavery is characterized by a complete loss of freedom, being owned and controlled but unloved. Adoption is characterized by the complete freedom of belonging and being loved. Slavery calls out "Yes, master" in fear and trembling. Adoption calls out "Abba, father" in confident acceptance. Are you a slave? _____

Thrust and Parry

It's so easy to fall back into fear and into a slave mindset that fears judgment and punishment. But, if you belong to Christ, you are His child and need no longer fear. Though man may at times break a covenant and end an adoption, God never breaks His covenant, ever. Scripture makes it clear that God's covenant with us is kept and held by Him alone.

Put a check next to the correct statement in each pair below. Each person is involved in the same activity. One statement shows the slave mindset and one demonstrates an adopted child's mindset.

☐ I must read my Bible every day or Satan will get me and ruin my day.
☐ I *want* to read my Bible, because it contains the loving words of my Daddy God.

☐ I want to go to church to be with God's family and to learn to serve God together.
☐ I can't miss church or I'll backslide.

☐ I choose not to watch that movie because my Father loves me and doesn't want my mind darkened by that kind of stuff.
☐ I refuse to watch that movie. Real Christians would never watch such junk and I'm a real Christian.

☐ I obey my parents and honor them because if I don't, my life will be cut short according to the Bible.
☐ I obey my parents and honor them because my heavenly Father loves me and desires me to be blessed with a purposeful blessed life.

☐ If I don't obey His Word, I'll be punished.
☐ If I don't obey His Word, I'll be disciplined and restored.

☐ I only listen to and sing worship songs and hymns because I can't think of anything more amazing to sing about than my Daddy God. I love Him.
☐ I only listen to and sing worship songs and hymns because I'm afraid of being tainted by the world and feeding my mind bad things.

You may have realized that in most of these scenarios there's nothing wrong with either option, but the point is that as part of God's family you are free to love and be loved by Him without fear. You follow Him and obey Him because He is captivating and delightful. He's your Abba Father, your Daddy God. He has your best interest at heart. As His precious child chosen by God, do you have any reason to fear? _____

Memory work: Copy 1 John 4:18 here: _____
_____
_____
_____

End with prayer: Ask God to take away all your fear of punishment and to find rest in serving Him as a beloved child.

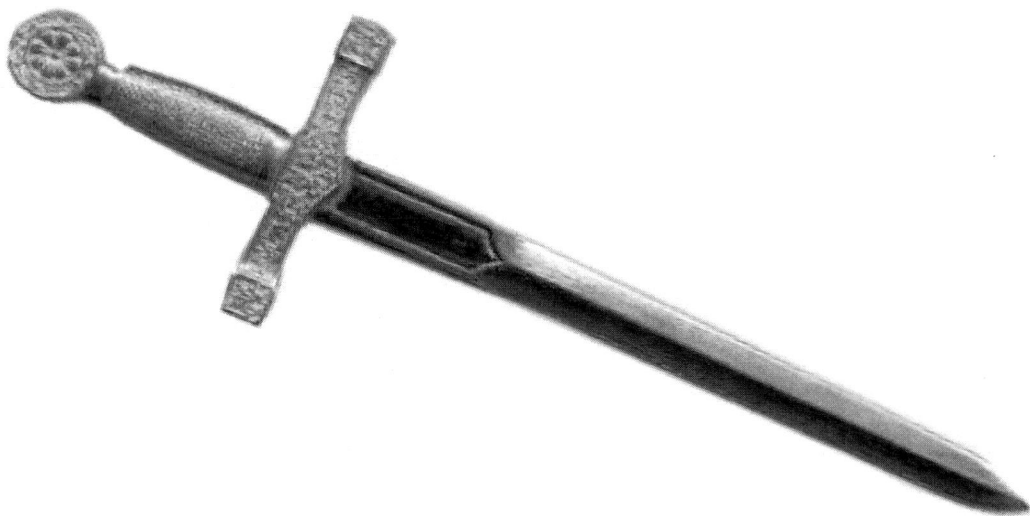

Day 90

Begin with prayer: Thank God for adopting you and for being your Father.

Sword Drill

Review the last nine books of the Bible:
H_ _ _ _ _ _, J_ _ _ _, 1 & II P_ _ _ _, 1, 2 & 3 J_ _ _, J_ _ _, and
R_ _ _ _ _ _ _ _.

Sword Play

The answers to the following multiple choice questions can be found in Hebrews 4:14-16. Place a checkmark next to the correct answer. According to Hebrews 4:14-16…

- This passage calls Jesus
  - ☐ An Angel
  - ☐ A carpenter
  - ☐ Just a man
  - ☐ A high priest

- Why is Jesus a different kind of high priest?
  - ☐ He sympathizes with our weaknesses
  - ☐ He has been tempted like us
  - ☐ He never sinned
  - ☐ All of the above

- In what ways has Jesus been tempted?
  - ☐ In every way
  - ☐ He can't be tempted
  - ☐ In some ways
  - ☐ None of the above

- Did Jesus ever sin?
  - ☐ Only when He was a baby
  - ☐ No
  - ☐ Yes
  - ☐ In His thoughts, but not in word or deed

- How do we draw near to God?
  - ☐ Only after we've done good
  - ☐ After we give an offering
  - ☐ With confidence
  - ☐ All of the above

- How is God's throne described?
  - ☐ Golden and covered with twelve jewels
  - ☐ The throne of judgment
  - ☐ The throne of grace
  - ☐ A comfortable couch

- What will you *receive* when you draw near if you've been adopted by Him?
  - ☐ Mercy
  - ☐ Discipline
  - ☐ An inheritance
  - ☐ Instruction

- What will you *find* when you draw near if you're His adopted child?
  - ☐ Jesus
  - ☐ Grace
  - ☐ Heaven
  - ☐ A choir of angels

- What will the grace you find there do for you?
  - ☐ Make us His child
  - ☐ Protect us from Satan
  - ☐ Keep us from sinning
  - ☐ Help us in our time of need

Fencing Practice

If you haven't already done so, turn in your Bible to Hebrews 4:14-16 and read it. For our final *Fencing Lesson*, we're going to look at how we approach or interact with God. In our last lesson (Day 89) we saw how our adoption gives us the privilege of calling God our Daddy rather than our master. If you've been adopted into God's family, you now hold the position of a beloved child.

The reality, however, is that God is still God, powerful and almighty. In Hebrews 4:16 we see that God is still sitting on _____. He is still King of kings, ruler of the universe. But thanks to Jesus, we get to approach God's throne differently. When an earthly king is sitting on his throne, there are many rules of etiquette that must be observed:

- An appointment must be made.
- A gift must be given to the king.
- A title must be respectfully used when addressing the king.
- Your hat must be removed if you're wearing one.
- No dirt, stains, or anything offensive is allowed on you in his presence.
- You must bow or prostrate yourself until given permission to rise.
- A petition may be made, but will only be granted if you manage to please the king.
- You may not question the king's judgment nor criticize his actions.
- Judgment may be swift and terrible, passed with just a thumbs down or a gesture of his scepter.
- Surrounded by warriors to do his bidding, absolute and swift obedience is required.
- You may not turn your back on the king when leaving his presence; you must back out of the room.

If you are not God's child, entering God's presence and approaching His judgment throne is a terrifying reality that will end in the worst possible way. But for a beloved child, even as the king is sitting on his judgment throne, it's an entirely different story! As a child of God, how should you approach His throne according to Hebrews 4:14-16? _____

Thrust and Parry

Picture a throne room with a mighty king on the throne. Picture the scene as one criminal after another is brought before him. The room is electrified by fear and pleas for mercy, swift judgment, chains and whips. Each judgment passed is just and true and deserved. People wearing their best clothes, bearing gifts, trembling, falling on their faces, longing for mercy.

Suddenly a door to his right bursts open and a mob of unruly children tumble through. The knot of princes and princesses make a noisy beeline for their father the king. They jump on his lap and kiss his face. He laughs at them with delight. Picture it.

Now picture yourself in the throne room. Do you picture yourself as one of the king's children or as one of those awaiting judgment?

After each statement on the next page, write "child" if it describes a child of the king or "slave" if it describes someone awaiting judgment.

- An appointment must be made and strictly adhered to. No additional time will be granted. _____
- Has instant access anytime day or night. Other appointments may be cancelled in favor of this one. _____

- May come empty-handed. His/her presence is enough. _____
- Must bring a gift in hopes of pleasing or appeasing the king. _____

- Must address the king with his complete formal title. _____
- May address the king as daddy. _____

- Must prostrate him-/herself and keep his head bowed. May not rise until and if given permission. _____
- May run to the king with joy, dance before him, and love him with abandon. _____

- May present a petition, knowing the king has no obligation or need to grant your request. _____
- May present a petition, knowing the king hears and answers every request, and his answers and gifts are always good. _____

- May enter his presence dirty and stained, knowing he'll love you anyway and will provide unstained clothing for you. _____
- Will be cast from his presence immediately if any dirt or stain is found on you. _____

- The warriors surrounding his throne are there *for you*, to do the king's bidding in protecting you. _____
- The warriors surrounding his throne are terrifying, poised to do his bidding against you. _____

- You view his throne as a place of judgment, where you will be punished for your failings. _____

- You view his throne as a place of grace, where you can climb on His lap and find a refuge. _____

Thanks to Jesus, you too can be His child – the child of the King of kings. Because the sinless savior took your place before the judgment throne, you now take His place as a child of God, climbing on your Father's lap as He sits on the throne of grace. Spend time in His Word, learning about your Daddy God. And with confidence of your full acceptance, draw _ _ _ _ to Him.

Memory work: Copy 1 John 4:18 here: _____
_____
_____
_____

End with prayer: Tell God you long to draw near to Him. Ask Him to make you hungry for His Word and His presence.

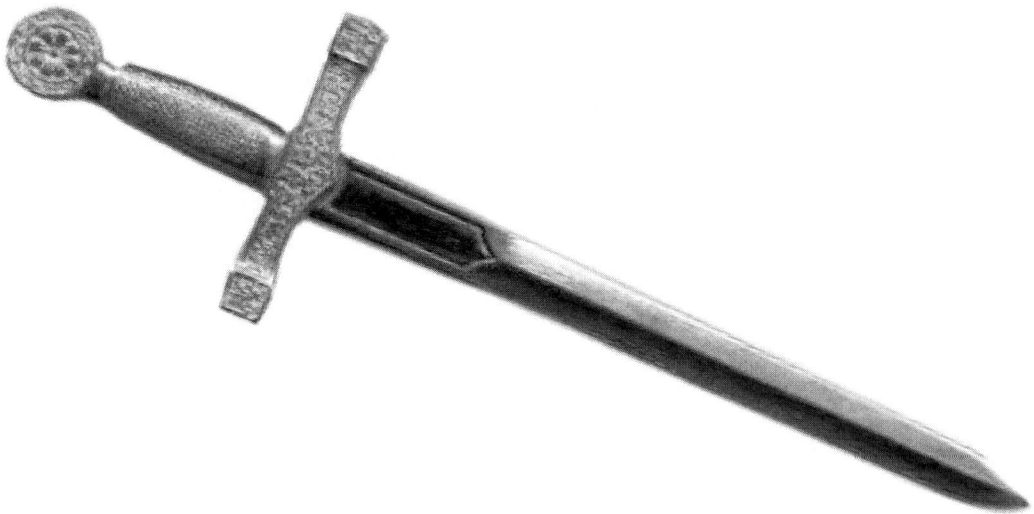